The Art
of
Art Therapy

By

Judith Aron Rubin

 BRUNNER/MAZEL, *Publishers* • NEW YORK
A member of the Taylor & Francis Group

10 9 8

Library of Congress Cataloging in Publication Data

Rubin, Judith Aron.
  The art of art therapy.

  Bibliography: p.
  Includes index.
  1. Art therapy. I. Title.
RC489.A7R83 1984   616.89'1656   84-9344
ISBN 0-87630-371-8

Copyright © 1984 by Judith A. Rubin

Published by
BRUNNER/MAZEL, INC.
19 Union Square
New York, New York 10003

MANUFACTURED IN THE UNITED STATES OF AMERICA

Preface

Although it may be presumptuous of me to think that I could describe "the art of art therapy," I want to be sure from the start that the reader knows of my own reservations about the title. This book is not intended to be *the* definitive, unalterable statement about how to do art therapy. In fact, one of my most secure convictions is that therapists of any sort need to find a style which is synchronous with their own personalities, and which cannot therefore be the same for all practitioners. Nevertheless, given inevitable (and appropriate) stylistic differences among clinicians, it seems to me that there are some general understandings necessary for effective art therapy with any age level and in any setting. Added to these "generic" foundations is the specific knowledge essential for work with particular populations in different contexts. These I hope to sketch out in this volume.

One motivation for writing this book was my frequent feeling of distress when hearing or reading about work in art therapy. Too often the clinician, while gifted or knowledgeable in one or more areas, seemed to be sadly lacking in others. Most upsetting was my impression—I think valid—that the individual was not even aware of such deficits. Perhaps, I reasoned, the necessary understandings for doing good art therapy had never been spelled out clearly for such people. This book is an attempt to do just that.

There is of course one potential pitfall, due to those characteristics of effective art therapists which have little to do with knowing any kind of information, and more to do with being a certain kind of person. For this reason, I have had to add to my statements of what one should know, some on how one should be, with the awareness that the particular form such being takes will vary among individuals. I am honestly skeptical about the teachability of such traits, though it is clear to me that they often become available to people after profound change experiences such as psychotherapy. At the very least, one can reinforce, reward, and support being open, flexible, creative, and caring. Whether such qualities can be transmitted in the same way as knowledge is less certain for me. In any case, since these attributes seem essential to good

work in art therapy, it would be wrong to omit them from such a book as this.

In a way, the whole book is an attempt to describe what goes into making a good art therapist, and no doubt is modeled on individuals I have known and admired in this and other fields. Among them are psychoanalysts, psychologists, psychiatrists, other therapists, teachers, and artists. Among them too are my earliest models of loving and caring—my father, my mother, and my grandmother—to whose memory this book is warmly dedicated.

Judith A. Rubin

Acknowledgments

I wish to thank Elinor Ulman, publisher of the *American Journal of Art Therapy*, for permission to reprint portions of Chapter Six which first appeared as part of a Panel Discussion on "Transference and Counter-transference in Art Therapy" (1982, Vol. 21, No. 1, pp. 10-12). I also wish to acknowledge the invaluable assistance of my colleagues, Linda Gantt (an art therapist) and Eleanor Irwin (a drama therapist), who waded through the entire manuscript and gave freely of their advice and suggestions for improvement. My thanks, too, to Frann Salley and Elaine Wade, graduate student interns, who also helped by reading, proofing, and xeroxing. I am most grateful to Gladys Agell (President of the American Art Therapy Association) and Irene Jakab (President of the American Society of Psychopathology of Expression) for agreeing to read and comment on the text prior to publication. My thanks also go to my editor, Ann Alhadeff, with whom it has been a pleasure to work. Special thanks to the support system provided by my employer, The Western Psychiatric Institute and Clinic (University of Pittsburgh), with excellent typing, word processing, and media services. The photographs were taken by: Jacob Malezi, Norman Rabinovitz, Sheila Ramsey, Norman Snyder, and the author. The book would not have seen print so soon, had it not been for the superb typing of the initial draft by Nona Rubin—and would not have been born at all, had it not been for the forbearance, tolerance, and support of Jenny, Jon, and Herb (my understanding family).

Note: While most of the photographs in this book are of actual patients and their art, some show normal children and adults in school or workshop settings and are used because they convey the intended idea. The self-portrait on the cover, for example, was indeed created by an anorectic teenager.

Contents

Introduction

In thinking about what constitutes the art of art therapy, it seemed to me that—to put it simply—there is an *Art* part and a *Therapy* part, both of which are essential. In elaborating these, it seemed that there was also an area I have called *The Interface*, in which the therapeutic evocation of and responding to the patient's art are central. The book therefore begins with these three main sections.

In the first, *The Art Part*, there are chapters on knowing the essential elements of art—materials, processes, and products—in regard to form, content, and the symbolic language of art. The second portion, *The Therapy Part*, includes the knowledge that any therapist must have: development, dynamics, and the conditions and process of therapeutic change. In addition to knowing therapy in general, the clinician also needs to know art therapy in particular, to know her* identity as a person and a professional. In the third portion, *The Interface*, there are chapters on knowing how to stimulate and then to deal with the art made and shared in therapy, including setting the stage, evoking and facilitating expression, and looking and learning from art.

In addition to the "basics" of art therapy discussed in the first three sections, there are also some "extras," of concern primarily to those who guide others in providing direct service to patients. Chapters on each area comprise the fourth portion of the book, *Indirect Service*, and include teaching, supervision, consultation, research, and theory. Although all of the aspects of art therapy discussed in the book seem applicable to all possible contexts, there are particular "knowings" and perhaps "beings" necessary for the best work in specific situations. These are detailed in the fifth section of the book, *Applications*, with chapters on different populations, settings, and modes of art therapy.

Despite the need for knowledge specific to each situation, I believe

---

*Since the vast majority of art therapists are women, I have chosen to use the feminine pronoun for the clinician in this book. My apologies to those men who use art in therapy. I trust that my decision will not stimulate an irrational "masculine protest," but rather a deeper empathy with anyone who might at times feel excluded.

the essentials outlined in this book to have virtually universal applicability. The "basics," and even the "extras," seem to be valid generalizations which can be translated in a variety of ways. In regard to population, they are true for work with children, adolescents, adults, the handicapped, and the elderly. In regard to setting, they are true for work in outpatient clinics, inpatient hospitals, schools, rehabilitation centers, and any other place where an art therapist might practice. In regard to modality, they are true for work with individuals, families, and groups. And in regard to theoretical orientation, they are true no matter where one might be on the continuum of art *as* therapy to art *in* therapy; and seem valid whether one's favored frame of reference is gestalt, humanistic, holistic, behavioral, or psychoanalytic.

I should hope, therefore, that this book would be relevant and helpful for all who use art diagnostically or therapeutically. I hope that it will say something useful to beginners as well as to advanced practitioners. While it is directed primarily to art therapists, it could be useful for any mental health professional who incorporates art into his clinical work, whether social worker, psychologist, psychiatrist, occupational therapist, or recreational specialist. It is not so much a "how to *do* it" book, as it is a "how to *think* about what you do" book. I suspect there is no one among us who cannot profit from thoughtful reflection on his clinical work. For myself, writing this book has provided just such an opportunity. It is my hope that it will provide the reader with a similar kind of stimulation, to think and act with increasing clarity about "the art of art therapy."

The Art
of
Art Therapy

PART I

The Art Part

The visual arts are a rich and complex realm, encompassing history, aesthetics, criticism, and the work of the artist in the studio. While it would be nice for an art therapist to know all aspects in detail, it is not really necessary to be an accomplished historian, aesthetician, or critic. Neither is it essential to be an accomplished worker in all possible media. Proficiency in any one of these can take a lifetime. There are, however, certain kinds of understandings and knowledge which matter more than others for a practicing art therapist. It is these that I will emphasize, with the awareness that it is always an asset to know more rather than less about any facet of the visual arts.

There are three chapters in this section, each one touching on a different aspect of the *Art Part* of art therapy, dealing with the basics: media, processes, and products. In each chapter, I shall try to focus on those elements most critical for the practicing art therapist, though I confess that, not being omniscient, I may well have omitted aspects which others would consider essential.

Art is, after all, the core of art therapy. It is my own belief that it can and should remain central, no matter how much training or experience a clinician has had in verbal psychotherapy. Sometimes individual art therapists who have gone on for further study in some other mode of treatment have moved more and more into words, with less and less use of art in their work with patients. I myself had some concern when I began studies in psychoanalysis that I, too, might find verbal psychotherapy more attractive. Much to my surprise and delight, I discov-

3

ered that my training in other ways of eliciting and viewing clinical material resulted not only in enhanced expertise, but also in a deeper appreciation of the value of expressive media and of the visual modality in work with other people.

I therefore begin this book with the *Art Part*, because it is that element which makes art therapy different from other forms of treatment. It makes art therapy more attractive to some patients and professionals, and more unattractive to others. It often enhances a person's self-esteem or his ability to express himself, though it can also be quite threatening in many ways. Whatever the assets and liabilities of art in work with patients, however, it is the unique and vital modality of the art therapist, no matter what the level of expertise. The three chapters in this section are interdependent, since there can be no products unless raw materials are transformed via a creative process into art.

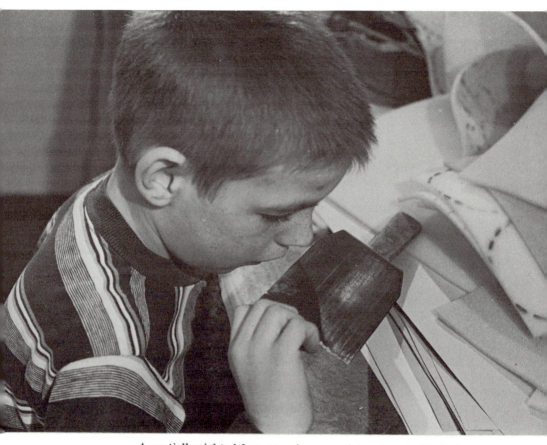

A partially-sighted boy examines a variety of materials before deciding what to use.

A young girl selects her working materials from a supply table.

Chapter 1

Knowing Materials

Without media and tools, there can be no art. While there is such a thing as mental imagery, and people of all ages do think in pictures, in order for such images to become art they must be concretized in some way. In the visual arts, this is done through the use of materials. Art therapists tend to prefer simple media and processes to more complex ones for several reasons. First, the more unstructured the medium, the more an individual will be able to project upon it. Since all art therapists hope to evoke personally meaningful creations, it would make sense that they would not wish to impose in any way on the patient's own natural imagery. To paint by the numbers or pour clay into molds is *not* an art activity, although art media are used. Such rigidly imposed tasks involve simply following directions—a laudable capacity, but not related to the essence or the goals of art therapy. Even the making of a pot holder or a ceramic tile trivet severely restricts the kind of imagery possible, despite the fact that there can be individual choice in colors and arrangement. While every art medium imposes its own intrinsic limits, there is in each the possibility of highly personal work by different individuals.

Another reason why art therapists prefer simple media is a practical one. Most art therapy sessions, especially in clinical settings, are limited in time. While it is possible in ongoing art therapy to work on a project which extends over days, weeks, or even months, such a plan is not possible in other contexts—as in a brief assessment, or with a group whose membership does not remain stable. There is much to be said for

7

media which permit the creation of satisfying products within the space of an art therapy session. This allows for consideration of the product as well as the process within a single time frame, when the impulses involved in the making are still very much alive.

There is yet another reason why simple, direct media appeal to art therapists, which is the fact that they can be used by individuals of all ages with little or no instruction. Because art therapists are often called upon to give technical help, they must know how to use materials effectively and how to convey that knowledge to others. Teaching, however, is a relatively small component of the role, used only in the service of being a better therapist for the patient. Thus, as patients will often tell us, it is true that we use materials which could be "used by a child," for beginners of all ages can quickly learn to successfully manipulate chalk, paint, or clay.

In addition to preferring materials which are *simple* and *unstructured*, art therapists should have sufficient respect for media to use only those which are *sturdy* and effective. This does not, as some people imagine, mean that the most expensive materials are the best. Indeed, the lowest grade of white drawing paper is quite adequate for most media, and the highest would be unnecessarily extravagant. Often, less expensive materials are more easily manipulable than more costly ones, which is true, for example, of different brands of oil-base clay or some colored chalks vs. some pastels. What does matter is that the material be strong enough to withstand normal pressures, and that it do what it is supposed to do.

Respect for materials is reflected not only in choosing those which are of reasonably good quality and which work predictably, but also in caring for all media and tools with concern. Brushes should therefore be washed right away, papers should be stored neatly, clay and tempera paint should be maintained at a usable consistency, and so on. Not only does such good care extend the value of limited resources, it also makes a statement to the patient about the value of the materials. This is analogous to the even more important message conveyed to the patient through the therapist's handling and storage of his products. Is it possible to be respectful of a person and to be at the same time careless about his creations? I think not.

Given these general requirements—for media which are simple, sturdy, and well maintained—what other things should concern an art therapist about materials? Most central, I believe, is sufficient experience with the use of those offered to patients, so that the therapist can assist in technical matters. Parenthetically, an art therapist should be aware of the unique capabilities of different media, surfaces, and tools, in order

to be able to offer adaptive solutions to a patient's problems in the actualization of his creative intentions. For example, if one does not know about the use of armatures to support three-dimensional modeled work, one cannot help a patient whose clay figure keeps collapsing with anything but his feelings of frustration. Similarly, if a patient wishes to build up the texture of his acrylic paint, it is important that the therapist know not only that it is possible, but also which available materials would work. Or, when a patient wants to represent overlapping with some transparency, it may be up to the therapist to suggest cellophane or tissue paper as workable ways to concretize such an idea.

The essential types of material with which any art therapist should be familiar are really rather few in number, though what is required is more than a superficial kind of acquaintance. There are the *surfaces* on which people may work, which include papers of various weights, surfaces, colors, and sizes, as well as cardboards of different kinds, canvases, masonite, and wood. The art therapist needs to be familiar with all of the commonly available kinds of paper, and to know the limitations and capacities of different types, in order to help the patient select the most facilitating size and kind of surface for his drawing or painting. Knowing the range of possible types can help the therapist to provide the patient with appropriate choices, without which there may be considerable unnecessary frustration.

As for *drawing materials*, the therapist should be familiar with all kinds of pencils—soft, hard, colored, charcoal, and those designed for normally resistant surfaces, such as transparency pencils or china markers. One must know too about different kinds of pens—those with a variety of nibs for use with ink, ball-points, felt-tipped, etc. There are many kinds of ink and watercolor markers now available, each with different possibilities, in various sizes and ranges of hues (and even odors). Then there is charcoal, both natural and pressed, and in pencil form. And as for crayons, there is not only the traditional wax variety in a range of sizes and shapes, but there are also others made of solid paint (like Craypas and Paintstiks) and those more closely related to chalk (like Conté crayons). Finally, there are chalks and pastels, which come in many different shapes and sizes, with varying degrees of softness. What is essential is that the art therapist be aware of the many potential drawing tools, and of the most appropriate surfaces for each.

There is a similar range of possibilities in *painting media*, where many varieties of each type are now available. Watercolors come soft in tubes or hard in pans; tempera comes in blocks, liquid, and powder form; and there are other water-base media as well, like gouache and casein. Finger

paint can be created in different textures, using a variety of available bases (such as soap flakes or liquid detergent or the many "cooked" types for which recipes are available); there is also the commercially prepared variety in moist or powder form. Finally, there are the more costly painting media, such as oils (which now come in a water-soluble form as well) and acrylics, available in tubes or as a liquid. Manufacturers continue to create new types of paint and other materials, such as "Liquid Crayon," a waxy medium which dries shiny and is water-resistant, an excellent surface for non-fired clay. As with drawing tools, it is essential for an art therapist to know about the many types of paints available.

Another central creative mode in art therapy is three-dimensional work with *modeling materials*. Here, one should know about clay—all kinds—from those which are fired in a kiln, to those which are designed to be baked in a kitchen oven or air-dried. In addition to natural or man-made clay with a water base which hardens, it is also necessary to know about oil-base clay, which does not get hard and comes in a variety of colors and degrees of pliability. Then there are the modeling doughs, some of which are commercially prepared, and many of which can be created using a variety of available recipes. As with papier-mâché, the range of possible consistencies and colors is great. Finally, there are commercial preparations in plastic or powder form with a wide range of qualities, such as "Elasticlay," which can bend after baking, or "Super-wood," which can be sanded and painted when hard. The art therapist needs to be familiar not only with the many types of modeling materials available, but also with the particular characteristics of each one, and with appropriate tools and surfaces for work with each.

There are also a number of other materials which can be used for *three-dimensional construction*, from stiff paper to wire, fabric, yarn, wood, and plastic. Again, it is important for the art therapist to be familiar with the possibilities, as well as with the particular tools and processes appropriate to each. Tools include such basics as scissors, brushes, and modeling tools, as well as different kinds of knives, staplers, string, and adhesive materials, such as tapes and glues. There is a wide variety available, each one with its particular capabilities and appropriate uses. If one works with wood, metal, or stone, then it is important to know about the special tools used with these materials and how they work best.

In order to keep up with new developments in creative materials, it is helpful for an art therapist to regularly receive catalogs from commercial distributors. Criteria for selection should include not only cost,

but also the kind of simplicity of use referred to earlier. When selecting or suggesting materials for anyone, the art therapist needs to consider the relevance of the medium to any creative intention, in addition to its ability to be used successfully by a particular person or group. In this regard, it is helpful to be aware of the degree of difficulty of the medium, as well as the patients' perceptual-motor capacities. Also relevant to one's decisions are management aspects, like the complexity of distribution or clean-up. Certainly, the amount of time and space available have to be taken into account, as well as the accessibility of water, soap, and other resources. Just as all art therapists do not have unlimited budgets for materials, so all do not work in optimal settings for art. It is often necessary to find a workable compromise between the ideal materials and those which are feasible within realistic constraints.

In a severely limited work situation, especially where an art therapist must be highly selective about what materials are made available, a wide-ranging awareness of possibilities is an essential condition for the best-informed choices. Such broad-based knowledge about materials cannot be acquired merely from looking at catalogs or reading books about what to do with different media. It is only available, I believe, through direct personal experience with the widest possible variety of basic media, tools, and processes. The art therapist need not be an *expert* with clay or paint or pastel, but she must have used the different varieties of each sufficiently to know their capacities, and to help another to work successfully with them.

Knowing the capacities of materials is also quite fascinating, for media and tools each have particular things they can and cannot do; and there are indeed more and less successful ways of using them. In addition, they have many qualities to which we respond emotionally as well as cognitively. Finger paint is not only smooth, moist, thick, and colorful; because of its abundance and texture, it can also be experienced as plentiful or messy, whether or not the hands contact it directly. Clay can stimulate feelings of disgust as well as feelings of pleasure; it can seem cold and unyielding, as well as soft and manipulable. While these possible responses are partly a function of what the patient brings to the experience, they are also dependent upon the particular qualities of the material.

Such projections occur in response to tools and processes as well as to media, so that a thick, long-handled brush can seem powerful to one person and unwieldy to another. Pounding a nail into wood can be felt as an exciting release of aggressive energy, or as an anxiety-provoking forbidden act. Sanding wood can be experienced as a loving kind of

caress, or as a hostile kind of attack. An exercise I have found useful with trainees never fails to demonstrate the capacity of materials and processes to elicit meaningful personal responses. In this experience, each person is asked to think about which medium, tool, or process he or she might be. Some wish to be paint because they want to feel fluid and colorful, while others identify with paint because they often feel out of control. It is important for an art therapist to be as aware of the symbolic qualities of materials as of their pragmatic aspects. Only then is she able to appreciate the full impact on patients of their encounter with different media and processes.

While it is tempting to go into further detail about the practical and symbolic aspects of each of the basic kinds of materials and tools used by art therapists, such information already exists in books and films which concentrate in depth on different media and processes. What is essential for the art therapist is to have not only a cognitive awareness of what is available, but also an appreciation of the "personality" of each medium, tool, and process—what it can and cannot do, and how it relates to developmental levels in terms of difficulty and symbolic meaning. Such an awareness can only be gained through substantial personal experience with the medium, tool, or process. Ideally, this experience should be under the supervision of an expert in the area, who can teach the essential skills needed to make the material do its work for the artist. Only an art therapist who can assist a patient in the use of a medium is legitimately entitled to offer it.

The challenge of how much to "teach" and how much to allow the patient to find his own way is one of many that call for clinical as well as educational judgment, a subject to be covered in later chapters. Meanwhile, no judgments will be well made if the art therapist does not have the "basics" under her professional belt, and all, I am sure, would agree that the materials with which we work are central. Equally important are the processes by which we transform media into products, the subject of the next chapter.

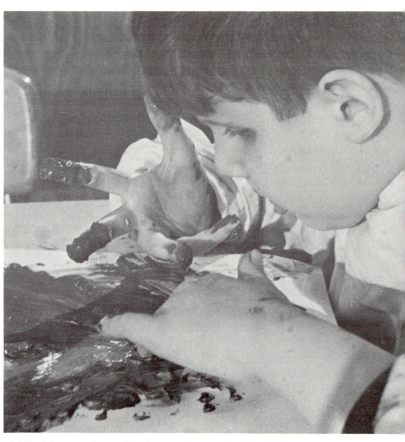

A blind boy explores the fingerpaint medium in all its richness.

Sometimes the process of working with materials requires very close attention and careful control.

Chapter 2

Knowing Processes

Without some kind of process, media and tools do not become art. A jar of paint and a brush do not become a painting until an individual uses one to place the other on a surface. Although the processes of working with different media are closely related to the physical characteristics of each, there is a wide range of possibilities. As with materials, it is essential that an art therapist be aware of these, in order to help patients to have the fullest and most satisfying experience with whatever is offered. The challenge here, as elsewhere, is to know when to give direct advice or instruction, and when to leave the patient to his own devices. Some thoughts about the creative process in a general way may help to guide this necessary decision-making act.

I believe that, whatever the age of the patient, the natural and organic way to begin with any material is to explore. Just as one experiments with a new toy or gets to know a new person, the initial step with a new medium is exploration. This is contrary to the common educational way of beginning, by instructing the person in how to properly use a material or tool. My own conviction is that therapy itself is an exploratory process, one in which the individual hopefully discovers and understands his own ideas and feelings, which eventually helps him to be more in charge of his life. One of the positive aspects of art therapy is that we can offer experiences of exploration and discovery through media as well as in words. I would hope, therefore, that all art therapists could become comfortable with inviting patients to explore materials they are encountering for the first time. In order for this to be possible,

15

the therapist must be comfortable with the idea that there may be no finished product, that some technical elements may be less than optimal, and that the patient is likely to experience some confusion with the ambiguity of not having a well-defined, goal-oriented task. Indeed, most individuals do find it necessary to create "something" at some point during their explorations with materials, since there seems to be a universal need to organize experience in a coherent way.

Some may object that an invitation to "explore," especially if it includes a playful component such as "fooling around" to see what will happen with the medium, is antithetical to the nature of art, which is to make a formed, finished product. Yet a quick glance at the literature on the creative process, whether by artists or psychologists, quickly assures us that this kind of playful experimentation is an essential element in genuine creative work of any sort. Perhaps more significant, it is also seen as an essential condition for gaining access to unconscious mentation by most psychodynamically oriented therapists, as in the free association of psychoanalysis.

Like free verbal association, exploring freely with materials is far from easy, eliciting many defenses and organizing phenomena in response to ambiguity and confusion. Some art therapy techniques have been specifically developed as a way of attempting to help patients to bypass these normal resistances, to get more rapidly in touch with less conscious kinds of imagery. These include such approaches as modeling with a blindfold on, or the use of a scribble as projective stimulus for a picture. I often ask workshop participants, after doing a scribble drawing, whether they think they would have come up with an image like the one they developed, had they been given a blank sheet of paper and asked to draw anything they wished. Almost universally, the answer is in the negative. When asked what they might have done if a free drawing had been requested, most think of either abstract designs or well-practiced schemata, often stereotyped and impersonal. The opportunity to "find" an image in a scribble is also a welcome excuse for most to feel less sense of responsibility (and therefore shame) for what emerges.

There are many such ways to help individuals to enter a more relaxed, free process of creation. The possibilities are limited only by the imagination of the art therapist. My own preference is to utilize them only when necessary, as in short-term workshops or some diagnostic interviews, and in therapy only when an individual or group seems "stuck" in some way. What seems most natural to me, in order to help patients to experience a genuine creative process, is to create a physical and

psychological environment in which such freedom becomes truly possible. Then, encouraging the kind of exploration and nonjudgmental playing with the possibilities of what materials can do can enable a most meaningful experience.

The conditions essential for such a "framework for freedom" include sufficient, organized, predictable space and time, as well as a trusting, interested, accepting, supportive attitude on the part of the clinician. Only if the therapist is honestly convinced of each individual's potential creativity in art is it possible to convey such confidence. Moreover, such an open approach to the creative process can evoke a good deal of anxiety in some, so that the therapist also needs to be able to help patients to deal with the stresses and frustrations of relative freedom. What is essential for an art therapist, however, is an understanding that the creative process for anyone must grow out of such a free exploration of possibilities. While this is most important at the outset, it is also true for many moments later in time—when a patient may have mastered the use of a medium, for example, but has not yet permitted himself to freely explore its full expressive potential.

In every creative process of any worth, there is also a time for "incubation," for allowing the mind to work preconsciously (and perhaps unconsciously) on the creative problem at hand. The art therapist needs to respect this phenomenon, to permit putting work aside for a period of time, or simply looking at it without making any changes, in order for this kind of problem-solving to occur. Not only can one allow such periods of reflection, but one can also promote them in a variety of ways, especially when the patient's anxiety creates pressures for premature closure.

And, more familiar, there is the need in any creative process for organizing, putting together, arranging, and elaborating the finished work. Materials vary in their ability to be reworked, so that there may be greater value for art therapy in those that permit change over time (such as clay kept moist), as opposed to those that do not (such as wood, once carved). In any case, while there is often value for a patient in having to make irrevocable decisions (such as where to saw or carve the wood), it is always the art therapist's task to monitor the technical progress of the work, so that its development will permit maximal modification by the artist until it has reached a satisfying finished state. This would involve such a simple intervention as suggesting that someone arrange parts of a collage or construction before gluing them down, in order to be able to rearrange them if so desired before the final decisions are made.

Here one might ask if the aesthetic judgment of the art therapist ought to be part of what is given to a patient. There may be situations where it would be helpful to suggest that a patient look only at a portion of a larger work (covering the rest visually), or perceive the product from a distance or a different perspective (such as upside down). I would conceptualize such acts on the part of the therapist as facilitating the patient's ability to make aesthetic decisions about what is "best" or "right."

This is analogous to my feeling about technical assistance—that it be offered only when needed to help the patient make a personally meaningful and practically durable product. Thus, it is unfair to let a patient use a material on a surface to which the therapist knows it will not adhere permanently, or to model a form which she knows will crack in the drying process. Similarly, it seems somewhat inhumane for the clinician to silently allow a patient to struggle to cover a huge surface with a tiny brush or marker, when she knows that a larger brush or marker is available for such a task. With respect for the patient as artist, however, the art therapist's role is the sharing of such information, not the mandating or prohibiting of any specific act, regardless of practicality.

So far, this chapter has emphasized the creative process using art media in the most general sense. There are also some specific aspects of creative thinking and acting which are highly relevant for art therapists. These are the capacities found by psychologists to be characteristic of creative people, whether studied anecdotally or experimentally. These traits usually include fluency, flexibility, elaboration, and originality. Each of these can be promoted and encouraged in a patient's experience with art in therapy, and each relates rather significantly to the larger task of creative problem-solving in life.

Fluency refers to the capacity to generate many ideas in relation to a problem, such as how to combine particular shapes or colors or figurative concepts in a work of art. While a large number of ideas is not essential for an artist, being able to play with multiple possibilities for dealing with life problems is helpful to all people, and is often a dilemma for patients, who tend not to see the many alternatives open to them. Perhaps the very experimentation with art, with no reality dangers or consequences, can be a preparation for a more courageous exploration of possibilities in real life. Certainly, the more ideas generated for solving the artistic problem itself, the more solutions from which to choose.

Flexibility refers to the ability to perceive the same thing in different ways, to shift gears from one frame of reference to another, and to deal with unforeseen events with minimal frustration. It is intimately related to most notions of mental health, where the extremes of both rigidity

and fluidity are signs of illness. To be able to be flexible in one's use of materials and tools in art-making processes is more likely if it is valued by the art therapist, who can actively reinforce instances of such behavior by the patient.

While *elaboration* may be the least intimately related to mental health—the primary goal in art therapy—it is still relevant and worthy of both encouragement and reward. Like fluency, the ability to elaborate—to extend, decorate, and refine—can result in not only more beautiful art products, but also a more adaptive response to life challenges. To be able to stick with a problem or piece of art once the initial inspiration has passed enables the momentary "high" to be translated into something lasting. And, in most situations, it allows the individual to achieve greater success and fulfillment than are given to the most "inspired"—but undeveloped—ideas and products.

As for *originality*, this is the aspect of creativity most often thought of by most people. Yet, as Ecclesiastes pointed out so long ago, there is rarely anything new under the sun. Every artist, great or amateur, has been inspired by the work of others. This is true even of the so-called primitive or naive painters. What seems most critical in art therapy is that the patient be enabled to find his own "true self," by discovering and developing preferred media/style/thematic modes. Even though the artwork may remind the historian of one or another well-known artist, what matters is that the work feel right and authentic to the patient, whatever the mix of outside inspiration and inside generation that went into its creation.

This is an area fraught with hazards for the practicing art therapist, who cannot help but have media/style/content preferences. What is essential is to be aware of these hazards, so as to avoid influencing the patient either overtly or subtly with one's own "taste." There is a striking similarity among the artwork of different individuals in some publications. One cannot help but assume that the worker, probably unwittingly, has influenced the art of the patient or student. In order to help each individual to really discover and develop his own genuine style, one must become as neutral as possible about the aesthetic elements therein, with the highest value placed on the authenticity of the art for the person involved. I believe this is the only position consonant with respect for the individual, his worth, and his art as an extension of himself.

As for processes of work with art media per se, there are two aspects which I feel are critical for art therapists. The first concerns the possibilities inherent in any material, which are never limited to those known

as most common or usual. Such a flexibility in thinking about art processes becomes especially vital in work with the disabled, for whom
modifications of media, tools, and surfaces may be essential conditions
for creative work. Even with those who are not handicapped, an openness to unexpected possibilities of work can be an asset for the art
therapist. Such a stance is helpful, whether responding to a child's
spontaneous impulse to use oil paints with his fingers, or trying to figure
out a way to make it possible for a person to draw with paint when he
cannot control a thin brush (but could manage a long-handled cotton
swab).

The other area that seems important for art therapists is a sensitivity
to the temporal and spatial aspects of the art process engaged in by
another. While some attempts have been made to classify such aspects
of creative work, such as deliberate vs. spontaneous types of artists
(Burkhart, 1962); close observation by educators and clinicians indicates
a rich and variegated range of possibilities in the rhythms of any individual's work during the course of a single session and over a period
of time (cf. Rubin et al., 1983). There seems to be more awareness on
the part of most art therapists of whether an individual uses a medium
"appropriately," than of more subtle qualitative aspects of the art process—differences in cognitive and creative styles.

While some such aspects of the working process are reflected in the
finished product, many can only be seen through close observation of
the doing itself. This includes what precedes and follows the work with
respect to materials, as well as associated behaviors during the use of
media. It involves words, facial expressions, body movement, and tone,
and the interaction of all of these in the gestalt of an art-maker's behavior.
It includes such aspects of being as activity/passivity, tension/relaxation,
awkwardness/coordination, impulsivity/deliberation, distractibility/
involvement, all in relation to the art process itself. Even such dimensions as rigidity/flexibility, compulsivity/freedom, or constriction/openness
can be thought of not only in relation to products, but also in regard to
the working process.

Similarly, attitudes toward the process can be reflected in the way in
which the individual engages with the materials. Reactions of disgust
vs. pleasure or reluctance vs. eagerness can be inferred through facial
expressions, body movements, and associated verbalization, including
that which appears unrelated to the ongoing art-making. The point,
which is difficult to articulate since it involves largely nonverbal phenomena, is that the art therapist ought to be attentive to all aspects of
the patient's working process. The reason for this is simple: all are

diagnostic data which are available and should therefore be attended to and understood throughout treatment, not only at the time of assessment or evaluation.

Those relatively unsubtle and easily specifiable aspects of process such as the sequence in which items are made, are not necessarily noticed automatically. The therapist must learn to record and to retrieve such information through practice, until recalling the order of creative events becomes a truly autonomous ego function (Hartmann, 1958). It is not too difficult to learn to note a product's place in a series; and it is possible, especially in individual art therapy, to note the sequence of acts within a single work of art. If one believes in psychic determinism (that all behavior is lawful and unfolds in a psychologically comprehensible way), such close observations become extremely valuable for understanding both the patient and his product.

Since detailed notation of all behaviors associated with a creative process is indeed demanding, it is no wonder that art therapists might sometimes shrink from this difficult task. One compensation for the high level of attentiveness necessary, however, is that the payoff in ultimate understanding is considerable. Being an active observer can also be a great deal of fun. If one is to make use of an individual's working process as part of one's data base, then one must learn how to observe accurately and sensitively, and on many dimensions simultaneously.

Turning one's energies toward active observation also lessens the likelihood of one of the greatest abuses in the field of art therapy—the therapist's intrusiveness during the creative process. It takes a good deal of experience and trial and error with each patient to find the optimal level of intervention over time, as well as during any particular creative act. What is essential is that the art therapist have sufficient respect for the patient's creative process not to interfere with its organic evolution. Ironically, this is more likely to happen in groups because of the impossibility of intervening with everyone at once, although the difficulty of observing the kinds of subtle aspects of process noted earlier is also greater. The clinician must make choices—with a family, for example—whether to observe an individual's working process, or to focus on the interactions between family members. In either case, however, I believe that time spent observing carefully is time well spent for learning and understanding, and which is the therapist's responsibility. Observation also allows the patient(s) to engage without interruption in a natural kind of creative process.

Am I suggesting that one never intervene when a patient is working quietly? Not at all. There are times when such an intervention is called

for, as when a neurotic patient is using his absorption in the art process primarily as an escape from difficult issues in the transference; or when an isolated member of a group is unable to initiate contact with others, yet needs some affirmation from the therapist. I am simply suggesting that art therapists err more often on the side of intrusiveness, perhaps because they mistakenly think they are not doing their proper thera-peutic jobs if they remain silent. I once saw a book, however, with the lovely title, *Art is a Quiet Place*. And so it is, or at least it should be.

In summary, the creative process itself is an essential element of art therapy, regardless of the clinician's particular theoretical orientation. In order to make such an experience available to patients, the art ther-apist must not only know the specific processes of work with particular media, but also know and respect the conditions essential to genuine creative activity. One needs to provide both a "framework" for artistic freedom, and a consistently facilitating presence during the activity itself. And in order to fully comprehend (and therefore fully assist) any patient, the art therapist must learn to observe the working process on many, often subtle dimensions simultaneously, and to intervene in a way that promotes its fulfillment.

REFERENCES

Burkhart, R.C. *Spontaneous and deliberate ways of learning*. Scranton, PA: International Text-book, 1962.

Hartmann, H. *Ego psychology and the problem of adaptation*. New York: International Uni-versities Press, 1958.

Rubin, J.A., Schachter, J., & Ragins, N. Intraindividual variability in human figure draw-ings: A developmental study. *American Journal of Orthopsychiatry*, 1983, 53, 654-667.

Active involvement in a creative process often means "letting go."

Feelings about the self are involved in the making and showing of most creative products.

Chapter 3

Knowing Products

Knowing products is simple, according to some. One just learns the meanings of different elements and can then translate the messages in patients' art, saying with conviction, *"This* (shape, color, or subject matter) means *that."* Of course, there are meanings in products, in formal qualities, and in content; but they are not to be found in neat formulas or simple recipes. Those generalizations which are in current usage are useful as an indication of possibilities, sometimes probabilities, but never certainties. Human beings, after all, are complex creatures, and so is their expressive behavior and the products that arise therefrom.

There exists a strong emphasis in art therapy, however, on products which are the visible, concrete outcome of any creative process. While I do not subscribe to the notion implied by some that there can be "art therapy" without art materials (with the patient as medium and the clinician as artist?), I do feel that an overemphasis on the product can deflect the therapist's attention from the person and the process by which he creates it. At times, this concern with the product may not only create observational blind spots, but also lead to nontherapeutic interventions, like working on a patient's creation in order to "improve" it, thereby devaluing the person.

Despite the tendency of art therapists to sometimes overemphasize products with both patients and other professionals, learning to read the language of art as expressed in products is essential to good art therapy. Indeed, without a psychologically trained eye, the art therapist does not really deserve to be thought of as a clinician. Psychologically

sophisticated vision is needed to be able to decipher issues related to development, deviance, and dynamics, and to use all components of the language of art—form, content, and the relationships between the two.

Art therapists have much to contribute as well as to learn about both development and dynamics. A knowledge of normal development in general and in art specifically is, of course, critical for accurate diagnosis and eventual treatment. Since art therapists work with all expressive media, and with many populations deviating in complex ways from the norm, we have much to discover regarding the "mapping" of normal and deviant art development, beyond what is already known about such limited expressive activities as human figure drawing.

We probably also have a good deal to add to the growing knowledge base about hemispheric dominance, and the functions of different parts of the brain. We can contribute little, however, if we have not fully digested and integrated the many bits and pieces of developmental knowledge about art expression already available. This is a difficult task, because the information comes from a variety of disciplines, like child development, art education, psychology, and psychoanalysis. Any well-informed art therapist ought to be aware of what is already known about art development, and ought to have integrated such knowledge into a clinical vision, so that developmental determinations can be easily and securely made.

As for psychodynamics, the art therapist might have much to say about the operation of various coping mechanisms, and about their relationship to internal strivings and to both internal and external constraints. There is even more to be clarified in the realm of symbolic meaning, choice of imagery, and the relationship of particular images to the creator and the conditions of creation. However, in order to "read" anything at all from patient art, the clinician must know well both sides of the diagnostic coin, i.e., have a basic understanding of all aspects of development (not just art), and a clear comprehension of at least one coherent theory of psychodynamic functioning. The clinician must also be able to perceive and to decipher the language of art itself, before it can be translated into any kind of meaning or significance.

There are two essential ways to regard any art product, whether one is thinking developmentally or dynamically: in terms of form and of content. There is also, as with art and therapy, an *interface* between the two, where form itself becomes the content of the work of art. Some art therapists have an unfortunate bias in this regard, focusing primarily on one or the other element. While emphasizing one item at a time may

be useful as a learning exercise, it cannot do justice to the richness of any art product, which necessarily includes both, each with vital messages for the clinician.

KNOWING FORM

The formal elements in art are many, and include not only general ones (such as organization), but also those specific to particular media (such as color or shading). There are some elements that apply to work in all materials. These include: the degree of organization, clarity, completeness, originality, age-appropriateness, expansiveness, simplicity, activity, and balance of the work. The first five items are related primarily to quality, while the last four relate more to style. Yet even such dimensions as these, while applicable to all two- and three-dimensional products, are manifest in distinct ways as a function of the medium involved.

Specific to different media are additional formal qualities, all of which should be part of the mental checklist of any competent art therapist. Pencil drawings, for example, can be considered in terms of line quality, which itself includes such distinct variables as darkness, thickness, sharpness, smoothness, and the relationship of the line to other formal elements (such as mass or space). With the addition of color in a drawing medium (whether pencil, crayon, or chalk), the art therapist can also assess such aspects as hue and intensity; and with a fluid medium (such as marker or paint), the quality of the strokes becomes relevant, with categories somewhat different from those appropriate to pencil or crayon. The interaction between these formal elements must also be considered. Are some colors linear and others in masses? How do they relate in space? Do they touch or are they separated, and, if separated, by space or by line? What are the relative sizes of different elements, and their sequence in the making of a product? And so on. . . .

While the artist considers all such formal elements in relation to aesthetic criteria, the art therapist is also concerned with their possible significance in terms of development, personality style, coping strategies, and symbolic meaning. Thus, each aspect of a work of art is rich in multiple messages. A mass of yellow paint can be seen not only in terms of its intensity or solidity, but also in regard to its placement on the page, its relationship to other elements in the painting, its relative size, its particular shape, and its symbolic meaning for the individual. Does it imply flatness or three-dimensionality, lightness or heaviness? Is it meant to be something, or does it resemble something when re-

garded projectively by the artist? When in the context of the entire sequence of events does it get placed in the picture space? Is it modified in any way by the artist in the course of completing the work? What developmental level is suggested by its form in the context of the whole? From what developmental level are the thematic issues it represents? Does it seem to be primarily expressive or primarily defensive? And so on. . . .

KNOWING CONTENT

The content of a work of art would seem at first glance to be a fairly simple matter; but upon reflection it, too, becomes complex. For content in any communication can be considered in at least two ways—manifest and latent. And, if one embraces the psychoanalytic theory of mental topography, content can be thought of as emanating from either conscious, preconscious, or unconscious levels of the mind. While these two ways of categorizing content levels are connected, that relationship, too, is not as simple as it seems. For manifest content, while presumably conscious, is not always something of which the maker is aware. In fact, what is "visible" can even come as a surprise ("Oh! I didn't realize I had drawn a bird here!"), suggesting that it emanates from a preconscious rather than a fully conscious level of mental awareness.

It is also useful to think of content in terms of the themes therein, which can be classified developmentally (e.g., oral, anal, phallic), and can also be thought of dynamically (e.g., aggression toward others, toward the self, etc.). In order to make such determinations about the meanings inherent in the represented or projected content of a work of art, it is best to have observed the sequence involved in its creation, and the many associations, both verbal and nonverbal, expressed by the artist. The art alone is never enough, yet in its associative context (like the dream) it is a rich source of understanding. This context includes behaviors directly related to the particular product, as well as those which precede and follow it. The repetition of either form or content is a signal that something is significant to the patient. Repeated images within a product or in different products alert the therapist to the intensity of the artist's message, though a single subtle "slip" of form or content can be equally important, albeit less comfortable for the person to perceive or express.

Content can be quite logical, making conceptual as well as perceptual sense. It can also be quite illogical, either perceptually (Escher) or conceptually (psychotic art). While both form and content may be parallel

on the logic continuum, they can also be diametrically opposed—as with an orderly, clearly depicted drawing, painting, or sculpture of creatures that are pure fantasy. It is sometimes said that images are the main language of primary process thought, while words provide a tongue for the secondary process. Yet either words or images can express either primary or secondary process thought, as in neologisms (primary process words) or surrealistic art (secondary process imagery).

So content is not simply a matter of identifying the "what" of a deliberately depicted image or a projected visual idea, and then classifying it developmentally or symbolically. This is just the first stage of understanding, and even at that level, one must also consider the spatial and temporal relationship of one aspect of subject matter to another. A wild animal baring its teeth alone on a picture space is a far different statement from the same animal shown inside a cage. Even an animal plus a cage is a different equation, depending on whether the cage or the animal is created first. And in this complex area of form/content relationships, one must consider what is usually called "style," whereby the manner itself, in which formal elements are expressed, carries a kind of symbolic meaning. Style is often thought of in human and dramatic ways, such as "voluptuous," "passionate," "cold," "detached," "loose," "fussy," etc.

While all of these elements of art are visible in the finished product, anyone who has observed the process from start to finish knows that much of the drama therein is hidden in the final outcome. To be able to get the richest and most therapeutically useful understanding from products, it is optimal to observe the entire process of their creation. Such aspects as sequence, tempo, rhythm, and associated verbal and nonverbal behaviors are indeed associations to the elements in an artistic product. Unlike a dream, revealed in consciousness but produced in sleep, art is created while awake, its very development visible to both artist and therapist.

Because I believe that the deepest understanding for anyone comes from within, it does not make sense for the art therapist to impose either form or content on the patient. Only when what has been created comes as completely as possible from the individual can its meaning be fully valid for understanding that person. Of course, there are exceptions, which will be discussed in the *Interface* section of the book. But for the purpose of knowing people by their products, our comprehension is most valid when based on something emanating as fully as possible from the person himself.

PART II

The Therapy Part

This section of the book is rather generic, in that the subject matter is probably relevant for all kinds of therapists. However, since the term "therapy" is so casually bandied about with so many different meanings, it may be helpful to note those aspects of psychology, psychopathology, and psychotherapy that are most critical for art therapists. As with the *Art Part*, it never hurts to know more, and specific settings or populations may demand further understanding in one or another area. Any art therapist has an ethical, as well as a professional, responsibility to gather that additional knowledge in order to do the job properly. Just as a painter may need to learn more about wood sculpture in order to reach troubled adolescents who are easily "turned on" to that mode of expression, so a therapist who has worked primarily with individuals may need to study family systems and therapy, if asked to do family art evaluation or therapy at a child guidance center.

There are, however, some basics, as with art, that every art therapist should know—basics that do not enter one's head through intuition or osmosis, but which require some kind of study, formal or informal. These basics are the subject matter of the first three chapters in this section. The initial one deals with development, both normal and abnormal; the second deals with deviations and dynamics, both individual and interpersonal; and the third deals with therapy, focusing on the necessary framework, the relationships therein, and the process of treatment over time. In each, general understandings are briefly noted, along with some specific issues relevant to art therapy in particular.

31

A final chapter deals with knowing art therapy and being an art therapist. This includes becoming clear about one's identity, through understanding the relationship of art to other action therapies (such as activity, occupational, and recreation therapies), as well as to other creative therapies (such as music, drama, and dance therapies). In addition to knowing how art therapy is similar to and different from related disciplines, attention is also given to the beliefs seen as necessary for the effective art therapist. Finally, there is a brief description of some of the personal qualities that seem essential for a good art therapist, including knowledge of the self. With the foundation laid in the first two sections of the book, it will then be possible to go on to the art therapy situation itself, which is the subject matter of the third portion, *The Interface*.

*At different stages in his art therapy, this boy used drama spon-
taneously. Here he responds to a Greek sculpture in a museum
by "telling off" the adult.*

Mother-child art activities help clarify developmental issues.

Chapter 4

Knowing Development

Knowing normal human development is vital to the practice of good art therapy. While one might suppose that the most important aspect of growth for an art therapist is what happens over time when people use art materials, by itself that is far from sufficient. Although a detailed knowledge of development in drawing, painting, and modeling is essential in order to recognize deviations from the norm, art expression cannot be arbitrarily divorced from the totality of human growth. Art therapists, while they deal with and through art, are ultimately responsible for understanding and helping the human beings who become their patients as whole people.

One might also suppose that a detailed knowledge of normal development is vital only if an art therapist works primarily with children. While that may seem superficially valid, many believe that no adult can be fully understood without an awareness of the historical roots of his or her problems. Although there are some theories of personality and psychotherapy that place little or no emphasis on the genetic origins of behavior, it is my own conviction that dealing only in the here and now is—like dealing solely with the art—unnecessarily narrow and limited, and ultimately unfair to the patient.

Whatever the age of the person one treats, it is best for any effort at understanding or helping to know about his development over time, including "roots" (history of parents, grandparents, extended family, etc.). The old dichotomy of nature vs. nurture has slowly been supplanted by a more complex understanding of multiple causation.

Whether thought of narrowly in terms of birth order, or broadly in terms of socioeconomic/cultural matrix, any individual's development reflects a dynamic interaction between genetic givens and environmental influences. Both kinds of information are relevant when the therapist takes a historical, developmental perspective, regardless of the patient's age at the time of referral.

However, reading or taking a developmental history is as limited in usefulness as requesting or seeing a drawing, if the art therapist does not know how to make sense out of it. In order to classify, categorize, and fully comprehend historical information, it is necessary to have a frame of reference, i.e., a clear conception of normal and abnormal development. At the risk of oversimplifying, I should like to suggest that there are some aspects of development which matter more than others for the practice of good art therapy. In addition to knowing normal artistic progression, an art therapist needs to be familiar primarily with social and emotional development, and secondarily with those specific cognitive functions involved in both making and perceiving works of art.

In other words, while it is helpful to know all of the expectable ages and sequences for the mastery of all developmental tasks, it is especially important for an art therapist to be familiar with what usually happens in the areas of sensory and perceptual functioning, as well as in reality testing and synthesizing. This becomes critical if an art therapist works with handicapped individuals of any age, who often require some pre-art preparatory or remedial activities of a sensory/perceptual nature in order to be able eventually to use art materials creatively. Similarly, though it is helpful to be familiar with all aspects of normal motor development, it is vital for an art therapist to know in detail about the specific fine motor behaviors involved in physically working with materials.

But physical development cannot really be understood independently of psychological growth (any more than cognitive development can be looked at independently of emotional growth). In fact, a growing body of evidence about the intimate relationship between soma and psyche seems to validate many dynamic hypotheses about the possible psychogenesis of such "physical" disabilities as asthma, allergies, and many kinds of learning problems often thought to be organically based (cf. Alexander, 1965). Even when there is no question about the reality of a physical handicap, the interdependence of mental and physical functioning is so great that the degree of impairment may be greatly magnified by psychological variables.

I find myself thinking of a number of children with whom I have worked who suffered from what psychologists call a specific learning disability, and who did indeed test as deviant from the norm in such areas as auditory or visual processing. Yet many of these children, after a period of successful art therapy, turned out to be able to learn mathematics or reading at a much higher level and faster rate than was earlier thought possible. That does not mean, by the way, that the minimal brain damage presumably involved in the specific learning disability was magically reversed, or that the children tested any differently on diagnostic instruments. It does mean, however, that the psychological problems which compounded the physiological ones, once removed, no longer inhibited the full use of the child's mental capacities—including his ability to benefit from the remedial teaching of compensatory learning strategies. I think, too, of many blind youngsters, whose sensory handicap could not be undone, but who after therapy were able to learn more easily and to move more freely than before. It was not the blindness alone, but the inhibitions caused by the maladaptive coping mechanisms used by these children, that had made the mastery of braille or mobility so very difficult.

It is not uncommon for apparently appropriate remedial efforts to be made in regard to specific problems, which eventually turn out to be psychological in origin and therefore require a different kind of therapy. I think of an almost mute girl with a severe articulation disorder, who was referred for art therapy after a painfully long history of evaluations, diagnoses, and treatments by doctors, developmental specialists, and speech therapists. Although she had suffered several convulsions, and there was indeed some mild retardation, her dramatic response in expressive therapy revealed that the blocks which had stood in her linguistic and intellectual path were largely psychological. Within less than a year of weekly individual sessions, she was talking more clearly and with fairly well-organized language, surprising all who knew her—her parents, her teacher, her former speech therapist, and myself as well. While she had also progressed several grade levels in basic skills during the year of treatment, she was still better off in a special class where she could get the greater personal attention that was optimal for her. But she no longer required speech therapy or medication, and was able to move along quite normally into adolescence.

There have even been some instances in my experience where almost all of an apparent handicap turned out to have been psychogenic. A boy of 18, who had been in classes for the retarded throughout his academic life, had scored consistently low on tests of intelligence. However, after

a little over a year of individual expressive therapy (stimulated by a period of suicidal depression), not only was he feeling happier and more outgoing, but he was also moved into the regular high school program in his school, on a normal educational track for the first time in his life. Perhaps the fact that he was also blind and had a seizure disorder affected the ability of diagnosticians to see the latent intelligence in this boy. This case, while tragic and ironic, is also profoundly instructive and serves as a reminder that the arts are often able to elicit the healthy capacities of patients, where other modes cannot. Whether it was the working through of his rage, the pleasure in his own creativity, or both, the experience with expressive therapy for this youngster revealed what had been seen as a genetic given (his retardation) to be a functional developmental delay.

Professionals and parents are used to thinking of some physical symptoms (like enuresis or asthma) as possibly or probably psychological in origin. This seems to be less true, however, for inhibitions in learning or motility, which are often seen as physiologically based. As we begin to understand more fully the functioning and flexibility of the human brain, it is likely that a treatment such as art therapy might be useful, not only because it deals with psychological conflict, but also because the very nature of the modality involves the activation of different parts of the human mind. Given the need for integration and synthesis in organized thought and action, a visual *and* verbal modality, which involves translation from one mode into the other, has tremendous potential for the promotion of higher and healthier mental functioning.

It is, after all, primarily mental functioning with which any psychotherapist is concerned. It therefore makes sense that the most important aspect of development for an art therapist to be knowledgeable about is mental—both cognition and affect. I find Piaget (Gruber & Vonèche, 1977) and Freud (1939) to be the most useful guides to intellectual and emotional growth, respectively, as well as some of those who have elaborated on and extended their original findings. Erikson (1964) is especially helpful because he includes more of the sociocultural matrix, while Anna Freud's (1965) work is useful because she has helped to delineate the various lines of development involved in normal maturation, and has suggested a coherent way of organizing data (the diagnostic profile). To consider both cognition and affect seems quite compatible to me, and I suspect we will see further attempts to integrate them in the future, as in the work of Greenspan (1980). Although early developmental study emphasized childhood and adolescence, it is also

useful to supplement one's frame of reference with investigations of infancy and the years of adulthood.

This book is not the place to restate specifics about psychological development that are detailed elsewhere. But, as with media and processes, it might be appropriate to remind art therapists of the importance of *all* stages and phases, and of the special significance of certain aspects of normal development. For example, with a child patient it is important to inquire about the meaning of the particular pregnancy and child to both parents, especially the mother. Also critical is the way in which the child, as an infant, adjusted to the stimuli and demands of the physical and social world. What kind of temperament was inborn, and how was it perceived and felt by the mother, especially in terms of her own way of being (cf. CIBA, 1982)? Was there a comfortable "fit" between mother and child, or was there tension and dissynchrony (cf. Lewis & Rosenblum, 1974)? And, as the child became aware of his separateness, how did both partners in the symbiotic twosome deal with the tasks and subphases of the separation-individuation process?

When the world changed for the child from a dyadic to a triadic one, how did he deal with the challenge of incorporating beloved but inherently rivalrous others (father, siblings) into his life space? Was he able to venture and explore as his universe expanded? How did he relate to those beyond the family circle: peers, babysitters, teachers? What were the school years like in regard to learning, social behavior, and all of the developmental tasks of childhood? What happened in adolescence—that period of massive change, inevitable instability, and potential for both pain and pleasure? And so on, through the primary psychosexual and psychosocial tasks of young, middle, and late adulthood. Whatever the age of the patient, it is important to ask for childhood recollections in general; it is also very useful to inquire about the person's earliest memory. Whatever is recalled is sure to be significant, and often one image of the distant past will stimulate others.

The reader may be wondering why it seems so important to know a patient's history in order to understand his or her problems. Whether the person in distress is a child or an adult, the very fact that there is an inability to cope with the demands of life in the present means that at some point or other, his development did not proceed in a completely "normal" fashion (with the possible exception of "reactive" disorders). If one thinks of human development as similar to building with blocks—something like a pyramid, in that so many vital tasks occur in early childhood—then it makes sense that if there are weaknesses or

gaps at any point along the line, they will create a structure with an inherent vulnerability to stress. Even though certain developmental tasks may not have been fully accomplished, the biological maturational thrust of succeeding stages will demand dealing with other tasks, which the individual is poorly equipped to master. In other words, a person who has not fully resolved a separation-individuation process in early childhood has many difficulties with succeeding phases, and is unable to master later challenges, such as the oedipal conflict or the definition of his or her sexual and personal identity.

Many of the clues about developmental lags, fixation points, or arrests are available in the patient as he presents himself in the present. His behavior and his artwork both give indications of unresolved issues and the developmental levels to which they belong. A history is very useful, however, as a way of validating one's clinical "hunches" about *when* things went off a normal track. Making sense out of a history, therefore, requires more than a coherent sense of development. It also requires an ability on the part of the art therapist to relate what she has learned about a person's past to the hypotheses she has developed based on what goes on in art interviews—behavior, images, and associations.

While an art therapist ought to know in depth and detail about normal psychological development, it is especially important to be familiar with what is known about the particular mental functions involved in creative work. There is some evidence from the investigations of psychologists that intelligence and creativity, as they are currently defined and measured, are independent capacities (Getzels & Jackson, 1962). So, in addition to understanding what is known about the overall development of the intellect and its ability to solve problems, it is also important for an art therapist to be familiar with what is known about the growth and development of creative thinking abilities. Related, but not identical, are the areas of fantasy, imagination, and play, all of which are necessarily involved in any creative act. The growth over time of the capacity to think and act symbolically, as well as to differentiate fantasy from reality, are particularly critical for art therapists, working as we do in a symbolic mode.

Of equivalent interest to art therapists, then, is a person's creative history, as far back as the individual (and, if a child, the parents) can remember. What kind of play activities and materials were preferred in infancy, early childhood, latency, and adolescence? If an adult, what is the current place of the arts in the patient's recreational life? And, whatever the age, what is the role of fantasy, imagination, and daydreaming for this person? Art therapists are naturally interested in the patient's

past and present relationship to art, both as maker and viewer. Attention should also be paid to the patient's propensity for "visual thinking" in general.

If an art therapist is involved in the diagnostic evaluation of a patient, in addition to being able to discover much through both process and products, it is also possible to use art to look more "directly" at a person's history. Many ways of asking patients to represent themselves over time have been suggested, usually as a pictorial or abstract representation of feelings, events, and/or people over the life span (perhaps on a long roll of paper). As with a verbal history, what is selected and how it is expressed are both significant. Another approach is to ask for representations (pictorial or abstract) of self or others (such as family) at one or more moments in the past, in the present, and perhaps in the future as well. The powerful, expressive language of form and color adds another dimension to the usual history-taking exercise.

Whether or not art is involved in the data-gathering process, when all of the available information on someone's life story is in, then the clinician can begin to organize that information for a fuller understanding of the problems bringing the person to therapy. My own theoretical bias is psychoanalytic, and I therefore find the Developmental Profile to be an extremely useful way of organizing clinical data, including historical information (Eissler et al., 1977). There are, of course, other formal and informal ways of conceptualizing the past and its influence on present functioning. What matters most is not the specific frame of reference used, but that there be some coherent framework in the art therapist's mind for making psychological sense out of a patient's developmental history.

Even if one does not believe in a theory of mental functioning that sees conflict as dynamically rooted, a clear image of normal development is essential in order to identify any kind of distortion or deviation therefrom. Although definitions of abnormality vary considerably from one orientation to another, and there are many who find diagnostic classifications inadequate, one cannot function in a psychiatric setting without some understanding of psychopathology and of the terms used to categorize different kinds of psychic disorders. Similarly, one cannot function in an educational setting without a clear comprehension of the current understanding of different types of exceptionality.

When development goes awry at any point in a person's life, whether the disability is inborn or acquired as the result of some physical or psychological stress, then subsequent development is necessarily affected. In order to not only name the problem but also understand its

etiology, one must know its historical origins. Only with this kind of underpinning can a therapist know how best to help a patient. Whether a phobia is being treated by behavior modification or analytic art therapy, the clinician needs to know the history of the person, if only in regard to the symptom. I also believe that developmental understanding leads to the most meaningful kind of psychodynamic formulation, the area to be considered in the next chapter.

REFERENCES

Alexander, F. *Psychosomatic medicine*. New York: W.W. Norton, 1965.

CIBA Foundation. *Temperamental differences in infants and young children*. CIBA Symposium 89. London: Pitman, 1982.

Eissler, R.S., Kris, M., & Solnit, A.J. (Eds.). *Psychoanalytic assessment: The diagnostic profile*. New Haven: Yale University Press, 1977.

Erikson, E.H. *Childhood and society* (2nd ed.). New York: W.W. Norton, 1964.

Freud, A. *Normality and pathology in childhood: Assessments of development*. New York: International Universities Press, 1965.

Freud, S. An outline of psychoanalysis (1939). New York: W.W. Norton, 1949.

Getzels, J.W., & Jackson, P.W. *Creativity and intelligence*. New York: Wiley, 1962.

Greenspan, S.I. *Intelligence and adaptation: An integration of psychoanalytic and Piagetian developmental psychology*. New York: International Universities Press, 1980.

Gruber, H.E., & Vonèche, J.J. (Eds.). *The essential Piaget: An interpretive reference and guide*. New York: Basic Books, 1977.

Lewis, M., & Rosenblum, L.A. (Eds.). *The effect of the infant on its caregiver*. New York: Wiley, 1974.

A little girl models with play dough during her individual art therapy as an outpatient at a child guidance clinic.

Monsters of all sorts are one way for children to give artistic form to aggressive impulses and ambivalent feelings.

Chapter 5

Knowing Dynamics
and Deviations

Knowing dynamics, as I am using the term, has to do with knowing why people function as they do, i.e., understanding the psychological causality of behavior in a broad sense and of symptoms (deviations) in a narrow one. As with development, an art therapist ought to be familiar with all of the major theories of personality and psychopathology currently in use, as well as deeply and thoroughly knowledgeable about at least one. Despite tremendous strides in recent years in the understanding of the neurobiological substrate, which has revolutionized the treatment of serious mental disorders, the experts are still far from being able to quantify all of the influences and outcomes in this complex area (cf. Wender & Klein, 1981). Existing theories represent useful hypotheses about why people act and think as they do, and are important to be aware of in order to not only communicate with colleagues, but also to further one's own efforts at understanding and helping patients through art.

Although there are significant differences between different theoretical approaches, there are also many commonalities. In fact, my own belief is that they are rarely mutually exclusive and are more often complementary. Each can be conceptualized as one of numerous blind men examining an elephant, focusing on one aspect of human psychology more than another. Or they can be thought of as propositions which vary, because the angles from which they sight their subject are not the same; or as different stains on a microscope slide, which enable different aspects of the phenomenon studied to become clearly visible. The ex-

citing challenge for an art therapist is to integrate these partially perceived truths from the particular perspective of art therapy itself, and the creative process which is its core.

Pragmatically, an art therapist cannot function in the mental health world of today without an awareness of the major theoretical approaches to understanding and modifying human behavior: behavioral, cognitive, nondirective, humanistic, existential, Jungian, Freudian, and all of the many formulations based on the latter, especially those of Perls (Gestalt) and Sullivan. Similarly, an art therapist in an educational setting must be familiar with different theories/explanations of learning problems and their remediation. An art therapist also needs to know and understand the labels for psychopathology and exceptionality in current usage.

Although it is somewhat artificial to separate theories of psychodynamics from questions of nosology, I do so largely because art therapists experience frequent confusion in this area. So often there is a defensive use of diagnostic terminology, as if by labeling a patient with a word we automatically understand why he behaves as he does. Whether the label is one describing overt behavior (such as "oppositional"), or implying causality (such as "passive-aggressive"), having defined the problem, the etiology seems to be assumed as simple and known, or, for some clinicians, irrelevant to the treatment. This confusion seems even greater when the label is one which has multiple referents, and conjures up a constellation of both symptomatology and etiology, such as "borderline" or "schizophrenic." While it is true that art therapists have a responsibility to comprehend the diagnostic terminology in current usage, the desire for simple formulations may be as pervasive in this area as in that of understanding patient artwork.

Although they differ as to the importance of etiological understanding for the patient himself, all current theories seem to agree that people with psychological problems are unable, for some reason, to deal comfortably and effectively with the tasks and stresses of their lives. Whether the disorder is pervasive and extensive or narrowly confined to some particular area, all approaches try to define as specifically as possible the reason(s) why the patient is unable to cope in a healthy, adaptive way. Naturally, the therapeutic approach depends heavily on one's understanding of the causes of the problem. Some feel that maladaptive behaviors are learned and can therefore be unlearned, as in behavior modification or cognitive therapy. Others are convinced that overt symptomatology, although possibly modifiable, is but the tip of an internal, conflictual iceberg, which itself must be resolved in order for the person to function freely, as in psychoanalytic therapies.

Whether the patient is seen individually, as part of a group, or with his family, an art therapist needs to have some way of understanding what goes on inside of him and why. As with developmental theory, I have found the psychoanalytic approach to dynamics to be the most useful in my own work. The notion that there are different parts of the personality which can be in painful tension seems to "fit" the clinical data of both people and their art products. That there are drives or strivings in all of us and that successful living involves finding ways of satisfying our yearnings that are acceptable to ourselves and our environment make good common as well as clinical sense. Perhaps it is the comprehensiveness of analytic theory that makes it seem so useful, though I suspect that there are other reasons why I and many art therapists find it so congenial.

For example, any artist knows from direct experience of the process that the source of creativity is rarely clear or articulate at a conscious level. Sensing that the imagery and gestures they employ come from some place within, artists have always been like depth psychologists, exploring and expressing the inner self. It makes sense, then, that art therapists would be attracted to depth psychological theories which postulate a dynamic unconscious, like those of Freud and Jung. I have had the rare personal advantage of undergoing full classical (Freudian) psychoanalytic training with both children and adults—a rich experience involving simultaneous personal analysis, didactic instruction in theory and technique, and closely supervised clinical work with patients. Since the children I see in analysis use art media extensively, it has been possible to apply the theoretical understanding of psychodynamics to patient art as well as to other forms of expression, like dreams and mental imagery. There is no question that, having invested so much time, energy, and money in the study of psychoanalysis, I am far from unbiased. But it is also relevant that I was drawn to study that particular approach, because the supervisors who were most helpful to me in my first decade as an art therapist were all analysts.

Despite my own bias for understanding dynamics in terms of id, ego, and superego, I do respect other orientations when the art therapist fully understands what she is doing. Many early studies of the effectiveness of psychotherapy concluded that the most significant variable may not be the theoretical orientation of the therapist, but rather the ability of that individual to empathize and to relate to the patient (cf. Wolberg, 1977). Although this would imply at the extreme that it is not knowing about art or therapy but being the right sort of person that really matters, that is a rather foolish conclusion. While such findings

do validate the importance of personal qualities in effective therapy, they do not thereby nullify the need for understanding and helping in a clearly conceptualized fashion.

As I look back at my earliest work with patients in art therapy, when I had little formal knowledge or training, I think that any success I may have had was due to the healing power of the modality, along with some relevant personal qualities. But I also believe quite firmly that, had I known then what I know today, I could have done a much better job of helping those early patients. Although I have learned much through supervision and other experiences about both theory and technique, it seems that the most useful learning for my work in art therapy has been in the area of psychodynamics, primarily in a richer and clearer under-standing of intrapsychic functioning within a developmental frame of reference.

In addition to general issues of psychodynamic functioning and its development under normal and pathological conditions, an art therapist needs to know in some detail and depth about the particular dynamics of creative behavior, especially in the visual arts. Admittedly theoretical, like all hypotheses of psychodynamics, those notions about why human beings are motivated to create are most relevant to our work. As with other aspects of psychology, it is important to be familiar with all of the most common theoretical formulations. Whether one agrees with the-ories that regard the creative act as primarily compensatory or with those that see it as a striving for self-actualization is not as important as being aware of different ways of perceiving its motivation and meaning.

Moreover, since human beings do not grow and develop in isolation, but in relationship to others, it is impossible to think about psychody-namics without considering interpersonal relationships as well. Even those who are convinced that psychological problems can become in-ternalized do not deny or disavow the importance of interpersonal dy-namics, whether in the family, the peer group, or the therapeutic dyad. Although some theories give more weight to environmental effects than others, and some approaches intervene directly with the interpersonal matrix (like family therapy), all ways of understanding psychological functioning and stress include both the individual and his relationships with others.

It is therefore essential for an art therapist to understand interpersonal as well as intrapsychic dynamics. In addition to reading and learning about how and why people relate as they do, it is extremely helpful to have the experience of being a member of an unstructured group which examines its own process. Whether the group is thought of as a learning

experience or as psychotherapy, an absence of predefined structure allows group dynamics to emerge quite naturally, organically, and dramatically. Anyone who has been involved in such an intensive group experience, like that modeled on the work of Bion (1959), knows much more about the powerful forces at work than any amount of reading alone can convey. Although individual dynamics and developmental considerations are relevant to understanding group process, there are additional ways of conceptualizing families and other systems that take into account the forces among and between multiple individuals.

As with a developmental history, art materials can be used in many ways to elicit meaningful data about the family, the group of origin. Most approaches to family art evaluation include a request for some open-ended work from each member (free product or one developed from a scribble, initial, or other stimulus), some representation of the family by each member, and some joint art task in which all participate. In addition to the interpersonal dynamics which become evident in the symbolic content of the products, behavioral data are also available for the art therapist, who can observe the many formal and informal reactions to one another among family members.

While comprehending group process and dynamics is vital for group art therapy, and knowing about family systems is essential for family art therapy, these understandings are equally relevant for the art therapist who sees individuals. For even in a one-to-one situation, there is in fact a group in the room. In reality, it is the therapist and the patient; but, in "psychic reality," there may be others "present" in varied and complex ways. Since the understanding of what is going on in a therapy situation and why has some elements specific to that very unique and special event, the following chapter on therapy itself will deal with knowing the framework, the relationship, and the nature of the therapeutic process over time.

REFERENCES

Bion, W.R. *Experiences in groups.* New York: Basic Books, 1959.

Wender, P.H., & Klein, D.F. *Mind, mood and medicine: A guide to the new bio-psychiatry.* New York: Farrar, Straus & Giroux, 1981.

Wolberg, L. *The technique of psychotherapy, Volume 2* (3rd ed.). New York: Grune & Stratton, 1977, pp. 55-59.

Art therapy involves helping a person not only to create something, but also to reflect upon it thoughtfully. Here the therapist is writing down the child's story about her collage.

Chapter 6

Knowing Therapy

One area often neglected in art and other therapies is that of the framework—the physical and psychological conditions one establishes, within which therapy becomes possible. Only in a certain kind of clearly bounded and conceptualized frame is an individual of any age able to fully and freely let go of his usual inhibitions, whether verbal or artistic. A feeling of safety and continuity is an essential condition for revealing to another the private aspects of the self. A secure and predictable environment is also needed in order for an individual to be able to create freely and authentically with art media. Such conditions for creative work have already been alluded to in the chapter on processes.

Physically, the art therapist must create an environment which has a minimum of distraction and a maximum of conditions facilitating creativity. The latter would include adequate lighting, seating, working surfaces, and a clear and attractive arrangement of a variety of art media, with materials for drawing, painting, sculpting, and constructing. All of these should be kept as constant as possible, thereby creating a feeling of security, as well as the possibility of independent functioning on the part of the patient(s). As for space, it is ideal if there is the possibility of both closeness and distance, openness and privacy—that there are sufficient options so that the patient can be next to or far from others. Although the therapist might under certain conditions (such as a brief evaluation) want to structure the space so as to maximize the possibility

of observing the patient while he works, in general it is best to allow the individual some freedom in determining the degree of closeness, especially in the beginning.

With a family or a group, similar considerations are valid. Again, it is important to have adequate lighting, working space, and a variety of clearly arranged materials, all of which are consistent from one session to the next. On the other hand, the clinician might also want, for diagnostic or therapeutic reasons, to structure the situation so as to maximize interaction (such as sitting at a round table, or restricting materials so that sharing becomes necessary), without necessarily mandating it (as in a request for a joint project). In general, in art therapy over time with both families and groups, I have a personal preference for flexibility within the framework. This means providing options in working spaces as well as media and themes, in order to allow individuals to determine their own distance and degree of interaction with other patients as well as with the therapist.

I suspect that such a preference for an open-ended approach is another reason why I find psychoanalysis so congenial. For one of the assumptions of that technique is that patients will, given maximum freedom (of verbalization), express what is needed in order to understand their focal concerns and conflicts. Although the art therapy situation is radically different from that of adult analysis, where the patient is on the couch and restricted to verbalization, the basic premise that free expression (association) is the optimal route to the repressed (which is causing problems) still holds. This is, in fact, the essential technique in child analysis, where an open-ended kind of stance invites the youngster to play, draw, or talk, as the spirit moves him.

The framework in art therapy need not be as explicit or rigid as in psychoanalysis, but it must be as clearly understood and provided by the therapist in order for the patient to feel fully secure. This is more difficult in the psychological arena than in the physical, where the pressures for a variety of responses are inevitably strong, regardless of the age of the patient. For this reason, it is essential that the art therapist be very clear about her own boundaries, which necessarily reflect her conceptualization of the nature of art therapy and the consequent role of the clinician.

Although these notions differ from one individual and theory to another, what matters most is that the therapist be consistent. This applies to all behaviors in the presence of and regarding the patient, and requires being clear about one's own set of "rules and regulations." These "rules" refer to considerations such as limits—limits on patient behavior (such

as prohibiting destruction of property), as well as on therapist behavior (such as not becoming socially involved with patients). They refer in a broader and more complex manner to the ways in which the therapist continually monitors verbal interventions, whether running commentary, inquiry, confrontation, or interpretation. And, in art therapy, the clinician also needs to be clear in her own mind about guidelines for nonverbal interventions as well, especially in regard to the art process and products.

Some think that the best therapeutic stance is being spontaneous, free, flexible, responding intuitively to the patient and his art. While that may seem on the face of it to be creative, such behavior is really quite undisciplined, unthinking, and—more important—untherapeutic. For whatever her theoretical persuasion, an art therapist ought to know in general what position she takes in regard to a patient at any stage of the therapeutic process. It seems to me that the artistry of good therapy lies in being flexible, but within certain guidelines, rather than being either rigidly unbending or fluidly unpredictable. Neither of these extremes represents a useful model to a troubled patient, who requires an image of freedom with order, energy with control. Neither chaotic freedom nor constricting control represent anyone's notion of mentally healthy functioning. All psychotherapeutic theories and techniques aim, ultimately, at enabling people to be in charge of and able to use the energy and abilities they possess.

In addition to the romanticized notion of the "spontaneous" art therapist, there is another image which I find equally untherapeutic (despite its popularity with some existential clinicians)—that of the "authentic" art therapist who shares her "real self" with the patient. While there may be times and places and patients where it is appropriate to convey personal information, this is the exception rather than the rule. The main reason is that the sharing of such information reduces the usefulness of oneself as an object of projection (transference) on the part of the patient. A secondary reason for thinking it is unwise to become personal is that it is often exhibitionistic and self-indulgent, although a clever therapist can usually rationalize that it is done in the patient's interest. After all, an art therapist is supposed to use her time and skill in the service of the patient, not of herself. This seems so obvious that it shouldn't need to be said; but I feel a grave concern about some reports which suggest that some therapists are meeting their own needs as well as (or even instead of) those of their patients.

Of course, no one would enjoy being an art therapist if the work did not fulfill some genuine personal needs. But one should still be able to

remove one's selfish strivings from the actual therapeutic arena. This is often difficult because the patient may demand—may even plead for—behaviors on the part of the therapist which would be gratifying to both (like asking the therapist to work on his painting or to go out for coffee after a session). It is important to remember that therapy is not primarily an arena for gratification of either patient or clinician, despite the fact that in order to sustain the tensions and frustrations of the work there must be some genuine pleasures for both.

KNOWING THE RELATIONSHIP

A therapist cannot work with a patient over any substantial period of time without establishing some kind of working relationship. Whether formalized in a contract (written or oral) or informally agreed upon, whether explicit or implicit, therapy must be a partnership if it is to endure the inevitable stresses and strains of any internal change process. Some have called the establishment of a solid working relationship a therapeutic or working alliance, a useful concept. For, despite the therapist's striving for neutrality in regard to what the patient presents, the work of therapy implies that both partners are allied in an effort to help the patient to get well and to live better. With a group or a family, there must be alliances with all members individually, as well as a kind of working agreement with the unit.

Although most writers have emphasized the task of involving the *patient* in this pact, I believe that it takes time for *both* partners to make a genuine commitment. The patient, it is true, needs to overcome any distrust and anxiety he may feel about this new person, and strange new venture. But the *therapist* also undergoes a progressive understanding of the other person, his needs and his potential, which enables the clinician to fully invest in the mutual task. Both therapist and patient are likely to experience anxiety, frustration, discouragement, and even despair over the course of any sustained treatment. The alliance enables both to endure such strains, and also defines the relationship, even in its darkest hours, as a mutual partnership based on a fairly high level of trust and commitment on both sides.

Art therapists are in a rather favorable position in the establishment of an alliance with patients, since what we offer is not only ourselves but our modality as well. In a sense, then, the patient forms an alliance over time with both the therapist and the creative process. While art materials can be threatening, it is also true that they don't talk back, and that with increasing skill a patient can learn to make them say what he

wants them to. He learns, too, that they can help him to both express and understand himself, that they are part of what is offered by the art therapist, who also offers her clinical as well as her creative expertise. The patient gradually becomes attached to art as well as to the clinician in an unconflicted, goal-directed way, as a means to get well.

Parenthetically, art media are probably useful in the establishment of an alliance, because they are intrinsically pleasurable in a sensory/manipulative way. They may even minimize the pain involved at many stages of the therapeutic process, from assessment through treatment to termination. Also, for the patient who is able to learn to use materials to make products of which he feels proud, there is yet another aspect: Because creative activity has its own rewards, there are continual reinforcements of the patient as artist, which go beyond sensorimotor pleasure and provide genuine enhancement of self-confidence and self-esteem. All of this reward, intrinsic to the art process, adds a continual, intermittent reinforcement feature to art therapy. Such a schedule is known to be the most likely to promote continuation of the associated behavior, so that it is not surprising that a patient's commitment to the creative process and to art therapy itself tends to grow over time. Not only is the therapist seen as the person providing these opportunities and therefore someone positive, but also the opportunities themselves have sufficient built-in gratification to enable an alliance to form relatively rapidly and to become increasingly firm.

Of course, it is well known that any kind of therapy (even a behavioral or cognitive treatment) stirs up less rational kinds of feelings and wishes in the patient (transference) and in the clinician (countertransference). As I have written elsewhere (Rubin, 1982), I believe that the concept of transference is an especially congenial one for art therapists, since it parallels what we already know about symbolism in visual expression. Just as a color or image can stand for something because of an individual's past experience, so do people project ideas and feelings onto other human beings. Given the need to make sense out of experience, people tend to fill in what they don't know about any new person, just as they tend to complete a visual gestalt. Moved by both the need to organize the outside world and the pressure of inner conflicts, all human beings tend to perceive new people on the basis of past experience with significant others and in relation to still-active strivings.

The conditions that facilitate transference reactions are much like those that foster the emergence of personal material in art. For the latter purpose, unstructured media are presented in a bounded but free situation, encouraging individuals to find and express their own imagery. In a

similar fashion, the therapist can present herself in a relatively neutral way, so that the patient can project feelings and ideas reflecting unresolved conflicts upon her, just as he projects his inner world onto the art materials. Art therapists can make good use of that tendency to distort what is perceived in terms of what is inside, to see the present through lenses colored by the past. Since there are many kinds of gratifications and nonneutral behaviors inevitable in art therapy, these will of course influence the kind of transference that develops.

In giving a patient materials, for example, an art therapist is a "feeder," offering supplies that may be experienced as good and plentiful or as bad and insufficient. The expectation that a patient will use materials to make a product may be viewed as unreasonably demanding or as affirming the person's potency and creative powers. Encouraging a patient to think for himself may be felt as supporting his autonomy, or as abandoning him unfairly. The art therapist offering potentially messy media in a permissive setting may be perceived as a benign parent who allows sensory play, or as a seducer who invites the patient to engage in forbidden pleasures. In limiting destructive uses of materials, the therapist may be experienced as a restrictive policeman or as a helpful guardian controlling dangerous impulses. When teaching about a medium or process, the art therapist can be felt as generous or as interfering.

In looking at the artwork, the therapist may be experienced as encouraging either voyeurism or exhibitionism, and in either case can be seen positively (as giving permission for desired acts), or negatively (as inviting forbidden behavior). When asking questions, an art therapist may be perceived as an intrusive prober, worming her unwelcome way into the patient's private, creative world. Conversely, such inquiries can be experienced as an affirmation of the artwork, an indication of the importance to the therapist of the patient and his productions. In all of these functions, essential to therapy through art but not through words, the art therapist is responded to in both realistic and distorted (transferential) ways, reflecting both the role and the patient's reactions to it.

Another unique aspect of transference in art therapy is the likelihood of a distorted response not only to the person of the therapist, but also to the media, the processes, and the products themselves. Materials such as clay or fingerpaint, for example, can evoke pleasure but can also arouse disgust. A process like the hammering of nails into wood can lead to a feeling of potency, or, if aggression is too threatening, can be invaded by anxiety. The products also take on meaning in relation to the state of the transference. A creation offered to an art therapist can as easily be a "bomb" as a "love-gift." A patient can feel narcissistic pride, but also shame, in the showing of his self-creation to another.

The presence of art also makes possible a range of concrete, sometimes even creative, ways of expressing the transference to the therapist. As with putting an idea into words, putting an idea into a gesture or a form can also reduce the pressure to act out directly either loving or hostile impulses. Clay, for example, can be caressed with affection or pounded with hostility. It can be formed carefully or impulsively and can be lovingly decorated or angrily stabbed. Anger can be expressed by refusing to use materials or by insisting on hiding the product from the eyes of the therapist. Transference wishes or fears may be represented in more or less disguised ways, as in beautiful or ugly pictures of the therapist or another authority figure. The treatment itself can also be represented—as a prison when the artist feels trapped, or a haven when he feels comfortable. And, instead of acting out his wishes, the patient in art therapy can create images of happy marriages or violent battles, with any degree of disguise necessary for him at that stage of treatment.

At times, such representations may provide sufficient indirect gratification and may successfully bind anxiety to such an extent as to be justly termed sublimation. A mark of successful sublimation is that it frees further energy for constructive work. Some art therapists believe that the promotion of transference via an art therapist's relative neutrality lessens the likelihood that sublimation will be achieved. Sublimation may indeed be interfered with by transference at moments when interpersonal pressures become overwhelming. However, a more insidious hazard lies in the failure to recognize subtly manifested transference reactions which can create formidable resistance to the treatment process.

An awareness of transference reminds the art therapist that behavior with art materials, or the style of the work itself, can defend against unwelcome transference reactions as easily as it can express them. For example, a patient might use insufficient paint in order to deny his strong urge to take it all. Or he might try to please a defensively idealized therapist through "pretty" or self-consciously "expressive" productions, thereby avoiding awareness of conflicted, anxiety-provoking impulses. What is essential here, as with more direct externalizations of transference reactions, is that the art therapist be aware of the patient's hidden instinctual/defensive agenda.

Equally important is an awareness of countertransference, that is, the distorted responses to the patient, his art, or both, that emanate from the therapist's own unresolved conflicts. As with transference, there are factors peculiar to the art therapy situation. Since an art therapist is also an artist, she must be careful not to let her enthusiasm for the quantity or quality of a patient's products influence her unduly. Art therapists

need to be on the side of the patient's creative self, but should neither exaggerate nor denigrate a person's productions. The challenge is to support and express appreciation of authentic work, without explicitly passing judgment on its aesthetic quality. Indeed, one hazard for an art therapist is letting the subtle promotion of her own favorite media, content, or style interfere with facilitating the patient's own mode of expression. Similarly, it is often difficult for a creative artist to be providing expressive media for others while unable to use it herself, which can stimulate frustration and even envy.

Knowing oneself well enough to spot one's countertransferential distortions is probably the most difficult area of all, despite one's familiarity with the topic. Knowing oneself internally—knowing how one functions and why one feels and thinks and behaves as one does—is a lifelong and difficult task. Unless the therapist is as gifted as Freud or Jung, who were able to analyze themselves, she will probably need some help from a more objective clinical other. Although my own preference for self-knowledge is the detailed journey through the mind provided by psychoanalysis, I would not recommend that route for every art therapist. But I have come to feel that anyone taking responsibility for modifying the psyches of other people through the powerful modality of art has a responsibility to undergo some personal psychotherapy. The primary reason, of course, is so that the art therapist's own conflicts, distortions, and characterological as well as conflictual hangups will not interfere with her ability to fully empathize with and help her patient(s). Just as transference reactions are helpful symbolic routes to the patient's inner world, so countertransference responses, promptly identified and understood, can often provide useful clues to the patient's transference or other aspects of his personality.

Unlike a strictly verbal clinician, an art therapist can also use her own artwork as an aid to self-understanding, in addition to helping the patient. Portraits of patients made outside the therapy session can, for example, help an art therapist to identify and comprehend countertransference responses, especially when explored with the help of one's own therapist or clinical supervisor. During a session, the art therapist can communicate in a variety of ways by means of her own creative imagery, whether working jointly, in turn, or alongside the patient. As with any other intervention, it is essential that the therapist who chooses to converse with a patient through art consider what it means to her to do so, and the probable impact of her activity and imagery on the person she is trying to help. Most important, the art therapist who uses her own

creations must be especially alert to the transference and countertransference implications of such potent nonverbal interactions.

I personally feel that trying to limit the transference in art therapy is futile, though modifying its expression is often essential to productive work. Distorted reactions to the therapist, both loving (positive) and hostile (negative) are powerful and, when attended to, can be used for understanding and as an agent of change. The greatest danger for art therapists lies in ignoring or minimizing presence of transference, for, unanalyzed, it can cause intense resistance and can bring about premature termination as easily in art therapy as in psychoanalysis. The wisest course is to encourage its expression and to do one's best to understand its manifestations. Only then can the therapist make an informed decision as to whether it would be best to manipulate, to interpret, or even occasionally to gratify a particular transferential wish.

Margaret Naumburg, analytically oriented art therapy pioneer, implied that the transference in art therapy was lessened in intensity because of the degree of libido invested in the art object itself (1953). In a sense, the product functions as a kind of transitional object, and it is, like the toddler's blanket, an object of transaction between patient/child and therapist/mother. I do not believe that the artwork dilutes the transference, which inevitably develops more or less rapidly in any kind of therapy. I do feel, however, that the presence of the product modifies what occurs and that there are pressures toward certain *forms* of transference in art therapy, as suggested earlier. Because there is so much gratification, for example, the likelihood of an initial positive transference is great. In a study comparing art and drama interviews with 24 youngsters, it was found that the art products tended to have more positive content, with a higher frequency of nurturance themes, while the majority of the dramas had more negative content, with a higher frequency in them of injury to the self (Rubin & Irwin, 1975). The "feeder" aspect of the art therapist's role, as well as the admiring "gleam-in-the-eye" mother—who approves of controlling one's (anal/art) products and applauds one's (phallic/art) display or performance—combine to produce a high frequency of maternal transferences in art therapy, especially in the early stages of treatment.

KNOWING STAGES OF THERAPY

In any therapeutic journey, whether relatively long or relatively short, whether fairly intense or rather superficial, there are certain predictable

stages or phases. This is true whether one is working with an individual, a family, or a group. Just as it is important for an art therapist to be aware of the framework and the relationship in therapy, so it is useful to know what is likely to happen and the sequence in which it normally unfolds. Most books on counseling and psychotherapy are rather global in this regard, talking about a clearly defined opening or initial phase, a more variable middle phase, and a differentiated termination or ending phase. While these three major segments are always present, I believe that they can be further broken down and that to do so is helpful to the practitioner. Not only does it sharpen one's ability to assess where the patient is on the ladder or road of therapeutic progress, but it is also helpful as a guide to what one can expect and potentially promote as the next likely stage of the treatment. As with normal development, there is always regression as well as progression; there is always over-lapping and the constant potential presence of all stages throughout the entire process. Nevertheless, the steps outlined in an earlier publication on individual work with children (Rubin, 1984), also seem applicable to work with all levels and combinations of people, though there are ad-ditional issues peculiar to groups and families at each stage.

In the beginning of treatment, the therapist's goals are primarily the establishment of a good alliance and, secondarily, the gaining of a fuller understanding of the problems patients bring, even if there has been prior diagnostic work. In order to make the beginning phase as com-fortable and appealing as possible, the clinician is generally more sup-portive and less demanding or confronting than would be appropriate later on. Fortunately, minimal intervention works equally well for the gathering of diagnostic information, the assessment of the particular issues causing problems in the individual, family, or group. The only structure that might be imposed during this first stage is that which the art therapist feels necessary to enhance the comfort level of the patient(s). For the patient, the initial stage is primarily one of finding out what is expected of him, getting to know the clinician, the media, and the pe-culiarities of what happens in art therapy. It is also a period marked by a kind of testing of the waters, in order to be clear about the nature and boundaries of this particular situation. In the area of limits, it is best, as noted earlier, to be clear, firm, and open about them. Such a stance is immensely useful to the patient, who needs to develop trust in the framework, as well as in the clinician and the modality.

If things go well, the patient gradually feels secure and comfortable, and begins to develop a feeling of trust in the therapist, the most sig-nificant index of a valid alliance. Trust becomes evident in art therapy,

not only in how people behave and what they disclose verbally, but also in what they are able to express visually. As with testing, the development of trust is rapid for some and slow for others. Only when there is sufficient trust, however, can the patient begin to take risks, revealing verbally and nonverbally those wishes and fears that have been hidden, from self as often as from others. As the communication process unfolds, and the patient is able to risk new ways of creating as well as conversing, there is the possibility of facing the issues that have emerged. To face that which has not been acknowledged before is difficult for anyone. The very anxieties which led to keeping the threatening ideas out of consciousness are restimulated as they begin to unfold.

These fears, usually out of proportion to the stimulus, cause many natural protective reactions, so that defensiveness and resistance, which may seem to have been reduced since the initial phase, return in full force. It is my conviction that without such self-protective reactions there is probably not any kind of useful therapy going on. That is, it is only when a person is able to come close to the disabling areas of conflict that he or she is likely to ever overcome them, whether the treatment aims at an educative or an insightful kind of learning. In any case, periods of resistance in art therapy are marked by all of the defenses characteristic of verbal expression, including an unwillingness to create, the use of impersonal imagery, a turning to (cartoon) humor, a regression to earlier forms of (art) behavior, and a compulsive fussing over details. There may be a willingness to create, but an unwillingness to reflect on either process or product. There may also be a superficial compliance with both doing and discussing, which masks a stubborn inner refusal to divulge anything personal or affect-laden. Whether the unwelcome impulse is focused on the therapist (as in transference resistance) or on some other person (like emerging hostility toward a child, spouse, or parent), the ensuing resistance should be understood as a natural defensive reaction. It is the patient's way of protecting himself from what appears to be an intolerable outcome (such as annihilation, loss of boundaries or of control, loss of a significant other or of that person's love, violent retaliation from a rival, or an overwhelming sense of guilt) should the impulse be expressed.

It is in the process of risking the communication and the subsequent confrontation of previously denied ideas and affects that much of the change in psychotherapy occurs. Such change seems to take time for most people, and it is best if the therapeutic contact can continue long enough for a genuine working through to take place. This involves looking not just once but looking many times at difficult issues—learning

about not only the feared impulses, but also one's habitual ways of coping (defenses), some of which have not worked well in the past. During this period there is usually a sharply intensified feeling of cyclicity in the therapy, of an "open" session followed by a "closed" one, or of a series of relatively free meetings succeeded by several marked by inhibition and/or regression. It is almost as if the psyche has to continually balance disclosure with closure, as if the need to maintain equilibrium operates not only momentarily but over time as well. Sometimes resistance can seem like an endless stalemate and can stimulate powerful countertransference in the therapist. What is most helpful during this period of facing, understanding, and eventually accepting what has been feared is a sustained empathic awareness of the depth of the patient's anxiety. Sometimes an aptly timed and well-worded interpretation can help to move things forward; sometimes one must simply wait and deal with one's own frustration. Only if the therapist can sustain the tensions of the working-through phase is there much likelihood that the patient will be able to tolerate them.

The penultimate stage is in the development and integration of a new image of the self, in both a passive and an active sense. To see oneself as a separate, integrated person (good-and-bad) and as competent (able to work, to play, and to love) is only possible if one is able to actualize those self-perceptions in behavior. From thinking, which is a kind of "trial action," to doing usually takes time. And it often requires support from the therapist, who helps the patient's newly developed self to take its "first steps" safely and effectively, as would any good parent. Needless to say, such a new image and sense of self is only possible if the patient has been able to give up maladaptive coping mechanisms, to fully accept what he has discovered in the facing and understanding stages of the therapeutic process. Accepting is very different from knowing about. It is as much an affective event as a cognitive one. Just saying the words is meaningless; behaving and feeling differently are the only valid indices. In the process of accepting previously denied or devalued aspects of oneself, one must also give up old ways of being in the world.

Between the disruption of old structures and the formation of new ones, there is usually a period that can be quite threatening, where old coping mechanisms are no longer available but new ones are not quite ready for action. This is a painful, often empty-feeling time, where the threat of loss of self or of control can seem overwhelming. No matter how unhappy the patient or family, the renunciation of old ways of perceiving, feeling, and behaving is immensely difficult. I believe that the inertia which seems to accompany any significant change process

is never laziness or even the pull of entropy, but rather a self-protective clinging to the known, the familiar, the predictable. For the unknown is always fraught with danger, despite its exciting appeal for the venturesome. Even the people who attend personal growth art therapy groups, who are highly motivated to improve the quality of their lives, who suffer normal discontent rather than crippling illness—even such relatively healthy and secure individuals inevitably discover a good deal of internal resistance to change during both art expression and reflection. Whatever the source of the anxiety about change, it is ubiquitous and accounts for the time it takes for people to not only practice new ways of being, but also become comfortable with them—to fully integrate them. There is also a necessary mourning—of the loss of old fantasies, goals, and images—which takes time too. Giving up impossible or inappropriate strivings is just as difficult as letting go of old defense mechanisms.

The biggest loss, inevitable in any therapy, lies in the loss of the therapist—the termination process, where the separating task becomes preeminent. Art therapy, like any other form of therapy, helps patients to separate fact from fancy, fantasy from reality, and, in a deeper sense, to separate from their illness and any secondary gain it may provide. In order to help people to accept all such separations, there must be a strong attachment to the therapist, both as a real person and as a transference object. The separation-individuation process between a patient/child and a therapist/parent is a powerful potential learning and reworking experience, and a painful and intense one as well. Attention should always be paid to the significance of termination, especially when the patient has been seen as part of a group or in a milieu setting. While the transference may not be as intense, it may be just as powerful (and, with very needy patients, is often instant). Even if there has been relatively little transferential involvement with the therapist, there is still a need to pay attention to all of the feelings, fantasies, and especially fears involved in saying good-bye, in letting go.

Sometimes the patient has little choice. The treatment ends, not because all goals are reached, but because of some extrinsic factor: The insurance money runs out, the therapist is leaving the facility, the program has been discontinued, the parents decide to withdraw the child, etc. With the more ideal conditions available in some outpatient settings and in private practice, it is possible to involve the patient(s) in setting the termination date. I believe this is best, though there is often much ambivalence and indecision around the task. Even when the setting of the date is out of the patient's control, the individual(s) should be en-

couraged to say something about *how* the ending period should proceed. Deciding what to do on the last day, for example, can provide an opportunity for some active mastery in the otherwise helpless situation of having to end, though not feeling ready.

Art products, it seems, play a special role at the time of termination. If they have been stored as part of the treatment, they provide a splendid and vivid basis for re-viewing the therapy, whatever its duration and scope. A patient may choose to keep all or some, and to give all or some to the art therapist. In either case, the product becomes a transitional object for both partners in the therapeutic adventure. It carries in it a piece of the treatment for the patient and a piece of the person for the therapist. Another unique aspect of termination in art therapy is that the patient, ideally, does not just identify with the therapist's clinical perspective, as in all forms of treatment. From direct experience as well as through identification, he may come away from art therapy with a strong sense of his own creative potential as an artist. He will also have learned, through practice and imitation, to look at his personal "visions"—his dreams and imagery as well as his art—and to use them as a way of further understanding himself. Any tolerance he has learned from his therapist for his own forbidden fantasies or wishes should also be felt for his artistic inadequacies. Whether he feels talented and desires further training, or has simply discovered that he can express, enjoy, and understand himself through art, he may very well want to continue in this modality, as well as in the kind of self-therapy which should be the outcome of any successful treatment (the ability to monitor and be comfortably in charge of oneself).

So another way to help a patient to terminate art therapy is to facilitate the likelihood that the person will be able to continue his creative growth (as well as continue to reflect and understand himself—a goal of all psychotherapy). Perhaps the means will be a good-bye gift of art supplies for the patient who is too poor to buy his own or is exceptionally needy of some concrete evidence of the therapist's concern. Or perhaps an art therapist will provide information to the patient, the family, or the referral source about where to buy appropriate materials or how and where to get further instructional or recreational art experiences. Perhaps it will seem appropriate to make referrals to specific teachers or art centers, just as one might refer a patient to another therapist. Because of the nature of the modality, the patient can carry on concretely with the creative work on his own or with the help of a professional who is an artist or teacher, not necessarily a therapist. In this sense, the patient can carry over into his real life an activity which, although it was a

means of inpatient or outpatient treatment, can continue as a normal, creative way of sustaining balance and finding fulfillment as a healthy, productive human being. In that way, art therapy can sometimes make the separation involved in termination not only easier to handle, but also more likely to be successful.

REFERENCES

Naumburg, M. *Psychoneurotic art: Its function in psychotherapy.* New York: Grune & Stratton, 1953.

Rubin, J.A. The role of transference and countertransference in art therapy. *American Journal of Art Therapy*, 1982, *21*, 10-12.

Rubin, J.A. *Child art therapy: Understanding and helping children grow through art* (2nd ed.). New York: Van Nostrand Reinhold, 1984.

Rubin, J.A., & Irwin, E.C. Art and drama: Parts of a puzzle. In I. Jakab (Ed.), *Psychiatry and art, Vol. IV.* New York: S. Karger, 1975, pp. 193-200.

Blowing ink with the air from straws enables two classmates to "play" at an oral level, and to create something artistic as well.

Chapter 7

Knowing Art Therapy

As suggested earlier, being an artist and a nice human being is not enough to make someone a good art therapist. In order to permit the fullest possible use of art for the purpose of healing, an art therapist must *know* certain things, must *believe* in others, and must *be* a certain sort of person. Only if these three conditions are met, is it possible to achieve *artistry* as an art therapist. Before one can function as an art therapist with patients or clients, one must know a good deal about *art*. Most important are the understandings and information necessary about materials, processes, and products, as detailed in the first three chapters. In the area of *therapy*, one needs to know a good deal about development (normal and abnormal), about dynamics (individual and group), and about the therapeutic process (the framework, the relationship, and the stages).

In order to begin synthesizing what one knows about art and about therapy, it helps to be clear about one's identity as an art therapist. This is as necessary for private work with patients as it is for public interchange with colleagues. Since art therapy is itself a hybrid discipline, it is superficially similar to a wide variety of other fields, from art education to play therapy to occupational, recreational, and activity therapy. Since all of these may involve the use of art materials by individuals or groups, they can look strikingly alike to the naive observer. Even the clinician's behavior may be similar, whether helping someone to use

materials appropriately or asking questions about process or product. Nevertheless, art therapy is different from all of the above, despite some overlapping areas with each.

While there are often superficial similarities between art and the other action therapies (recreation, activity, and occupational therapy), there is a deeper affinity between art and the other creative therapies (music, movement, drama, poetry, and phototherapy). Although the primary modality in each is quite distinct, it is also true that human beings, especially in a situation which promotes freedom of expression, often move spontaneously from one mode to another. Children frequently create dramas while they draw or sculpt; adults and adolescents sometimes write poetry on their paintings. Such spontaneous shifts have led me in my own work to a multimodal approach, especially appropriate for the very young, but also applicable to adolescents, adults, families, and groups. I do not see it as "expressive therapy" either. I prefer when possible to work with an expert in another modality, since my own skills are quite limited in creative areas other than art; but I feel quite comfortable with permitting or even encouraging a shift of mode during the working process. I think of myself throughout as an art therapist, not an expressive arts therapist, or a play therapist, or an activities therapist, for the art process is always at the center of my work.

Issues of identity in a synergistic discipline such as art therapy have naturally been of concern from the first. It is necessary to not only relate the two components (art and therapy) in a way that makes sense, but also differentiate art therapy, as noted above, from its activity cousins and its creative arts siblings. There are even times when one needs to clarify, for a colleague or a patient, the distinctions between art therapy and the use of art by other kinds of clinicians (as in the diagnostic drawings requested by some psychologists, or the paintings used by some psychiatrists). When a psychologist, psychiatrist, social worker, or counselor uses art extensively in his work, is that person then an art therapist? This is a difficult question, since it is highly likely that anyone using art a great deal is something of an artist himself, such as Gestalt therapist Joseph Zinker, psychiatrist Mardi Horowitz, or psychoanalyst Marion Milner. Nevertheless, even for those who have a sincere affinity for art and who employ it clinically, if their primary identity is something else, art is then seen as an adjunct—used when perceived as useful or appropriate, but not always or usually central to the individual's professional work as a therapist. By contrast, the art therapist's primary modality is art, despite the fact that the talking time may occasionally exceed the doing time, or that there may even be sessions where the pressure

to talk is so great or the depression so profound that the person does not create with media. These instances are the exception, however, and the "rule" is that in most art therapy, all or part of every meeting is spent creating and/or looking at art. Whether the art is thought of primarily as a vehicle for sublimation (healing through the creative process) or for communication (art in psychotherapy), the art process and product always occupy considerable time and space.

In addition to the ongoing task of defining one's own use of art in therapy, it is most helpful to become informed in some detail about those related disciplines mentioned above. Only then can distinctions be clearly made, both for oneself and for the society in which one works professionally. While it is necessary to know what art therapy *is*, it is also, and perhaps even more important, to know what it is *not*. One can only be clear about how one is different from one's professional relatives if one also knows a great deal about them, so it follows that an art therapist ought to be knowledgeable about her closest professional relatives, especially the other arts and activity therapies. Only by knowing how art therapy is similar to and different from occupational or recreational or play therapy can one discuss intelligently with colleagues or patients what art therapy in particular has to offer.

WHAT ONE NEEDS TO BELIEVE

Belief is not the same as knowledge, despite the fact that most people try hard to justify their convictions on some rational basis. The beliefs that I feel are essential for an art therapist concern the need, the right, and the ability of every human being to be creative. Only if one is convinced of the need can one motivate those who at first appear apathetic or resistant. Only if one is convinced of the right, can one work effectively with those severely handicapped populations for whom fully formed art may never be possible, but who deserve the opportunity to develop to the utmost whatever sensory and creative potential they have. Finally, only if one is convinced that every person has the ability to be a creative artist can one sincerely strive to find the song in the soul, the poetry in the person, whatever the medium or modality. I suppose another belief that is necessary is in art therapy itself, which probably involves a sincere conviction that both art and therapy can help people—and, on a personal level, that one can really enable that to happen.

Unless one really believes in art therapy, one will be tempted to engage in the kind of clever or naive mislabeling, which often serves short-term personal or political goals. If the clinician believes that she is not doing

therapy until she is trained to be a therapist, then she is not likely to masquerade as an "art therapist," even though she is offering art to a deviant population or in a treatment setting. It is not a matter of where the therapist works or whom she serves that makes an activity art therapy. What does matter is the goal (therapy) and the use of art as the primary modality in the pursuit of that goal of human growth in a more than momentary way. Even when that is the case, there is often a temptation to call what one is doing something else, because of the pervasive anxiety attendant upon the word "therapy." The common fears of patients about being harshly exposed or manipulated in a painful way may be confirmed whenever anyone calls herself an art therapist without the requisite background. This is unfortunately the case in many settings, where administrators seem strangely comfortable with calling an art school graduate with no psychology background a *therapist*, despite the fact that they would never allow such an individual to give psychological tests or to draw blood. While this situation is of concern primarily to trained practitioners and their professional association, hopefully it will become the concern of all who believe in the healing power of art and the creative rights of each human being (cf. Reamer, 1982).

WHO ONE NEEDS TO BE

More important than believing in oneself is being the right sort of person. There is no single right sort of personality for good art therapy, any more than there is only one right way to behave as an art therapist. But some characteristics do seem to be essential and are probably potential in most people, though sadly undeveloped or inhibited in many. These necessary qualities include some related to creative thinking, such as fluency, flexibility, originality, an ability to take risks, to tolerate ambiguity, and to regress in the service of the ego. Certainly, one must have experienced the creative process oneself in order to be an effective art therapist. I do not believe, however, that one must be an actively practicing, exhibiting artist; rather, what is essential is that one has known, in some depth and at a personal level, what it means to create with art media—the pain as well as the pleasure, the tension as well as the release.

Incidentally, I find it intriguing that art therapists do not always behave *creatively* in their clinical work, despite the fact that most are practicing artists. How is it that people can be comfortable manipulating essentially unpredictable materials, enduring and even enjoying the inevitable tensions of the creative process, yet so often seem unable to

adopt the same attitude in regard to their work as therapists? Perhaps, having identified themselves as artists before they became therapists, they are understandably cautious about tapping what they know to be powerful, but not easily controlled, inner energies in the service of this new identity. Indeed, they are right to be cautious; for while it is necessary to gain access to those potent resources, it is also essential to control their overt expression and to do so within some clearly bounded framework. In art, this framework is provided largely by the medium, shaped by the artist's intent; in therapy, it is provided by the treatment context and the role of the clinician within that frame of reference.

Given that caution, and with sufficient knowledge about both art and therapy in one's mental storehouse, I submit that an effective art therapist is a person who enjoys the challenge of using creative thinking in the service of the therapeutic task at hand. I believe this is true whether the clinical questions are about the *what* of symbolic meaning, the *why* of behavior, or the *how* and *when* of intervention. The persistent search by some art therapists for simple answers to complex questions suggests that they are not yet comfortable with using their own creativity in finding their own solutions. Yet the challenge of understanding and helping each new human being, of solving the mystery of how to help each person to find and enjoy his creative potential—in art and in life—is for me, and for many others, the source of continuing stimulation and pleasure in the work of art therapy.

Though it goes without saying, one cannot be any kind of a therapist if one doesn't genuinely like other people, and the kind of people who end up in treatment are not always easy to like. So it is necessary to be the kind of person who enjoys relating to those who may be resistant or inhibited as human beings, as well as in their art. One also needs to be genuine, to behave in a real and human way. I am often surprised by the comments I consistently get from trainees after I conduct a family art evaluation with one of them, that they "never knew it was possible to be *so natural* with patients." One can be authentic and friendly, without being either seductive or effusive, and one can still maintain a good deal of therapeutic distance and neutrality in regard to one's private self.

As for one's private self, as noted earlier, it is vital to get to know and accept as much of oneself as possible, whether one ends up exploring one's inner world through art therapy or some other form of treatment. Such self-knowledge is essential, partly because one can never fully empathize with patienthood until one has experienced it and, more important, because one cannot use oneself well as a therapeutic instrument in the service of another, when one is responding unconsciously

to one's own "unfinished business" (unresolved conflicts). I don't have strong feelings about when in one's life such an undertaking is best; but I do think it helps to be in therapy while one is practicing art therapy, so that the ways in which one's own conflicts affect one's work can be examined directly. I am increasingly convinced that it is only through a capacity for empathy and for truly following the patient that really artistic work can be done. I suspect that it is not possible to allow oneself to "feel with" another in any depth, unless one is genuinely comfortable with all aspects of one's own psyche.

I am also convinced that no amount of the right knowledge alone is sufficient to make a person a fine clinician. This knowledge, while an essential condition, must still be applied with conviction in work with other human beings. The artistry involved in outstanding therapy through art may depend, in the final analysis, as much on personality as on technique. For no amount of scientific knowledge will make for good art therapy if it is not applied in a sensitive and artistic way by a human being who can relate effectively to others in the special fashion needed for successful treatment.

While all of these concerns about what one knows, what one believes, and what sort of person one is may seem peripheral to the topic (the art of art therapy), they are really the bedrock—the foundation on which good art therapy must rest. I do not mean to imply that they are accomplished in any sort of neat chronological sequence: that one learns, believes, and becomes in some sequential order, according to a prescribed plan of action. Rather, it is necessary for growth to be continuous and ongoing in all of these areas throughout one's lifetime. Learning and knowing about both art and therapy should expand and deepen over time, just as a developing person will naturally expand and deepen his values and himself as a human being. Nevertheless, I am convinced that one cannot be any more artistic as an art therapist than one can be as a painter, if one doesn't *know* the "basics," if one doesn't truly *believe* in human potential, and if one doesn't have the *personality* and the ability to sustain all aspects of the role. These are the necessary conditions for artistry, which does not, despite the mythology, spring full blown from anyone who is not properly prepared.

REFERENCE

Reamer, F.G. *Ethical dilemmas in social service*. New York: Columbia University Press, 1982.

PART III

The Interface

The Interface is that area where art and therapy meet, the synergistic core of the work of the art therapist. It is best if it takes place within a matrix of knowledge about art and therapy, as outlined in the first two portions of this book. In order for art therapy to occur, however, the stage must be set: first in the institution, then with the referring individual(s), and finally in the art therapy room itself. The first chapter of this section describes all aspects of setting the stage—moving from the larger to the smaller arena, from the preparation distant in time to that immediately before and at the outset of the art therapy session. The second step in the work of the art therapist is evoking expression—stimulating the individual or group to use creative media in some way. This involves not only asking patients to do something with materials, but also deciding in advance as well as on the spot what to request, suggest, or offer. These issues are dealt with in the second chapter in this section.

While people are working, the art therapist's primary task is one of facilitating expression—helping the individual or group to work most productively with the materials available. This task of enabling patients to create during the working process is examined in the third chapter in this section. When the working time is over, the therapist's task lies primarily in looking and reflecting—helping the patient(s) to learn about self and others from the product(s) that were created. This aspect of the art therapeutic process is discussed in the fourth chapter of this section,

which focuses on the perception and discussion of art for therapeutic goals.

Each of these facets of the art therapy process is treated in a separate chapter, which may imply that they always occur in the sequence in which they are discussed. It is often true, however, that two or more will be happening simultaneously, or in an alternating sequence, for any individual patient. Within a group, of course, different people will usually be at different stages in the creative process at the same moment in time, and this will shift throughout the session. For any single art therapy product/process, however, it is always true that the stage must be set, the expression evoked, facilitated, looked at, and understood. In all of these activities, the art therapist uses what she knows about art and therapy in a way that helps patients to grow.

How an art therapist accomplishes each of these tasks is a measure of her artistry, her ability to synthesize what she knows in the course of each clinical moment. It is easy to talk in generalizations about how to be a good art therapist. The challenge is to be able to integrate one's knowledge sufficiently in order to respond with genuine spontaneity and in a way that is optimally in tune with the patient's needs. That, of course, is not so easy. It takes time, practice, close supervision, personal reflection, and, most important, a flexible approach to one's work, and an openness to the lifelong possibility of improvement. The best clinicians I know tend to be the most modest, both about their technique and their theoretical formulations. They are the least doctrinaire and the most open-minded. They tend to make good supervisors, teachers, and consultants, as well as good therapists. I think this is true not only because they know a great deal and are able to communicate it well, but also because they are secure enough to be comfortable with the notion that they can never know it all.

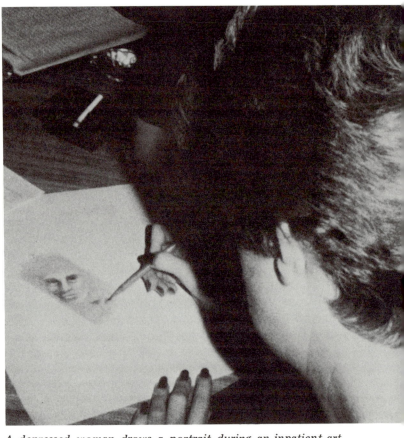

A depressed woman draws a portrait during an inpatient art therapy group session in a psychiatric hospital.

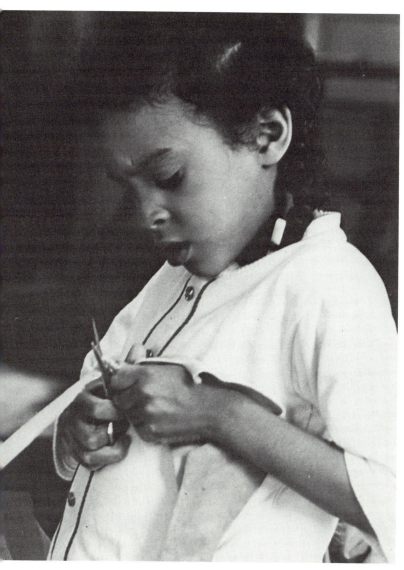

A well-set stage makes possible intense concentration.

Chapter 8

Setting the Stage

The first step is setting the stage for the art therapy encounter. But before art therapy can occur anywhere, there must have been some prior groundwork, which involved getting the agency to a point where it was willing to support the work of an art therapist. In dealing with institutions, it is necessary to think, as one does with families or groups, in terms of the entire system. Entering a system and harnessing its energies in a way that is conducive to the growth and development of an art therapy program require more than tact and knowledge about art therapy. As in working with a family, it helps immensely if the art therapist can look intelligently at personnel and program in a larger context, which means knowing systems analysis. When one is able to identify the values and the power structure of an institution, one can then develop a plan for moving in the desired direction. As with the assessment of individuals and families, both a historical (developmental) and a dynamic perspective are useful ways to conceptualize any social system, such as a hospital or school.

Having recently moved from direct clinical work with outpatients to the administration and supervision of therapy with inpatients, I am acutely aware of the many differences between the two kinds of settings. The strategies which worked for program development in a child guidance center are not necessarily best for growth in a psychiatric hospital. But in both cases, understanding the development, dynamics, power, and values of the system with which one is dealing is highly relevant. Although getting past the front door is a long way from working with

a patient, the way in which the art therapist deals with administrators in terms of such issues as space, time, supplies, and relationship to the rest of the setting can determine what is then possible in the face-to-face encounter.

Another principle which makes pragmatic sense in therapy also makes sense in institutional change. It takes time for any substantial transformation to occur, and even more time for it to become integrated. If one has a fairly clear sense of how and why the system currently functions, and an equally sure sense of the kind of art therapy program which might eventually serve its needs, it is possible to start where the system is (as one starts where the patient is) and to work toward the goal, dealing with resistances on a collective basis, just as one does with an individual or group in therapy.

In any case, once the green light has been given for art therapy to occur, the first step is planning for the actual encounter. Whatever the situation, the art therapist is probably going to be talking to somebody—the referral source, the patient, the parents—about the reasons she is being asked to see the person or group, and their expectations of what she can offer. This is a delicate transaction, requiring artistry on the part of the art therapist outside the art room. While the specifics of what one might say will vary from one situation to another, a good general principle is to be very careful in listening to what is being requested, covertly as well as overtly, and to ask any clarifying questions one might have in a clear and diplomatic way. If it is the patient or parent who makes the initial contact, then this interaction is really the beginning of the treatment process and needs to be handled with as much care as the initial meeting. In general, I attempt to avoid any more telephone interaction than seems necessary to discuss the facts involved, and to make a judgment as to whether seeing the person is appropriate, preferring to reserve as much as possible for the face-to-face encounter.

Setting the stage with a referring professional is a somewhat different matter, for often this person, like a parent, will be presenting the recommendation to the patient or family, so that some education may be necessary about what to say and what not to say. How a patient is prepared by the art therapist or someone else will certainly affect how he approaches art therapy, at least initially. In some situations it is necessary to remain silent where one might otherwise prefer to speak, since too much information might confuse or frighten the individual—whether referring clinician, parent, or patient. It is important in early stage-setting encounters to be as unthreatening as possible,

to listen carefully, especially "between the lines" or with one's "third ear," and to form as much of a beginning "alliance" as seems feasible with the person who makes the initial contact.

Some decisions which may need to be made in advance concern time and space. In both, there may be realistic constraints which limit the options, though usually, if one or another seems essential to the endeavor, the art therapist will be able to explore creatively, with the others involved, a "good enough" solution to the problem. Though this may seem minor, I include it because I am often surprised at how passive and helpless some art therapists seem to feel about issues of time or space. While it is true that one often has to make do with less of either than would be optimal, it is my impression that being clear in one's own mind about the necessary minimum helps considerably in making workable arrangements. For example, it is simply impossible to conduct a meaningful family art evaluation in less than one hour; one-and-a-half- or two-hour sessions are much more fruitful time spans. I would never, therefore, agree to do an evaluation in a half hour, though I might agree to have a family work together on a mural and discuss it, as a way of getting a single glimpse of their interactive style. But I would also make it clear to the referring clinician that the longer period would be much richer, since the hypotheses generated by any single task might then be confirmed or refuted by behavior in others.

The issue of time is an important one, though it is sometimes seen by art therapists as either insignificant or inflexible. Naturally, the optimal length of an individual or group session will depend on many relevant variables, including the attention span of the patient(s), the number of people involved, and the goals of the art therapy activity. It is best to be open-minded and flexible in one's thinking about time, though it is also necessary to be firm about whatever boundaries are established. Nevertheless, a recent experience, in which we found, much to our surprise, that hospitalized schizophrenics were able to become deeply involved in a creative process and discussion lasting as long as three hours, has reminded me once again of the need to avoid rigidity in one's thinking and expectations. Length of sessions should be thought about and planned as realistically as possible, but with an openness to modification as indicated, such as the gradual lengthening of the group time, which occurred with the schizophrenics. Frequency of meetings is also significant and should be approached with flexibility and imagination. In establishing an inpatient program with a wide variety of populations, we have had the luxury of being able to experiment with group and

individual work at varying intervals, from daily to weekly, and to explore some of the benefits, especially in short-term work, of seeing patients more often.

The amount, location, and kind of space available are relevant when setting the stage for art therapy. Sometimes the worker is offered only one option, sometimes many. When I consulted to a school for the deaf, a room was suggested for the pilot art therapy program which seemed best to the administrators. Upon exploration of the entire building, how-ever, another room was identified which seemed to me more appropriate for the activity (ample daylight, a "cozier" space for individual work, proximity to a water source, etc.). On many of the inpatient units at the psychiatric hospital in which I work, the art therapists have ended up working in a space which at first seemed ridiculous—the kitchen. But on most floors, the kitchen is a spacious room with a large round table and several smaller ones, good lighting, ample storage space for supplies and patient artwork, and easy access to water. It has been necessary to work with the staff in order to reduce unnecessary and irritating inter-ruptions, like people going to the coffee machine or refrigerator, or using the washer and dryer. But on the whole, much to my surprise, the kitchen turns out to be the location of choice for inpatient art therapy groups in this particular institution. Even a well-equipped art studio would present significant problems, since those patients restricted to the unit could not participate, and there would be constant scheduling conflicts among the three full-time art therapists currently employed. In other words, one needs to be open-minded about space as well as about time, to be flexible in one's thinking in general, but also, paradoxically, to be firm about one's minimal needs (e.g., sufficient light, work area, storage space, and time for art therapy to be possible).

Once time and space have been agreed upon, the most critical artistry of "stage setting" occurs: the actual arrangement of furniture, easels, and art supplies within the available space. This should be done thought-fully and as consistently as possible from session to session. In general, the space should be arranged in such a way that the patient(s) can most easily do what is expected. The precise decisions about the setting of each specific art therapy "stage" depend on the goals of the particular session, as well as on the capacities of the person(s) involved (devel-opmental level, degree of pathology, etc.). The ideal is an environment which is both orderly and stimulating, which looks and feels safe, as well as inviting. Clean and organized is always more appealing than dirty and disorganized, even when it is the same chunk of clay or box of water colors.

Having observed a good deal of art therapy in a great many settings, I am convinced that even greater attention could be paid by many art therapists to the "re-creation" of the physical environment in which they work. There are, of course, exceptions, where the thoughtful arrangement of space and supplies is most impressive. But in many instances, especially when the space used for art therapy must be shared with others (as is so often the case), the clinician is often remarkably casual about how things are set up physically, as if it really didn't matter. I have the impression that this may matter more early in the treatment process than later, but that the physical stage which is set by the art therapist has a much more significant effect on what happens during the session than is generally supposed.

An example of a recently observed session comes to mind, in which the art therapist, highly skilled in relating to her elderly psychiatric patients, had pushed four small tables together—creating a nice, large working surface about eight feet square, where each group member could easily see and relate to the others. However, she selected the largest size of paper to give each of the eight patients around the table, despite the fact that there simply wasn't enough space available for everyone to use such a big sheet (18" × 24"). For these disturbed older people, this presented a serious problem, solved by a few who folded the paper, but, for the others, frustrating their efforts to paint throughout the session.

Although this dilemma sounds minor, the art therapist was so involved with her presentation to the group, which was meant to motivate them to paint, that she was quite unaware of the frustration she had unwittingly stimulated. Had she simply offered a smaller size of paper, the concerns about working area would not have interfered as they did for almost all of the patients, unnecessarily draining mental and physical energy from their creative task. Although it is helpful to most patients to expect and to promote independence in creative work when feasible, for those whose energy resources are already limited, it does not make much sense to divert any of it from the art activity, where it needs to be invested.

Even when the space is sufficient, I have often observed art therapy situations where the working surface is unnecessarily complicated by multiple supplies and extraneous items, which inevitably distract and may even interfere with a patient's ability to get started or to stay focused. If art therapists were to think about the arrangement of space and supplies as a creative task, one to be approached with as much care and artistry as layout on a page or placement within a collage, the

resultant order would probably have a significant effect on patient ability to be creative. For though a facilitating physical framework can offer options in space and materials, it should also provide uncluttered and undisturbed possibilities for concentration on the art activity.

Setting the stage for different kinds of art therapy sessions will naturally reflect their distinctions. Certainly, there are different requirements for a group setting designed to evoke independent decision-making, and one where the art therapist wants to present a specific task in order to motivate and engage the group in thinking about a particular theme or activity. If one wants patients to make a personally syntonic choice, a variety of media need to be available, set out in a clear and organized fashion; and there should be uncluttered work spaces, with options for privacy or closeness to others. However, if one wants to engage a group's attention and interest in a motivation, seating everyone around the same table with no distractions on it makes the most sense, at least as an initial configuration.

Similarly, if one needs to observe closely the process of a patient's work with materials, then it is logical to set up the space so that observation is possible, e.g., to make sure that the patient will be sitting and working within view of the therapist, whether or not there are choices of location. Or, if one wants to observe subgroups and alliances within a family, it is helpful to have things set up to allow movement in space, so that customary interaction patterns can be easily manifest in a natural way. Setting the stage for the motivation portion of an art therapy group session, might be quite different from the setting offered for the working time in the same session. A group first seated around a table for an introduction to a task might well be invited to move to any appealing working space, at alternative tables or easels, in order to make the creative process most comfortable for each individual. On the other hand, if the goal of socialization is a high priority for a particular group, then keeping the patients around the same table during the working time is more likely to promote informal interchange while they create.

Of course, the stage-setting for the discussion and reflection segment of any art therapy group might well be different from that which best suits either the motivation or the working period. I once observed a group in a fascinating setting created by a colleague, where each patient worked at a wall easel on his individual painting, the physical setup facilitating individual involvement in the work with minimal interaction. When finished, the patients brought their paintings to another section of the large room, tacked them up on the bulletin board wall, and sat in a semicircle of comfortable chairs, where the discussion took place

when all were assembled. This setup made it possible to view all of the products at once, as well as to focus on individual pictures in the course of the discussion led by the art therapist.

As with other phases of an art therapy session, there can be a surprising lack of attention given to creating an optimal viewing/reflecting situation. Holding up pictures individually is awkward and frustrating, since the artist cannot simultaneously show his work to others and see it himself. An easel at the side of the table is one possible solution, if it is considered best to view each product independently of the others for discussion purposes. If it is seen as more productive to have all of the pictures simultaneously visible, then some kind of larger surface makes more sense, such as a movable blackboard, display wall, or bulletin board wall. Of course, it may be necessary to modify the seating of some or all patients, in order that all products may be viewed by all members of the group. While this may sound unnecessarily fussy, I believe that the therapeutic effectiveness of each facet of the art therapy session is, at least in part, a function of the environment and its facilitating or inhibiting effect on the desired behavior.

Finally, an important part of setting the stage with any new patient(s) is to explore openly any expectations—wishes as well as fears—about the art therapy session. What do they imagine will be "seen," and what do they think will be asked of them? It is important to encourage any questions they might have, as well as to elicit their fantasies about why they are there and what is the purpose of this event. Although I always ask for these patients' ideas first, since what they imagine is so useful diagnostically, I also answer, as honestly and openly as I feel is feasible, their very legitimate questions about what is going to happen to them and why. This is especially important if they themselves have not participated as fully as they might have in the decision-making about coming for art evaluation or therapy.

Probably the most common anxiety is that the art therapist will be able to "read" things about them from their artwork, things of which they themselves are not aware. The popularization of the use of projective drawings and the many cookbook approaches to art interpretation certainly encourage this misperception. I believe quite sincerely that there is no truly valid "meaning" to be gleaned from patient art, without clarification and confirmation by the individual's own associations. I can therefore say to patients with honesty that, despite their understandable fears, I am really unable to fully decipher their art without their active participation. I tell them that understanding the meanings of what they produce is a collaborative effort, in which their own thoughts and as-

sociations play a central role. And I tell them that I will share with them as openly as possible any notions I may have, which are based partly on what I "know" about visual symbolism, but are also based on what they have said about what they have created. Of course, hypotheses which might seem too threatening are not conveyed to any patient prematurely, especially if the idea is merely a hunch. With this possible exception, then, one can honestly reassure patients about the art therapist's inability to see through them on the basis of their creative products. Like any other kind of reassurance, of course, this may be minimally successful, in the sense that a patient might still be suspicious and fear being unmasked. Of course, a patient might also *wish* that the therapist would have all the answers, and be able to translate in some facile way the underlying meaning of drawings, dreams, or symptomatic behavior.

Another common concern for patients beginning an experience with art therapy is that they are incompetent, untalented, and just "can't draw a straight line." While very young children are usually confident, as are those of any age who see themselves as gifted in art, most people feel like klutzes when they take marker or paintbrush or pencil in hand—awkward and "dumb"—although they might feel intelligent in other realms. It is important, therefore, to bring this common anxiety into the open and to empathize with the difficulty of communicating in an unfamiliar modality.

It is important to state that the usefulness of art therapy does not depend on having talent in art—that, in fact, being a serious artist can sometimes make it harder to be genuinely "free" in visual expression. It also helps to acknowledge the inevitable feelings of discomfort or self-criticism that go along with feeling inadequate as an artist, and to sympathize with that. But the clinician can say, with sincerity, that it really doesn't matter, since art in therapy is art for another purpose than art itself. It is a way of understanding more about oneself and feeling more in charge of all of one's resources, including one's creativity. Depending on the age level and type of disorder, one can also try to explain in language that makes sense to the person the usefulness of the creative process as a paradigm of everyday experience, in addition to the value of visual expression as symbolic speech, saying things for which we may have no words. Since I believe quite sincerely in art as therapy as well as communication (as a vehicle in psychotherapy), I feel comfortable trying to "sell" a patient on both of these values, neither of which demand talent, skill, or experience in the visual arts.

On the other side of the coin, while patients fear looking inadequate and lacking in skill, most adults and adolescents dread anything that

appears childish or infantile. One way of dealing with this understandable resistance to regression is to select materials for older patients that
clearly look "grown-up," like charcoal, ink, acrylics, or stone. Even when
one wants to offer media that can also be used by children, it is helpful
to present materials in a way that looks and feels adult. Thus, one brand
of watercolor marker is best placed in neutral containers rather than in
its original box, with its grinning childlike cover. One can also choose
brands and types of crayons that look as if they were designed for use
by artists, as opposed to others that, while usable by anyone, are associated with grade school and childhood.

Despite care in the selection and presentation of materials, one must
often deal more directly with patients who object because the activity
seems babyish. As with other kinds of anxiety, it is helpful to encourage
them to elaborate just what it is about art that seems childish, and what
they might be worried about. After exploring their thoughts and associations and empathizing with any anxiety they might have about regression and potential loss of control, it is also useful to explain that the
"childish" part of creating art is not necessarily incompatible with being
a mature adult. I sometimes suggest that being in touch with one's
playful self, one's silly self, and even one's whiny or angry self can be
helpful in the larger goal of gaining access to all of one's resources and
feeling more completely in charge. Moreover, whether the goal is felt
as getting rid of that childlike part of the self or having easier access to
one's playful parts, the regressive aspect of art media and processes may
turn out to be useful. Although it can evoke anxiety, it need not always
do so. One can even promise that in time, as the patient becomes more
comfortable with the materials, the regression involved might actually
feel like fun.

It is foolish, short-sighted, and generally untherapeutic to attempt to
circumvent resistances, such as those caused by these common initial
anxieties. Perhaps some art therapists have translated the many writings
about the ability of visual imagery to bypass the usual mental censorship
as an invitation or license to attempt to cut through defenses in general.
While it is true that we sometimes do not subject visual imagery (mental
or artistic) to the same defensive maneuvers as verbal communications,
art is still much like a dream—a compromise formation between an
impulse and a prohibition. So it is naive to think that drawn or sculpted
form is without defense or compromise. It is similarly naive to think that
it would be good therapy, even if one were successful in getting patients
to use media without acknowledging anxieties and resistances. The art
therapist will get much further, in both the long and the short run, if

she pays attention to anxieties and inhibitions and the fears behind them, rather than attempting to seduce or pressure the patient into creating in spite of them.

Now the reader may wonder why I have put so much time and energy into describing the importance of setting the stage, as if a well-set stage will help to overcome normal, expectable anxieties and inhibitions. The two are related: To create a situation that makes good art evaluation or therapy most possible pragmatically and least stressful psychologically is as much a part of being a good art therapist as knowing art media or having interviewing skills. And it is true that setting things up in a facilitating fashion will help patients to feel less anxious and usually less confused. But it will not take away the fear of being seen through or the worries about looking inadequate or feeling infantile. These concerns are almost always present with adolescents and adults, and even with many children, including some who ought to feel good about their art—but who, because of their illness, are afraid to perform badly or to lose control and are as inhibited as older patients. These worries need to be examined and addressed as carefully and clearly as the setting of the physical stage. Dealing with them openly is also likely to lead to more comfort in subsequent work.

Of course, any anxieties and inhibitions the patient(s) may have at the outset will be present for some time. The art therapist does not make them go away instantly simply by getting them out in the open and exploring them. And they will be there, for most patients, throughout not only the first session but later ones as well. These anxieties need to be taken into account, not only in setting the stage, but also in the next major component of the art therapist's task, evoking expression, which is the subject of the following chapter.

Individuals find a congenial working space in an art therapy room that is set up to permit both isolation and closeness.

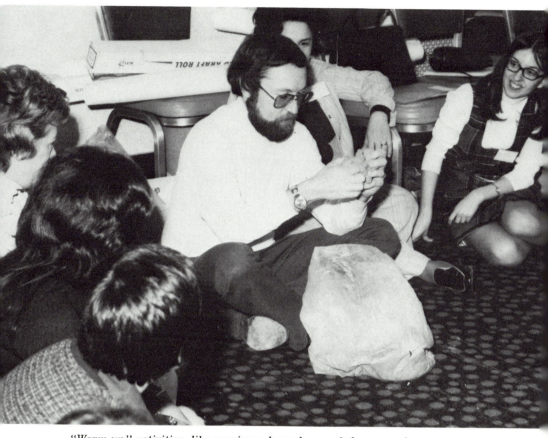

"Warm-up" activities, like passing a large lump of clay around a circle and working on it quickly in turn, can help a group to relax.

Chapter 9

Evoking Expression

Evoking or stimulating expression involves inviting the patient or group to make something, whether it be to choose freely or to do a specific task. The most difficult issue for many art therapists seems to be the question of *what to do*, what sort of opportunity or stimulus or task ought to be suggested to the patient(s) at any particular session. To my mind, the best activity for any art therapy moment is one which is possible within the time and space available, capable of being done by the particular patient(s), and likely to achieve the long- or short-term goal most focal in the therapist's judgment at the time. If there are any guiding principles beyond these, they are those of economy and ease—the simplest and least costly way (in time and effort) to accomplish the desired goal. There should be no need to use more materials, or to make the task any more difficult or threatening, then seems necessary.

The usual tendency in art therapy is to classify techniques according to the materials used, the nature of the task, or some other descriptive concept. Such approaches are not in themselves harmful, and can often be helpful, as in the conceptualization of an "expressive therapies continuum" (Kagin & Lusebrink, 1978), or the lists of activities provided by some clinicians (Furrer, 1982; Paraskevas, 1979; Robbins & Sibley, 1976). However, I believe that it is most helpful to think in terms of the steps involved in deciding what to do in art therapy, and the variables one needs to consider in making the final decision. Just as there are certain reality constraints (like time, space, or furniture) influencing the setting up of the physical space, or economic limits on what and how much

89

can be offered, so there are similar conceptual boundaries or guidelines, which form the context for decision-making about activities. The most important question, which needs to be answered as clearly as possible, is the *goal* of the particular art therapy session. Once that is evident, the sorting and brainstorming necessary for creative decision-making about what to do have some direction.

For example, if the goal of the activity is primarily *diagnostic*, the art therapist will want to maximize the likelihood of gaining whatever information she may desire in the shortest period of time. Thus, if one wants to find out how someone perceives his or her family in an individual interview, asking for a *representation of the family* makes more sense than any other topic. If the clinician is aware of some of the modifications others have thought of to amplify this theme, she will have them available as needed to facilitate the patient's ability to comply with the request. For example, thanks to Kwiatowska (1978), I often suggest an Abstract Family Portrait for those who are uncomfortable with drawing the human figure. Or, thanks to Burns and Kaufman (1970), I may suggest that the family be shown doing something (the Kinetic Family Drawing), in order to get an idea of the nature of the interaction within the group. Or, for someone who likes modeling better than drawing, I might use Keyes' (1974) idea of a Family Sculpture. If I sense a good deal of defensiveness and think it likely that some disguise will be useful, I may offer the idea of an animal family or the use of fruits or some other category intermediate between representations and abstract shapes. The media offered will depend on the time available and the nature of the patient, though it is always best to have some choice (of medium, paper size, or clay color), so that the individual can work in the way which feels most comfortable to him.

If one wants to assess someone's ability to function independently, however, a completely free choice procedure, with no instructions except to choose, would be most useful. The number of choices offered would again be a function of the time and space available and, to some extent, the age level and diagnostic classification of the patient. On the other hand, one might want to evaluate how someone works with others, like their family or a group of peers. In that case, it would make sense to ask people to make something together, possibly to discuss it first, then to do it as a group. Whether one limits space, size, location, time, medium, or topic will depend on variables such as what is available pragmatically and what one thinks matters most in understanding this particular group. One might end up specifying medium, as I have in family art evaluation, for very practical reasons—e.g., thick poster chalks

work well, because they cover large surfaces in a very short period of time. Or one might specify a topic, because one wants to see not only how the group interacts, but also how they respond to a particular theme, as in asking a group of inpatients to create a mural about the hospital.

If the art therapist is clear about what it is she wants to find out diagnostically, it is not so hard to decide what to do. Obviously, a request to determine whether or not a patient is organically damaged would suggest a different kind of art interview than a request to find out if he has a neurotically distorted body image. While the answer to either *might* emerge from an unstructured art session, I would probably include some specific tasks along with "free" ones, especially those which make sense in regard to the questions raised (like a copying task for organicity or a self-portrait for body image). If the request is more global, and one wants to find out in a broader way just what conflicts a person is struggling with and how he or she is coping, then an unstructured art interview (giving the patient a choice of media and topics) seems to work best, at least for me. I suspect other clinicians may be more comfortable with more structured tasks or sequences, and I cannot deny the advantage that such interviews are more easily comparable from one individual to another. However, the more unstructured interviews that one does, the more these too can be compared, and will yield the richest lode of data for most patients.

What matters is that the art therapist be clear in her own mind about what it is she wants to find out, whether for her own purposes or at someone else's request; whether at the outset of treatment, in the middle of the process, or at the time of termination. When the question is clear, and if the art therapist has stored in her mental "grab bag" an awareness of materials, ways of using them, and what one can tell from different approaches, then it is really a lot of fun to think of how to answer the diagnostic inquiry at hand. Most often there is no one *right* answer. The one that ends up being chosen is the one that not only seems appropriate to the circumstances, but also feels most comfortable to the particular clinician.

That matters much more than one might think, for I am quite convinced after a number of years of observing and training others that no one can "put on" an approach that doesn't "fit." Like clothes on a rack, there may be a number of activities (of the right size) which fit the needs of the patient and the question at hand. The one chosen should be, wherever possible, the one which is most appealing and comfortable for the individual art therapist who is going to do the actual work. As with

clothes, one is often concerned with the responses of significant others. Just as I might search for a dress which both fits me and appeals to my husband, so I usually use an approach in art assessment or therapy which is not only comfortable for me, but also acceptable to others whose support is necessary for the ongoing work.

This, of course, is as true for treatment as it is for diagnosis. Therapy, too, cannot be conducted in a way that is dystonic with the therapist's own style, or aversive to others involved in the treatment. Given that necessary requirement, one can think of the decision-making about what to do in art therapy when the goals are *therapeutic* as similar to that used for *diagnostic* aims. For example, if one's goal is to help someone to loosen up, one might consider arm and/or body movements, perhaps in the course of a scribble drawing, as in the approach described by Florence Cane (1951). Or one might think in terms of media and encourage a patient who always uses "clean" materials to try paint, fingerpaint, or clay, perhaps with a brush or tool as a first step. To relax the patient(s), one might use any of a number of warm-up activities, a variety of which have been described by numerous art therapists (cf. Rubin & Levy, 1975). In addition to considering approaches via the body or the materials, one might also explore topics or themes which would encourage playfulness and looseness.

The art therapist may have another kind of goal, such as increasing self-esteem, in which case tasks or materials with a high potential for success would be selected. I do not, by the way, mean paint-by-number pictures, molds, or kits, or any such impersonal and restrictive approaches. Not only are they not art in the truest sense, but I also believe that, despite their pervasive popularity with patients and staff, to put together someone else's creation can never give a person the same feeling of satisfaction and self-actualization that is available from his own authentic work, no matter how crude. There are, however, materials which are themselves intrinsically beautiful, like the exciting hues of cellophane or tissue paper. Cut or torn and glued on a white surface, it is almost impossible for either to appear anything but attractive. Similarly, carefully chosen oil-base clay can promote a "successful" outcome because of the beautiful, varied colors of the easily pliable medium, which look attractive whatever is done to or with them.

If the individuals with whom the art therapist is working need to make something "useful" in order to impress others or feel good about themselves, then it makes sense to teach fairly foolproof techniques, like coil or slab pots, or contour drawings. If the patients are so demoralized about their ability that it seems they need some kind of preformed

"crutch," then the challenge is to find one which will make them feel better about what they produce, but will not interfere with the product being their own. For example, plain white precut kites and Frisbees (which really work) are extremely popular with adolescents; yet each youngster's decoration remains his own personal picture or design. Another very popular activity among my patients is to draw a marker picture on a special round piece of paper, which can then be sent to the manufacturer and for minimal cost is made into a real (dishwasher-proof) plastic plate. A similar project involves drawing on a smaller round piece of paper, which is then made into a metal badge the patient can pin on his or her chest. In all of these instances, the artwork involved is entirely original and varies from one individual to another. But the final product is almost always a source of pride, because of the fact that it has a kind of utility (and therefore value) that a drawing or painting has in very few households, and unlike many "homemade" items, it works!

Another common goal in art therapy is to help patients to express or release strong feelings, like aggressive impulses. While catharsis alone is never enough, genuinely experiencing the expression of any affect and finding that it can be controlled and need not be destructive make for a very useful learning experience. It is one easily provided in art therapy, whether it is through thick crayons which can stand heavy pressure without breaking or the suggestion of specific activities which require aggressive energy, e.g., making something of wood which involves hammering nails or wedging clay by slamming it onto a board. If symbolic destruction is what the individual needs to safely experience, then sawing wood, cutting paper, or slicing clay might be a most satisfying art activity—not for its own sake, but in the service of creating something. Or, the art therapist might focus on theme rather than medium or process and suggest a picture about anger or a fight.

If one's goal is to uncover repressed material, it is likely that easily expressive media will work better than those which require more time and deliberation. It is sometimes useful to suggest a kind of free association in images, going from one creation to whatever comes next, trying not to be deliberate or concerned about any kind of logical progression (a procedure based on the verbal free association of classical psychoanalysis). With this kind of goal, as with one like helping individuals to discover their identity, a choice of unstructured media seems most likely to allow people the necessary self-definition and authenticity consistent with the aim.

On the other hand, one might have a very specific goal in mind which calls for a much narrower and more focused approach, such as helping

an individual to consider how he sees himself in relation to others. In this case a picture of his life space at that moment in time might be most appropriate. If one wants to help a patient lost in delusions to focus on reality, it is appropriate to suggest that he draw the still life placed before him, or do a portrait of the patient opposite him. Conversely, if the goal is to better understand the content and symbolism of a patient's hallucinations, the therapist can ask him to draw or paint what it is he sees or hears at delusional moments.

In working with a couple on becoming more aware of their communication patterns, one might suggest that they draw together on the same sheet of paper without talking, and then discuss afterward all that they thought and felt in the course of the exercise. Or, if the therapist wants to help two people to become aware of their misperceptions of one another, she might ask them to draw each other "privately" on opposite sides of an easel. They would then look at their partner's portrait of themselves and modify it as they wish, followed by a discussion of their perceptions both of themselves and their partner (a technique like that developed by Wadeson (1973) for art therapy with couples). Or, if one feels that two parents each perceive their troubled child in mutually incompatible ways, a request to represent that youngster independently and then to compare the portraits is appropriate.

Perhaps the goal is not one of changing perceptions or promoting awareness, but rather of facilitating some kind of needed experience that an individual or a group might be avoiding. Whether it is being playful and having fun, or being able to express aggression openly and directly, there are many possible activities using art media that might enable the patient(s) to have an enriching experience. As with all of the examples so far, once the goal is clear in the clinician's mind, she can use what she knows about art and therapy and the patient(s) involved to create a relevant activity.

But what if the therapist is not certain about what is needed at any particular moment in therapeutic time? Perhaps it is because I am rarely sure that I can always *know* best what patients need to see or to experience that I am personally more comfortable with an open-ended approach, where the choice of both materials and themes is up to the individual. The times when I have decided to suggest something specific are infrequent, usually in response to what is going on at that particular moment. On even more rare occasions, I have planned ahead, out of a strongly felt need regarding the patient(s), often based on the immediately preceding session. Planning ahead, however, seems risky, since one never knows "where" any individual, family, or group is going

to be in advance of any particular meeting, no matter how long one has been working with them.

What I am more likely to do is to have some thoughts about where the individual or group needs to go and some ideas of how to help them to get there. If anyone is unable to get started successfully, even with my help, I might then suggest as an option a particular medium, theme, or exercise related to the "plans" in the back of my mind. The only exceptions to this way of operating that make sense to me are diagnostic sessions and time-limited or theme-centered therapy. In the latter two, the inherent constraints make it more appropriate to zero in on whatever limited goals seem possible, rather than waiting for a more natural course of therapeutic events to occur.

While it seems to me that the structured approaches to art therapy, which are sometimes called "art therapy techniques" are often clever, creative, and probably harmless, I worry that in preventing patients from finding their own creative way with materials, we are also depriving them of the essence of a genuine art experience. I would like to be able to believe that the many delightful and stimulating techniques which are so popular serve mostly to enhance patients' abilities to be creative and communicative. I feel some concern, however, about what seems to me a kind of arrogance on the part of many clinicians who decide for patients what is best for them at any point in treatment. Such omniscient art therapists also have a regrettable tendency to specify themes and manner of working at moments when I would prefer giving the individuals more options. But many would say, "Isn't that part of our job? Aren't tasks the medicinal resource of the art therapist, who has a responsibility to choose from among the many creative activities available the one that is most needed by the client, just as the medical doctor is obligated to prescribe thoughtfully for his patient?" While those who subscribe to this position believe it to be their responsibility, I feel it is a perversion of the medical model, and am astonished at the certainty of those who practice primarily in a prescriptive fashion.

As noted above, there are times when choosing or creating a specific task makes very good diagnostic or therapeutic sense. But whether one values the art primarily as sublimation or as communication, authentic artwork by anyone requires independent decision-making about as many aspects as possible. I don't think I am a rigid art therapist in most respects; yet I feel quite stubborn about the importance of safeguarding personal choice in regard to art, whenever patients are capable of exercising such options. Parenthetically, it has been my happy experience that even severely impaired populations can be enabled to learn to make

their own decisions with the right kind of help. Of course, there are
times when the limited time or work space available makes it difficult—or
maybe even impossible—to offer any kind of choice at all. But I feel
convinced of the morality of the issue, that any human being has a *right*
to make his own choices, especially in such a personal realm as art.

Art therapists have many choices available in regard to media, task
specificity and structure, and the nature of one's own involvement. In
order to achieve whatever goal is primary at the time, we have options
about the *medium*: one can offer an open choice from two or more alternatives, specify the use of one class of material (e.g., drawing, painting, or modeling), or designate a specific one to be used. We have a
similar range of choices in regard to the *theme* or topic, which can be
quite open or more or less specific: We can request the drawing of a
feeling, or specify one like sadness or anger. We can also be more or
less specific about the *manner* in which the task is to be done: We can
ask someone to represent a feeling by using abstract shapes or showing
people expressing it. There is always a variety of ways of combining
medium, theme, and manner into a task for any particular situation.
The goal might be helping patients to work together cooperatively. However, the particular group involved might not yet be ready to discuss
and create a mural together, without severe tension and probable fight-
ing. The challenge, then, is to decide what degree of cooperation they
are capable of and to lead them in slow steps toward the desired goal
(the method of successive approximation).

For example, a group of disturbed youngsters wanted to work together, but were unable to do so when provided with the opportunity.
So the first step was to make a mural where each child created his own
building independently, cut it out, and placed it (one at a time) on the
common backdrop. The children then took turns drawing the "environment" around their individually created houses. Essentially the same
approach was subsequently used with a three-dimensional project, each
child creating a plasticine animal and placing it on a cardboard "ground"
which was later decorated with markers. During the discussions of each
activity, a good deal of attention was given to whatever open disagreements or silent hurts might have been present during the minimally
shared aspects of the task. The next step was for each child to work with
one other person on a joint picture, with adult assistance when necessary
in both the decision-making and doing phases of the project. Since the
children were able to do that with some success, it was decided to try
increasingly larger groups, each time paying attention during the dis-

cussion to the working process, how it went, where it was hard, and what alternatives might have been considered. The focus was on the interaction among team members, rather than on the product, which was primarily present as the concrete reminder and reflection of that interaction.

Quite a few sessions were necessary to help this group of troubled youngsters, with poor impulse control, to get to the point where they could work together in groups of four on the planning and execution of a joint project. They then exercised their teamwork on both two- and three-dimensional products and had learned a good deal by the time the series of sessions was over. What they learned had less to do with art and more to do with social skills; but their pride in the joint creations they were able to produce was great, and the amazement and admiration of the staff quite genuine (especially since these same children were much less cooperative in most other situations on their inpatient psychiatric unit). This experience exemplifies how the relevant variables (in this case, degree of disturbance in relation to the goal of cooperation) influence the decision-making about what is offered or suggested in art therapy.

These decisions are not really so hard to make if one truly understands the who and why of the patient(s), and the what of growth needs. Then the challenge is to provide the kind of artistic activity which will best meet those needs at that moment in time. While it is my own feeling that in most instances an open choice of media and theme is best, even in that context one is often challenged to help the patient(s) to make those decisions independently. When a structured task seems optimal, there is not only the pleasure of choosing or creating a relevant activity, but also the need to present it to the patient(s) in a clear, stimulating, and relatively nonthreatening fashion.

It is clear that one cannot make such decisions about what to do or how to do it without a wealth of background understandings and knowledge about both art *and* therapy. Otherwise, there is a temptation to latch on to cleverly creative activities provided by others and to use them in an imitative way, without fully understanding either their original intent or the needs of the patient(s) to whom one is responsible. I am not, by the way, suggesting that one should never use the ideas of others. Using someone else's idea in a way that is synchronous with its original purpose is indeed "a sincere form of flattery" and highly appropriate. Equally relevant, however, is feeling free to modify a good idea in order to suit one's particular situation, when the original format

does not quite fit the new context. Perhaps most pleasurable for the creative art therapist is dreaming up needed ideas as required in her own clinical work.

I feel we do our patients an injustice to approach them blindly, without knowing why we are doing what we are doing, and without a clear sense of how to deal with whatever arises from our evocation of patient expression. I am concerned that the use of stimulating materials and cleverly structured activities may sometimes mask an underlying confusion on the part of the art therapist about what is going on. Of course, patients often need help to get started, and some patients do need more help than others. No one expects a retarded or depressed or confused patient to be as self-motivated or independent as a neurotic one. But one does not necessarily have to deal with a lack of motivation by using lots of "turn-on" techniques. Yes, it is necessary to "wind up the mainspring" (Linderman & Heberholz, 1979) more actively with some individuals or groups before they are able to work productively. But there is a tendency to do this more often than is really necessary or helpful to the patient(s).

A recent experience with geriatric groups in a psychiatric hospital has again convinced me of the power of self-motivation when the right kind of stimulating stage is set for art, despite the very real handicaps of age, despair, and confusion. The art therapist, who had assumed for several months that these older patients required much structure (being told what to use, what to represent, and how to do it), was asked what she thought would happen if she offered them the same kind of choice she was making available to the substance abuse group, a younger and more independent population. She assumed they would do nothing. She was pleasantly surprised when she found that most of the older patients could decide for themselves, although they did need more help from her in order to make decisions about what to use and what to make, and often needed assistance in actually starting to work. Given such support, however, these patients made impressively varied products, which were much more personal and expressive than those they had done in response to the therapist's carefully designed lesson plans.

If I have a bias in the area of what to do, it is for *flexibility*. Given my conviction that an open choice is best for most therapeutic and diagnostic purposes, I also see the advantages, at times of assessment, short-term therapy, and theme-centered work of more specific task structure. I can even acknowledge the rare but real moments during work that is primarily open-ended when it is best to suggest a specific medium, theme, or task. One of the most critical aspects of presenting the idea (whether

open or structured) is the therapist's manner of doing so. How patients are invited to choose or to do may affect whether they are able to follow through more or less easily.

In general, the more comfortable and confident the art therapist issuing the invitation, the more positive will be the patient's expectancy of his ability to accept it. My own conviction is that, one way or another, it is possible for any person or group to use art media creatively. It may be necessary to shift gears several times in order to help someone get started, or to assist someone through the steps of the decision-making process; but with the expectation that everyone can find something congenial, it is usually possible to enable that to happen. Perhaps most important, there is no need to feel any great rush or pressure about how quickly that should occur, and often patients in groups or even individuals will spend a signifcant period of time observing, talking, looking around the room, or watching others before being able to plunge in themselves.

At moments like that, I sometimes adopt a Pied Piper approach, in which I use myself as a model, attempting to engage people in creative activity by doing so myself with evident pleasure. I rarely have to put into words the invitation to others to use the materials I have chosen; I just make sure that the equipment is accessible to them, and my activity itself seems to act as sufficient stimulation. Whether those who "follow" do so in a submissive, competitive, or imitative fashion is not the issue; what is important is that it is a most useful way of using one's artist-self in the service of a pivotal task in art therapy: evoking expression.

It is important to be clear about the request, and, if it seems indicated, to be firm—not to ask the patients *if* they would like to do something, but to say that they *will* do it, and then to offer to help them begin if they have any difficulty. Although some diagnostic or therapeutic goals might lead to a less supportive structure, there is little to be gained by making it unnecessarily hard for people to get started. The art therapist can always be helpful, especially when the task is a fairly threatening one. Moreover, presenting tasks or offering theme ideas can be done in an artistic way almost as easily as a heavy-handed one—it just takes time and thought to do so. But to my mind, it is the same as creating an inviting set of media and working spaces; it is part of the art therapist's overall job of evoking creative expression.

Of course, that is just the beginning of the creative process. Setting the stage, deciding what to do, and helping people to get started are the necessary events which initiate the central core of art therapy: the work with media. While people are working, whether individually or

in groups, the art therapist is still present and has an important and equally critical task: to enable the artist(s) to make a creative statement with materials. The complexities of this role, how it shifts and fluctuates in the course of a session as well as over time, are the subject of the next chapter on facilitating expression.

REFERENCES

Burns, R.C., & Kaufman, S.H. *Kinetic family drawings.* New York: Brunner/Mazel, 1970.

Cane, F. *The artist in each of us.* New York: Pantheon Books, 1951.

Furrer, P.J. *Art therapy activities and lesson plans for individuals and groups.* Springfield, IL: Charles C Thomas, 1982.

Kagin, S., & Lusebrink, V. Expressive therapies continuum. *Art Psychotherapy,* 1978, *5,* 171-180.

Keyes, M.F. *The inward journey: Art as therapy for you.* Millbrae, CA: Celestial Arts, 1974.

Kwiatkowska, H.Y. *Family therapy and evaluation through art.* Springfield, IL: Charles C Thomas, 1978.

Linderman, E.W., & Heberholz, D.W. *Developing artistic and perceptual awareness* (4th ed.). Dubuque, IA: William C. Brown, 1979.

Paraskevas, C.B. *A structural approach to art therapy methods.* New York: Collegium, 1979.

Robbins, A., & Sibley, L.B. *Creative art therapy.* New York: Brunner/Mazel, 1976.

Rubin, J.A., & Levy, P. Art-awareness: A method for working with groups. *Group Psychotherapy and Psychodrama,* 1975, *28,* 108-117.

Wadeson, H.S. Art techniques used in conjoint marital therapy. *American Journal of Art Therapy,* 1973, *12,* 147-164.

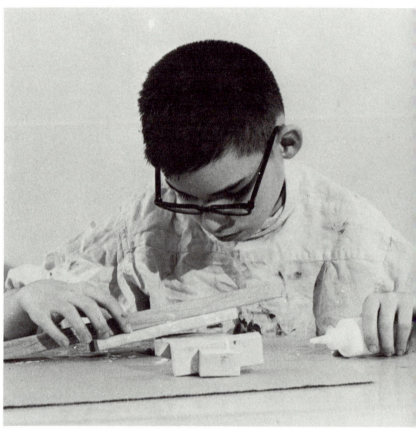

A boy who is retarded, cerebrally palsied, and legally blind can mobilize amazing energy and control when he has the chance to build with wood scraps and glue.

The art therapist helps a geriatric patient by teaching him how to mix paints in order to get the color he wants.

Chapter 10

Facilitating Expression

Facilitating expression goes on from the moment the patient has started to work until he is finished. And from the time of getting started, to doing all along the way, to deciding when to stop, a patient may be more or less independent. Those who can function well and creatively on their own need to have their autonomy, working space, and time respected by lack of intrusion. In this regard, it appears that some art therapists don't feel that they are doing their jobs if they are simply sitting and quietly observing the patient. But if they can learn to be comfortable on their observational toes, there is a great deal to be gained from watching facial expressions, body language, and the sequence in which things are created.

Although there is so much to observe that it is not possible to detail all of it here, it might help to note some typical aspects of a person's encounter with art media, whether seen individually or in a group. It is especially interesting to note how the individual makes his selection of medium and just how he takes the very first step with the materials. Is he slow and cautious, or does he plunge right in? And if he starts quickly, is it impulsive or deliberate? Does he seem selective or haphazard in his use of materials? Does he seem intent on making something, or is he more interested in manipulating? How involved does he become with the material and does that change over time? How absorbed is he in the working process? Does he seem to pay attention to the environment and to other people, or does he seem lost in his own thoughts? How intense and how long is his concentration span? Does

he seem distractible, and if so when and by what? Does the art activity seem to be a means to gain approval, to engage in social contact, or is it perhaps an end in itself?

While a patient creates, one can observe whether he works at a fairly even pace, or uses a lot of energy in manipulation of the material, body movements, or verbalization. What is his working tempo? Does it change over time, and if so, how? How much or how little energy does the person seem to have available over the course of the session? In the course of doing his artwork, does the person become progressively more free? Does he start in a disorganized fashion and gradually become more controlled? Or does he stay the same throughout? Is there any change in body movement, speech, or mood in the course of the work? What kinds of movements does the person use with the materials: free or tense? careless or careful? large or small? jerky or smooth? Are his body movements in general sure or unsure? rigid or relaxed? steady or uneven? slow or rapid? and so on.

If the person talks while he is working, what kind of voice tones does he use? How articulate is his speech? And to whom does he speak: the art therapist, other patients, or himself? Even apparently unrelated spontaneous verbalization during the working process is important to note, since it is inevitably connected with what is being done with the materials. If the person wants to describe or talk about the product or process while working, listen with respect and remain careful not to intrude on his creative work space. Observing what is actively rejected, as well as what is selected, and watching as closely as possible the sequence of steps on the way to the final product are both important in understanding the patient and his art. This is especially critical if a person is using materials which permit undoing (like clay or fingerpaint) or covering over (like tempera paint), where the messages visible in the process may be obscured in the final product.

With all there is to observe during the art process, there should be no need to initiate intervention for its own sake. After all, to intrude on a creative process is to disrupt the very event for which one has so carefully set the stage and prepared the patient. On the other hand, if a patient is asking, either verbally or nonverbally, for help at any moment, the art therapist should usually offer assistance, but in the least intrusive fashion possible. It is ideal if the help can be given in a way that enables the patient to discover the answer himself. The challenge to the art therapist is to act in such a way that the patient can find the problem and/or the solution. This may require a nonverbal action, like turning a picture upside down to help someone decide if it feels balanced overall;

or it may require a verbal intervention, like a comment or question which catalyzes some new awareness on the part of the patient. For example, a person might express despair or frustration about his artwork, that "it's not turning out right," or "it doesn't look good." Before one can help in any meaningful way, it is necessary to help the person to clarify the source of his distress. The art therapist might therefore ask the patient to tell her, as specifically as possible, just what it is that he finds distressing about his work. Once that has been defined, then the art therapist can ask other questions or engage in other actions, which will eventually enable the patient to decide how best to remedy the problem.

On the other hand, there are times when an art therapist knows some technical tip of which the patient is unaware. When it seems that the naive artist's life would be made significantly easier by the sharing of that knowledge, it seems inhumane not to do so. However, if respect for the patient as artist is genuine, the technical tip will be offered as an option, not an instruction or command. It is difficult not to insist that a person use a smaller brush or a stronger glue, when one knows that his chances of ultimate success are minimized by what he is using or doing. While it is an art therapist's responsibility to let the patient know the probable consequences of one procedure or another, it is also important to permit each individual to make the final decision for himself. One cannot prevent frustration for patients any more than one can protect one's children from pain. In fact, as with offspring, it is probably ultimately more useful for people to fully experience some negative consequences, in order to be able to freely change their own behavior. What goes on between therapist and patient in art therapy in regard to technical procedures is much like real-life learning experiences. But these occur in a protected situation, where the patient can safely find out what happens if he submits, opposes, or responds in some other way to the therapist's indication of an alternative way of working.

Facilitating another person's creative behavior is a delicate matter. Whether to be active or passive, to be physically near or far, to be psychologically close or distant, to act warm or cold, to comment or to stay quiet, to look or not to look—these are the difficult decisions which have to be made from moment to moment in clinical work. In making such decisions about when to intervene and how, one must be not only artistic, but also knowledgeable. It is in making these kinds of decisions that knowledge about both art and therapy becomes essential, especially one's understanding of appropriate goals for the patient(s). Intuition is simply not enough. Therapy is not something that can be done "by the seat of one's pants," at least not well. The challenge is to make one's

knowledge about art and therapy so integrated a part of oneself that it
is fully available in a spontaneous way. Clinically informed intuition is
quite different from following one's impulses; the former can usually be
trusted, so that one is free to act on hunches. And later, when there is
time, one can think about it deliberately and reflect critically.

Whatever the nature of one's intervention, whether initiated or in
response to an overt request, facilitating patient art can be thought of
in general as the provision of what has been called an auxiliary ego.
That means lending one's own ego (one's knowledge or organizing
capacities) to the patient, when one feels it would help him to actualize
his creative intentions. Sometimes lending one's ego is optional and
sometimes it is essential, as with severely handicapped or disordered
patients. But in either case, it is quite different from dominating or
deciding or doing for the patient, especially if he is capable, and simply
needs some help in order to be able to think or act on his own. Being
respectful of individual choice and artistic preference is essential—a reflection of respect for other people, no matter how damaged the state
in which they are seen. Such an attitude is also consistent with any kind
of genuine creative process, which has to be ultimately from the person
if it is to be truly his own. This is true whether one believes in art *as*
therapy or art as a means of communication *in* therapy. The more authentic the art, the more likely it is to be a true sublimation or an honest
communication.

Whatever the art therapist does, from the beginning to the end of the
working process, a guiding principle is that of the "least restrictive intervention." This is a paraphrase of a contemporary term in mental
health and special education—the "least restrictive environment." As
with the latter, what is unstated but implied is that one should provide
the most facilitating intervention or environment for that particular individual or group. It does take skill, artistry, and tact to find the least
restrictive or intrusive way to support a patient's creative efforts. Perhaps
what is most needed is a wordless gleam in one's maternal eye, or
perhaps an approving comment about the artwork itself, or about the
patient's behavior during the process. Sometimes it is necessary to offer
or to give more active assistance with the work, usually in response to
an overt or subtle request on the part of the patient.

However, if things are threatening to get out of hand, the therapist
needs to intervene without being asked in order to set limits on action
or words, and to help anyone losing control to regain it. Even this kind
of intervention is best done in the least restrictive/intrusive way possible.
One may be able to settle things down with just a glance, perhaps a

gesture, or maybe a few softly spoken words. Or the situation may require that one take charge in a more active way. This kind of limit-setting need not be seen as restrictive, however, despite the fact that the therapist is probably literally restricting one or another sort of behavior. Rather, the limit-setting can be viewed as a reestablishment of the very *framework* for free functioning that one has worked so hard to create. Whether silent or assertive, an art therapist needs to maintain an ever-watchful eye and presence throughout all moments of any art therapy session in order to use what she knows to help those in her care to experience both creativity and consciousness in a safe and secure context.

When she intervenes, she will strive to be not only correct, but also artistic in how she does it. It is probably in the *how* rather than the *what* of intervention that artistry is distinguished from mere competence, more a matter of style than of substance. Perhaps one reason why art therapists can make so many mistakes and still help patients to get better is that their manner conveys the sincerity of their wish to assist, even if the content or form of what they are doing or saying is widely off the mark.

An art therapist's behavior in the course of the working process is critical to the success of her work, but it is usually ignored or minimized in discussions of technique. As with stages in therapy, much attention is paid to the beginning phase (evoking expression) and to the final one (looking and learning), but what goes on in the middle is often a muddle. The range of possibilities for intervention is so great that it is difficult to make generalizations. Whether one is seeing an individual, a family, or a group, what one does and how one does it depend on an almost infinite number of variables, which are overwhelming to list, let alone quantify. But the kind of thinking which is relevant for setting the stage and evoking expression is also relevant for the task of facilitating art in therapy. That is, one ought to do what seems most appropriate at that particular moment in time for that particular patient or group in order to move the treatment along toward one's goals. And, in accord with the principle of least restrictive intervention, it should be done in the most subtle way that is likely to enable the patient(s) to reach the goal of the moment, as well as the long-term goals one has decided make most sense.

It is always necessary to disentangle patient needs from one's own—a task most easily accomplished if one has achieved some degree of self-knowledge—and to engage in continual self-monitoring. For example, it is important for an art therapist not to let her need for finished products

interfere with the patient's use of art media in the fashion most helpful to him at that moment in time. This may mean manipulation or even destruction, rather than a formed creation. For an artist, it is not easy to sit quietly by and observe something that seemed to be moving toward form begin to disintegrate. Though there are times when I would intervene in such an event, there are others when I would not, guided much more by my therapist-self than my artist-self.

If, as Kramer (1958) has suggested, an art therapist combines in one person the ability to be artist, therapist, and teacher, then one of the issues during the working process is how much one should use any particular aspect of oneself at any moment in time. My own preference is for flexibility in this area, as in others. I am convinced that the pendulum swings for most individuals from an emphasis on the art as sublimation to an emphasis on the art as communication, sometimes in the course of a single session, sometimes at greater intervals. I therefore feel a frequent need to shift gears, at times using more of my teacher-self in the service of a meaningful product, at others using more of my therapist-self in the service of understanding the messages therein. In both, I hope that my artist-self is available to facilitate and respond to the patient's creative work.

One can use one's artist-self in a variety of ways in art therapy. Perhaps the most important is in empathizing with what the patient is going through in the course of the creative process, from the initial decision-making moments, through the ups and downs of the work, to the time when he feels "finished." As noted earlier in the chapter on materials, this means actually working with all media offered to patients, allowing oneself to become engaged and to experience the peculiarities of each medium, tool, or process so that one can genuinely "feel with" a patient's attempts. Although I believe that one does not need to be an exhibiting artist in order to be a good art therapist, it is necessary to allow some time and space in one's own life to work with materials, whether for recreation or more serious aims.

It is also helpful to use one's artist-self as a tool for reflecting on what one is experiencing in response to any particular patient or group (including staff). Using art media to represent the individual(s) or the feelings and fantasies they evoke is a most powerful way of reflecting on one's inner experience. Whether or not one senses countertransference reactions, one should always try to keep in touch with whatever is stimulated by patients or colleagues. It is a source of further self-knowledge, but it is also a source for better understanding the people with whom one works. Whether one uses paint, chalk, clay, or cut paper

matters little; what is important is the use of all aspects of oneself, including the artist inside, as a means of understanding.

Perhaps the most common appearance of the artist-self in art therapy is in the use of media with patients for one or another purpose. The Pied Piper technique described earlier, as a way of stimulating others to use materials, is one possibility. Another reason one might choose to use materials alongside patients is to reduce their self-consciousness about being observed. I often find myself doing a scribble drawing, for example, as a way of demonstrating the technique to someone; and sometimes I continue and develop the scribble in order to promote interaction with a reluctant individual or to help family members in an evaluation to feel less uncomfortable. For similar reasons, I might casually manipulate a material that someone else has chosen, not so much to stimulate or even to demonstrate possible uses, but more often to reduce the tension many patients feel when they are working and the art therapist is sitting and staring at them.

Another way in which an art therapist can use her artist-self is in actually drawing (or painting or sculpting) with the patient. One such possibility is literally working together, as in the nonverbal dialogues used by several therapists with severely regressed and withdrawn patients. In my own experience, the only time I found myself wanting to become involved in a pictorial dialogue with a patient was in work with an elective mute in an attempt to connect with her, despite her intense resistance. This same patient also evoked in me an uncharacteristic desire to create several portraits of her, probably another attempt to establish a relationship.

On equally rare occasions, I have found myself using drawing as a way of clarifying an interpretation, such as showing a patient that he has put a "wall" between us, or has "boxed" himself into an isolated space. With families in ongoing family art therapy, I have occasionally drawn an image of how I see their interaction patterns, which is more eloquent and probably closer to the truth than I could achieve with words alone.

Also on rare occasions, it has seemed useful to work with a patient on a creation, usually when I feel that my involvement can enable a kind of artistic statement that the individual is too fearful to make without active support. There is yet another usage of the artist-self, through a technique called *closure*, which art educator Viktor Lowenfeld developed in his attempts to reach severely handicapped children (1957). It involved starting something (like a clay sculpture) by partially doing it, then giving it to the patient to complete. It is a kind of stimulus or starter, which

may be necessary for a person who is unable to organize materials completely on his own. A similar kind of starter approach can be used to help inhibited individuals to begin, though most often it is possible to help them to create their own scribble lines or ink blots. For some, however, a dot or line or shape on the paper supplied by the therapist seems to enable them to get started more easily. Whether it is related to a need for permission, a desire for oneness, or some other cause, it is yet another way in which a therapist, who is also an artist, can use those specialized skills in the service of treatment.

Another possible use of oneself as artist is in following instructions to create given by the patient. While I see this kind of technique as something of a last resort to be used when all else fails, it is really analogous to following a patient's directions in dramatic play, role play, puppet drama, or psychodrama. That is, given the fact that one has decided to use media oneself with a patient (who for the moment refuses), it makes more sense to use it in a way dictated by the patient than according to one's own whims. For example, a child I was once seeing wanted very much to be the boss of me in many ways. He pretended that he was a teacher, instructing me in how to draw a particular cartoon character. Not only did I get an A−, but we both experienced what a demanding and critical boss he was, which he then related to disciplinary experiences with his severely punitive mother.

One of the most risky yet most exciting uses of the artist-self with patients has been reported by art therapist Mildred Lachman-Chapin (1983). Her technique involves drawing or painting in a spontaneous fashion during the time that the patient is involved in his own work. Since the artwork for both follows an initial period of discussion and a decision about the theme for the day, each person is presumably focusing on that topic and its meaning for the patient. It represents another way of using one's preconscious thinking as a therapist, and reminds me of the mental images that run through my mind when I am with a patient, or the doodles I draw in my notebook while an analysand is on the couch. However, such a technique could be abused by those with insufficient self-awareness. Like Winnicott's (1971) use of squiggles with child patients, where he and the youngster took turns elaborating simple scribble drawings into images, it is something that seems appropriate only in the hands of a very experienced clinician. Nevertheless, given a sophisticated art therapist and a fairly sturdy patient, the approach has considerable potential as a way of using one's artist-self in an authentically creative fashion in one's work as a therapist.

There has been considerable focus on the use of the artist part of

oneself, largely because that is what is unique to art therapy as opposed to other modes of treatment. The educational function in art therapy may also be seen as distinct, if viewed specifically as teaching the patient how to use art media or how to look at and think about art products. Yet every kind of treatment requires some education of the patient on the part of the clinician, whether it is explicit, as in cognitive therapy, or implicit, as in client-centered or existential therapy. Whatever the "game" played by the particular therapist, the patient needs to learn its "rules" and how to play it.

One question that is relevant in art as well as in other therapies is how explicit to be about what is happening and why. Although I began in my work saying little and hoping that people would grasp the essence of art therapy by experiencing it, I have gradually become more open with patients, especially at first encounters. This parallels an increasingly direct way of dealing with issues in general, such as asking even a reluctant child why he has been brought to a clinic and what he thinks are his biggest problems. It seems just as relevant for the art therapist to tell him or a group why she is offering them art media, and why she is inviting them to choose or to do something in particular. Not only is such an open approach more honest and ethical, but it is also quite helpful to patients of all ages and diagnostic classifications.

The educational role of an art therapist should not, therefore, be limited to helping people use media or look at art; it should include helping them to understand the meaning and purpose of art therapy, for them and for their treatment. The natural resistance of most adults to using materials is more easily overcome if they are presented with a meaningful reason why such an activity will be helpful to their recovery. They can then allow themselves to regress, play, and create, because they can see the serious purpose of the activity and are less likely to be overwhelmed by feelings of foolishness or embarrassment. One of the most difficult aspects of this educational task is finding nonthreatening but understandable language with which to present the purpose of art in evaluation or therapy. Part of the "art" of being an effective therapist is being able to tune in to different age levels and views of the world and to communicate comfortably and effectively with all sorts of people through words. One of the assets of art therapy is that it gives the clinician and the patient yet another mode of communication, one which can be carried on in complete silence and, as described earlier, can be used to confront, to mirror, or in some other way to communicate with each other.

The art educator aspect of the art therapist is that of a teacher who

knows a lot about materials, tools, and processes, as well as looking at and learning from creative products. In teaching the use of materials, my own preference is to do so only when necessary. For most people, little or no formal instruction is required in order to use most basic media. For many, a minimal statement or demonstration may do the trick. In groups and families, individuals often learn from other members how to do something in art. An art therapist is not primarily a teacher, though clinicians in different settings have offered formal art classes to patients with great success; and that seems like a fine idea, as long as it is made explicit. In art therapy, the teaching of techniques seems relevant only when it is essential in order for the patient to be able to use the materials, especially to use them to say what he wants to say.

Thus, the teaching in art therapy is a means to an end rather than the central focus of the work. It is important to remember that the end is not art, but therapy, so that any teaching about art is always in the service of its therapeutic usefulness. For some patients, this may mean skill development in the use of a medium, learning specific techniques which enhance their comfort and facility. But the goal is rarely to make them into artists, although that may be a happy secondary gain. It is more likely that the goal is to help them to feel like competent individuals or to understand more about their inner selves. Only if the creation of increasingly refined products would seem to promote either goal does it make sense for an art therapist to use her teacher-self in the service of such an aim.

Having minimized the role of art instruction in art therapy, I also remind the reader that the first portion of this book is called the *Art Part*. I do feel strongly that no one can be an effective art therapist without knowing materials, tools, processes, and products—without knowing enough, in other words, to be able to teach any patient at any time what he needs to know in order to say what he wants to say during art therapy. The artistic component of this role is in being selective, in using oneself as a teacher only when necessary, and in providing there, as elsewhere, the least restrictive intervention. If one can help a patient to help himself, even on a technical matter for which one might have a quick and easy solution, it will be a better learning experience for him, and will promote his eventual autonomy as a person and an artist.

How does the therapist aspect of the art therapist's role become visible during the working process, when the main task is facilitation of the patient's artwork? On the surface, it might appear that the artist and educator facets are more central, especially during the time that people are involved in creating. But it is not that simple. In addition to the

active observation noted earlier as an important part of the working time for the therapist, an art therapist's primary identity as a clinician should really infuse everything she does. That is, when observing patients at work, it is with a clinically trained eye, which sees behaviors with art materials and other people primarily in psychological terms. Someone looking in the room during the middle portion of an art therapy session might easily see it as an art lesson or a recreational activity. While both learning and fun may well be part of what happens, neither is the primary aim, except as they relate to the goals of therapy.

Whether to interact with a patient and how to do it during the working process—whether to initiate, how to respond—these are the difficult clinical questions that are always present in art, as well as in other forms of treatment. It is only the therapist part of the art therapist's identity that can answer them, and hopefully a well-trained one which is able to do so in a thoughtful way. I believe that there are two main variables to be considered in answering these questions at any moment in time with any patient(s). The first has to do with the goals for the individual(s), both short- and long-term, and how best to reach them. If, for example, the clinician has determined that an individual needs to work on some reality problems which he is not representing in his artwork, then casually talking about them while he is working might be appropriate. The second variable concerns the readiness of any patient at any time to move in the direction one sees as relevant in any specific way. While some patients might be very comfortable talking while they work and it might even enhance the freedom of their art, others could find their creative process seriously inhibited by simultaneous conversation. However, the therapist cannot usually know or even guess in advance how talking while working will be for any individual who has not initiated it spontaneously. One therefore needs to try it out and see what happens.

Trial and error is a necessary mode in any work as delicate and multileveled as art therapy. Many clinicians seem afraid to fail. Indeed, one of my most common supervisory tasks is to support therapists in trying things they fear will backfire with patients. In most cases, the worst that could happen is that the patient will not respond at all or will do so with anger. Neither of these is disastrous, though it is wise to be cautious with those who have problems controlling physical aggression.

If the anxiety about failing is overcome, and the art therapist tries something that doesn't work, the creative clinician will learn from the experience and will go back to her mental drawing board, trying to find yet another way to achieve the same goal. If, for example, the patient

who needs to discuss a reality crisis situation cannot talk while he draws and does not bring up that topic when discussing his art, the therapist has to think of other options, like separating such news-of-the-week discussions in time from the rest of the session, either at the beginning or at the end. In other words, there probably is a workable way to help a patient to discuss crucial issues; the challenge is to figure it out through trial-and-error thinking and action.

Or, if the therapist feels that an important short-term goal is helping a patient to become freer and less stereotyped in his art, which has stayed largely defensive for some months, the creative clinician will try all kinds of approaches, until she finds one or more which "click" with the particular person. It might be doing a scribble drawing; it might be using a fluid medium; it might be thinking of mental imagery before using media—but whatever it is, the important thing is to keep on trying, to be open-minded and inventive in one's thinking about what might help. On the other hand, a therapist might try everything she can think of either to get a patient to loosen up or to discuss reality concerns, and still nothing works. So yet another part of the therapist's task is realizing her limitations, her lack of omnipotence, the need for consultation with a colleague, and the ever-present possibility of failure in this delicate discipline of therapy through art.

Deciding to give up, whether permanently or for the time being, is not always because of failure, but more often, one hopes, because of success. For any patient who is actively working with media, there is also the need to decide when any particular artistic product is done, finished, complete. For some this is easy, intuitive, and unconflicted; for others it is the focus of an intense, obsessional debate or block. For many, at least at first, it is an area in which they feel inadequate because of their limited experience with art. Patients often ask the therapist to tell them not only how they are doing, but also whether or not something looks finished. As with other judgmental questions, my own preference is to help the patient to make his own evaluation. One can be quite active in noting things to think about or ways to look at a product in order to decide if it is all right and if it is done, without ever making an explicit judgment. The artist in the art therapist must often bite her tongue at such moments, since it is impossible to avoid having an aesthetic response to a patient's work. But a good teacher, as well as a good therapist, can promote more growth by helping the person to evaluate himself than by doing it for him.

In learning how to be his own critic, the patient also learns at various steps along the way how to perceive his artwork in an informed fashion.

The final step in most art therapy sessions, whether individual or group, is looking at and reflecting upon the product and the process behind it. The therapist's task in this activity is helping the patient to do this so that both therapist and patient may better understand and learn. This is the subject matter of the following chapter on looking and learning from art.

REFERENCES

Kramer, E. *Art therapy in a children's community*. Springfield, IL: Charles C Thomas, 1958.

Lachman-Chapin, M. Empathic response through art: The art therapist as an active artist in the therapeutic relationship. In L. Gantt & S. Whitman (Eds.), *The fine art of therapy*. Alexandria, VA: American Art Therapy Association, 1983, pp. 80-81.

Lowenfeld, V. *Creative and mental growth* (3rd ed.). New York: Macmillan, 1957.

Winnicott, D.W. *Therapeutic consultations in child psychiatry*. New York: Basic Books, 1971.

Working silently together and later discussing it can be a power-ful learning experience about both art and human interaction.

Chapter 11

Looking and Learning
From Art

No matter what the age of the patient, there is value in both doing and reflecting in the visual arts. One of the ways in which art in therapy differs from art in other situations is that there is almost always some kind of reflection upon the art experience. Depending on the age of the patient(s) and the context of the work, it may be quite brief or fairly extensive, but it is an important component. It is more critical for those who see the art primarily as communication, and less central for those who value primarily the potential for sublimation through art. But even clinicians who subscribe to the art-as-therapy approach are interested in what people have to say about the experience and the products they create. Interviewing patients about either process or product seems to be the most difficult aspect of art therapy for the novice, whether dealing with an individual, a family, or a group.

Since most art therapists have a good deal of the artist in them, setting the stage and evoking and facilitating expression seem to come more naturally than looking at and talking about what has happened. Stepping back and reflecting aloud on either product or process is a new experience not only for the patients but also for art therapists-in-training, and requires learning new skills and sensitivities. Since defenses are such powerful forces, even though they may be partially bypassed in art, most patients make it very difficult for the interviewer to elicit really meaningful comments about their work. As with all of the other roles one plays, an adjustment must always be made to the disability and functioning level of the patient(s).

It is especially tricky to find the right "language" with which to enable different people to talk about their art or the experience of making it. Creative interviewing is, like much in therapy, an ongoing trial-and-error process, in which one needs to be willing to encounter many blind alleys and frequently frustrating responses from the patient. The challenge is to maintain one's enthusiasm and optimism, to continue trying hard to find a way that is comfortable and compatible, and to help every individual to reflect meaningfully on his art experience. One needs to be willing to try not only different verbal avenues, but also different expressive modalities. Dramatization with or about the art product, for example, can be a way to help a patient to associate, when other approaches have failed.

In a videotape of a diagnostic art interview I did some years ago, I see myself practically turning verbal somersaults, while trying to get something meaningful in the way of associations out of a very resistant girl of ten. I confess that it is mildly embarrassing to show the tape and that I usually excuse myself by telling my audience that I was under pressure because of the many observers at this demonstration interview. But the fact is that a child or adult like the one involved, always requires more activity on the part of the art therapist in order to elicit significant responses. Just as it is most artistic to ask the fewest and most open-ended questions of a fluent, freely associating patient, so it is equally artistic to move in with action and drama, when encountering resistance. Perhaps it is analogous to the sculptor's task: to chisel and chop with vigor when that is required by the material, but to sand and smooth with caution when working with another medium or at another stage of the process.

Lest the reader think I am comparing patients in art therapy to an artist's medium, to be molded or shaped according to the clinician's desires, let me restate the importance of each individual and his own authentic creative unfolding. So perhaps a better analogy than sculptor would be gardener: providing the proper environment, nurturance, and care to enable the person to flower best in his own fashion. This imagery can easily be applied to the tasks of setting the stage, and evoking and facilitating the patient's artistic expression. It may be a bit more difficult to see its relationship to the task of helping the patient to learn by looking at and talking about his art. But I believe that they are quite similar, since the challenge of creative interviewing is to help the patient say what is truly on his mind, to bring out into the open what is inside of him; just as in the art process one hopes to evoke the patient's own personal imagery and help him to give it concrete form.

Discovering meanings in patient art and behavior goes on throughout

the art therapy session. Observing selections, avoidances, images, sequences, and so forth requires that the art therapist learn to "watch with
the third eye." She needs to observe, as closely as possible, the manner
in which each individual proceeds and how he works. This includes all
steps on the way to the final product. It also requires learning to "listen
with the third ear" (Reik, 1948), especially to what may seem to be
unrelated spontaneous verbalization during the working process. Nonverbal expression can also be eloquent, like the pleasure in a patient's
face as he smashes a piece of clay hard with his fist. Sometimes the
person will want to describe or discuss the product or process while he
is working. It is important then to be receptive, but also to listen without
intruding. The really fascinating exploration of the product and the patient's responses to it, however, usually take place after the working
time is over, during the discussion part of the art therapy session.

While looking and associating and reflecting on products can, of
course, occur during the doing phase of a session, it is helpful to separate
the two kinds of behaviors in time and, if appropriate, in space. As
noted earlier in the chapter on setting the stage, creating a physical
situation, where an individual or group members can look at the artwork
with some aesthetic distance, enables a deeper and more focused kind
of learning from the experience. Placing the artwork in a location that
minimizes the need for eye contact with the therapist (or other group
members) can help in reducing self-consciousness during the interviewing process. Whether the product is on the wall, an easel, the table, or
even the floor matters little. What is important is that all those involved
be able to see it easily and that they can, if they choose, look at the art
rather than at each other.

From a visual perspective, it is important to set things up so that the
art produced in a group or by an individual can be viewed clearly and
coherently. Finding a location which is neither too close nor too far, as
well as one which is central to the viewer(s), is of course essential.
Another useful aid is some kind of framing, whether temporary or permanent. This need not be very elaborate and can easily be done by
simply suggesting that the patient find a piece of colored paper of the
next larger size on which to mount the product, choosing from among
assorted hues the one which most appeals. Another possibility, less
colorful but more professional in appearance, is to use a precut mat of
the appropriate size, which immediately gives a rather finished look to
the artist's creation. What is most important here is separating the art
product clearly from other visual stimuli, so that the patient(s) can really
focus on it in all respects.

The same considerations are true for three-dimensional work as for

that on a flat surface. Creating an attractive setting upon which to display the patient's sculpture can help immeasurably to enhance the viewing/reflecting/discussing part of the process. Sometimes the best "stand" is simply a piece of colored construction paper, setting the sculpture off from the table surface and the surrounding stimuli through shape and tone. Sometimes greater separation is needed, so that a tray of a size and shape appropriate to the product is best, perhaps on a raised surface; a modeling stand draped with a piece of cloth, for example, makes a very attractive and easily available sculpture mount. In some cases, it helps to present the three-dimensional work against a solid color background, light or dark, like a wall or board covered with some color of paper. In my office, putting a folded piece of construction paper at right angles to both wall and table at the point where they join makes a quick, attractive, and visually clear background for most work in clay, wire, or wood.

The challenge then is in how to invite reflection, since a request to talk about the art may easily get no reaction or a negative one. Although one should always respect a patient's right not to talk about his work, just as one should respect his right not to use art media, one can also try to encourage some reflection, just as one would attempt to stimulate some creative activity. The patient might want to talk about someone else's picture if he is in a group, or he might prefer to reflect on the experience of using the medium, rather than on the product. The message that should be given in the discussion portion of a session is similar to that sent when evoking expression: that the therapist expects and feels confident that each individual has something to say (verbally or creatively) and that her job is to find a way to make it comfortable for him to say it.

It probably helps if the initial suggestion is simply to look, to take as much time as is needed, and to see what thoughts and ideas emerge. It also helps to leave the invitation to reflect as open-ended as possible, so that different people can use the opportunity in the way most comfortable for them at any moment in time. Although one could suggest a specific focus on the process of creation, on the art elements, or on the representational messages, it seems more valid in this area (as in art expression) to allow the direction to come from the patient(s). It is for this reason that the initial question or invitation should be as unstructured as seems feasible, leaving considerable leeway to the respondent(s), such as: "Would you please tell me (or the group) about your picture (or sculpture)?" Or: "Does that have a story to go with it?" For

some highly verbal patients who want to share and who enjoy this kind of exhibitionism, an open invitation to talk may be enough to stimulate a veritable flood of descriptive/associative material.

For most, however, more creativity is needed on the part of the interviewer in order to help them to clarify and extend the ideas inherent in or stimulated by their art. This is more difficult than it may sound, since every art therapist has her own projective reactions to patient art and must guard against asking questions in such a way that she intrudes her ideas or in any way pressures the patient to agree or disagree with how she (the therapist) sees the picture. Whether the person has a need to be compliant or oppositional, or can respond freely, is never certain, so that any response to an implicit suggestion on the part of the therapist is automatically suspect.

The difficult but also pleasurable challenge, then, is to find ways to help people to talk about their artwork which are comfortable for them, yet do not in any way influence what they see in or say about their products. There are, fortunately, a number of rather specific questions one can ask, which do not give the answer or even suggest it, but which do help patients to be more articulate about what they have made. If the artwork is abstract, for example, one can ask if it reminds the artist of something, or what it looks like. In such a case, if there is still blocking, turning the picture or sculpture around so that it can be viewed from different perspectives may help to stimulate some projections. Sometimes covering a portion of the work helps a patient to focus on one part and to deal with it more effectively. Such visual techniques always supplement verbal ones throughout the evocation, facilitation, and discussion phases of an art therapy session.

If the artwork is representational but the content is still not clear to the therapist, it is safest to be open about that and to ask for clarification. To guess incorrectly can be distressing to the patient, who thought that the picture or sculpture looked like what he had in mind. While it may wound his narcissism a bit to know that the therapist cannot identify what he has made, it is probably less painful that if she thought it was something he never intended. Not knowing all the time what a person means to say visually is really quite human and in the long run admitting it is more helpful to a patient than appearing omniscient. This latter quality, while often feared, is also desired by most patients. Most yearn for a therapist who not only knows it all, but is also omnipotent, magically able to make their troubles go away. Confessing that one sometimes doesn't understand a picture, just as one sometimes doesn't

understand what a person is trying to say in words, is really helpful to the patient, who needs not only to see the therapist as less-than-perfect, but also to be able to accept his own limitations.

Once one has some idea of what is represented in or projected onto the artwork, one can try to engage the patient in the potentially pleasurable activity of getting ideas from what he has made, taking yet another creative journey with guidance and support. Ideally, interviewing someone about his artwork is an adventure for both clinician and client, a voyage through associations and ideas which often leads to unexpected realms. When trying to involve a patient in this process, one ought to give it validity by justifying its usefulness and relevance to treatment, just as one should be able to justify using art materials in therapy, especially with a reluctant or resistant individual. I feel comfortable telling anyone of any age that talking about art is a very interesting way to find out more about both the art and oneself and that it is also fascinating, since the thoughts can lead in so many possible directions. Whether one stresses the creativity involved or the importance of understanding symbolic communications will depend of course on the age, illness, and anxiety level of the patient. I think it is never appropriate to be dishonest, to pretend that the story a patient tells is not related to him, for example. But it is equally important to meet the patient where he *is*, which may mean respecting a good deal of disguise and distancing in his art or associations.

The most useful beginning questions, as noted earlier, are open-ended, allowing maximum leeway to the interviewee. However, it is also true that these often elicit either no response or a minimal one, so that the interviewer is then challenged to use her creative resources without influencing the patient's ideas. If there is a constant self-monitoring process going on, the risk of intruding one's own projections is minimized, and one is then free to explore different associative avenues with the patient. What probably matters more than anything else in this endeavor is being both optimistic and persistent. This combination of attitudes, if held sincerely, works as well for the interviewing activity as it does for the creative one. If the therapist approaches the discussion with the expectation that every patient has something to say about the product, the process, or both, she will work hard to find a way for each person to do so. If she does not get discouraged by blind alleys or dead ends, she will continue to explore new avenues of discourse in order to find a workable wavelength for any particular patient at any particular moment in time.

Of course, the art therapist may sometimes have to give up. But it is

my impression that many clinicians give up far too often and far too easily during the interviewing process, probably much more than they do in regard to the creative activity itself. Perhaps it is because they are more comfortable with art than with words. Perhaps it is because they see their primary task as the provision of a creative experience, with reflection as secondary and optional. My own feeling is that it is the combination of doing and reflecting that gives art therapy its special potency . . . that we do really engage both hemispheres of the brain in the expressing and thinking aspects of treatment, thereby enabling integration and synthesis. Moreover, we not only encourage the ego to use its full capacities to select, organize, and synthesize in the creative process itself, but also promote the development of its observational skill (observing ego) in the looking-at and reflecting process involved in viewing and discussing the art.

Having emphasized optimism and persistence, I should like to add creativity to the list of those qualities necessary for the art therapist as interviewer. There are many possible ways to elicit projective ideas through art, limited only by the ingenuity of the clinician and the resistance of the patient. For example, if a piece of artwork represents a setting of any sort, a question about what is happening there or where the patient would be if he were in that place can lead to rich associations. Or, if there is a representation of a living creature, the therapist might ask what the character would say if it could talk, eliciting either telling about it or actual role-taking. It is even possible to suggest that inanimate objects might talk and to ask what they would say if they could speak.

It is also useful at times to suggest that the patient imagine something moving or changing in the picture and ask how it would then be (if the person came out of the house, or if we could see inside). A broader question of a similar nature involves what happened just before the depicted or described scene and/or what is likely to happen next. A patient can be invited to say the first word that comes into his head, as he looks at different components of a work of art, perhaps with the therapist pointing to one item at a time (the "pop-into-your-head game" approach to free association). Or, he can be asked what a particular shape, color, or object reminds him of or makes him think of.

If talking *about* something seems too threatening, it is often the case that talking *for* it is less so; this is especially true with children, who frequently prefer talking *as* a character to telling *about* it, taking the role of a created creature with abandon and expressiveness. For those who have exhibitionistic tendencies (true of most who are not inhibited in this area), making a radio or television show out of the interviewing

process can be most useful, with a paintbrush or other suitable object as the microphone, and an invitation to the artist of the week to tell the listening/viewing audience about what he has done or made.

Another approach to interviewing the reluctant patient is to offer a choice between logical alternatives, which enables the individual to further clarify and elaborate his ideas about his creation. For example, if a person has drawn a human being and responds with the statement that "it's just a person," one can ask what sex it is, what age (or age group), and what it does most of the time. It is then more natural to ask questions about how the person (now defined by age, sex, and occupation or pastime) is feeling, where he is going to or coming from, what he might be thinking, or what he would say if he could talk. The more articulated the fantasy, the easier it is to follow it and for the individual to further elaborate it. Again, the tricky part here is not to impose or suggest one's own ideas, but to ask the kind of characterizing questions that help the individual to create his own story, and to always follow his lead as closely as possible.

Other adjuncts to successful interviewing are such props as real microphones and tape recorders, with the possibility of listening to oneself (and to others in a group) and reflecting at yet another level on the event. For the last several years I have had in my office a dictaphone with both a built-in and a hand-held microphone, either of which can be used for recording interviews about art. An especially useful feature is the playback, which can be private if set on low in the mike and held to one's ear, or the speaker playback, where one can vary not only the volume, but also the tone and the speed. But even without such fancy gadgetry, I have found, especially with children and some adults, that a portable tape recorder, with a microphone they can hold while they talk, can enable a much more fluent description of the product and of associations than seems possible without such an aid.

Some, on the other hand, find it easier to write than to talk out loud, and titles are probably the simplest kind of initial association or reflection on a product. They are also rather easy for most patients to come up with, especially if one is supportive of artistic titles that don't have to fit logically, but that come into the patient's head as he regards his artwork. If the patient can say it but cannot write it himself, that becomes the job of the therapist, an aide, or another patient—whoever seems clinically most appropriate. Poetry, which can be free-flowing and unrhymed, is another way to elicit verbal associations of a nondiscursive nature; it, too, like a title, can be written down or dictated by the patient. Another approach is to simply encourage patients to write—on the art-

work itself or on another piece of paper—some words which seem to them to go with or describe the art, the process of doing it, or the product itself. Stories are probably the most elaborate kinds of verbal associations of a literary sort and are quite congenial for patients of all ages. Group storytelling, perhaps of the round-robin variety, is easily stimulated by art produced by one or more members and can be quite playful as well as productive.

With children, puppets or miniature life toys come in handy and can even be used with some adults, who are either intellectually childlike or comfortable with being playful. The puppet or small figure of a person or animal can become the interviewer and is sometimes much easier for the patient to answer than the more threatening therapist. Or the dramatic play prop (puppet or figure) can be the one who answers the questions, posed by either another such character or the therapist. One little boy and I did a good deal of work during a resistant period of his analysis by using an owl puppet, who was quite willing to answer questions about his artwork and other topics when he himself was not. This same owl was also able to pose very useful questions to me and to other puppets about the boy's symbolic productions, which reflected in yet another way the child's concerns.

I suspect that there are countless ways to evoke people's associations to their artwork, limited only by the imagination of the individual interviewer. This is a similar situation to that which exists regarding activities, which are also probably infinite and require the spontaneous ingenuity of the individual art therapist. It may be that many art therapists do not trust their own creativity—their capacity to either design a relevant activity or to evoke meaningful comments. Given the necessary knowledge and understanding, however, and a substantial amount of flexibility and creative thinking, an art therapist can be as good a facilitator of verbal expression as she is of visual expression. With both, she must be careful to focus on the patient, her primary task being to bring out what is already inside or potential in that person. Even if she also sees her job as adding to or filling in (e.g., building structure or making up for deficits), it should still be undertaken in the service of what seems to be the most legitimate aim of art therapy: the development of the creative power and self-control of the individual.

To be a good interviewer, one must be something of a chameleon. This does not mean that one ought to imitate or mimic the person with whom one is conversing, nor that it is helpful to lose one's own identity in that of another. Rather, in order to get on a workable wavelength with another human being, one has to feel one's way, and sometimes

even take on some of the coloration of his communicative mode. The therapist may be echoing the rhythm of the patient's speech, mirroring his body language, using some of his more colorful vocabulary, or in some other way trying to be sure that she (the therapist) is both hearing and being heard. This is vital, because only when the patient feels heard can he begin to feel understood. Many bright clinicians, who in fact comprehend what a patient is trying to tell them, fail in communicating that understanding to the patient. The patient, in turn, does not feel that his message has been received, let alone understood, because the therapist's language and mode are so incomprehensible to him. Much of this chameleonlike activity on the part of the therapist is intuitive, and part of a total attempt to empathize with the patient. An art therapist must be comfortable enough with herself to do this, to let go her usual controls and even some of her characteristic style, in order to make real contact in verbal communication with another person who may be very different from herself.

Fortunately, the discussion phase of any art therapy session is preceded by the evoking and facilitating of expression, both of which entail much nonverbal, and probably some verbal, interaction between art therapist and patient. By the time the two start to talk formally about the patient's product, they have already established some sense of each other and have hopefully found some ways to communicate. Making sure that one touches base with each person in an art group, therefore, whether with eyes, hands, or words, is probably closely related to one's eventual success in evoking a spirited group discussion among all of the members.

One of the biggest questions on any interviewing art therapist's mind is whether or not to try and relate any of what the patient is saying about his art to him as a person. Sometimes the answer is provided by the patient, who spontaneously remarks on how a drawing or sculpture reminds him of something in his own life, or how his way of reacting to the disappointment he feels with his product is typical of him in all situations. But more often than not, the painting or sculpture is discussed on its own terms, as a separate object, which is one of the great assets of art in therapy. The art product becomes an intermediary object, perhaps transitional at times. It is always a concrete something, with meaning to both therapist and patient, on which each can focus in both the doing and discussing phases of a session. The difficult part for many art therapists lies in the question of making a bridge or connection between the art and the patient's reality.

One very simple rule, which makes good psychological sense to me,

is to stay at the symbolic level for as long as possible in discussing any particular product. It is best to stay with the disguise in the imagery and associations, to talk about what is in or projected onto the artwork, and to go as far as one can at a symbolic level. This is true because the more disguised the images, the more the patient will be able to safely and comfortably reveal. Only after one has, in a sense, "milked" the imagery, via storytelling or associations, does it seem sensible to explore in any kind of open fashion the possibility that it might represent something related to the patient.

As soon as a person becomes aware that he is talking about himself through his imagery, he naturally becomes more self-conscious and is only able to reveal that which is currently tolerable to his ego. The therapist may, of course, introduce the notion that there might be some connection, as in asking whether he sees any relationship between what he has said about his art and himself. If his response is negative, that is usually a clear signal that the patient is not yet ready to see the connection, and the best therapeutic response is to gracefully withdraw. On the other hand, the question may evoke a positive or quizzical re-action, in which case one is invited to pursue the notion, always asking questions in an open-ended way which allows the patient to be in con-trol, to take the lead, and to feel in charge.

Just as art therapists can seem unnecessarily timid when pursuing the asking of creative questions about the patient's art, so they may also seem unnecessarily intrusive when they finally get into the interviewing mode. This may be partly due to a certain naiveté about defenses, which are very "real" psychic phenomena. Frequently, what a person has said about his symbolic creation is so blatantly revealing to the art therapist that it seems inconceivable that the patient really did not know that he was talking about himself. But that, after all, is what symbolization is all about. A true symbol, in most depth psychologies, expresses in a disguised form an impulse which is not known by the artist. Its adaptive (defensive) power derives, at least in part, from the fact that the forbid-den or ineffable ideas it represents remain unconscious to the artist (cf. Jones, 1916).

This kind of symbolism is, of course, quite different from the patient's conscious labeling of colors, forms, or representations as standing for some person or feeling. I am not suggesting, by the way, that such deliberate use of the symbolizing properties of art is not valid. I simply wish to remind the reader that, with the exception of a psychotic who is really incapable of repression, for most patients those conscious con-nections are different from the deeper meanings which remain less avail-

able to awareness. What can be elicited through interviewing and brought to consciousness are only those thoughts, ideas, and feelings which are preconscious—not fully repressed, but not necessarily in one's awareness at all times.

If a therapist understands enough about symbolization and the workings of the wide range of possible defense mechanisms, a good background in development and dynamics can enable a clinician to hypothesize the unconscious messages disguised in patient art, just as an experienced analyst can often guess correctly the concealed meanings of a patient's dream imagery. With both, despite the reality of certain so-called universal symbols, whose likely significance may be hypothesized within a fairly narrow range of possibilities, it is essential to look at the patient's own associations in order to obtain any kind of valid understanding of the imagery. Even if it turns out that one's initial guess about meaning was correct, one should not assume that any image "always" means something specific, nor even that its significance is invariant over time for any particular patient. Because of the mechanisms of condensation, displacement, reversal, and symbolization, visual imagery is usually multiply determined, like other mental products. This very richness and multileveled quality of visual imagery is part of what gives art therapy its potency; and it is also something every art therapist must keep in mind, especially when she feels some pressure to find a nice, simple translation of meaning.

This multifaceted nature of visual symbols can also be taught to patients, some of whom learn to enjoy with the therapist the mental game of generating a variety of associations and attempting to make sense out of them. This leads me to think of interpretation, something misunderstood by many art therapists in concept, as well as in their work with patients. One reason for the confusion is that there are at least two important meanings of this term for an art therapist, which are not identical but are related. One is more narrow, confined to the art product, and has to do with interpreting the meaning of his *art* to the patient. The other is broader and includes any statement of an explanatory nature regarding patient dynamics, which ideally includes some genetic (historical) component as well. Even in psychoanalysis, where interpretation is considered the primary therapeutic tool, it is quite rare. Most of the analyst's comments are of a preparatory nature, such as "running commentary" or "restatement" in a clarifying fashion of what the patient has said. Even in a client-centered model, "reflection" to the patient includes making explicit those feelings or attitudes which have been implied but not stated. And if one feels that what the patient needs at

a particular moment is support, then such statements are also appropriate and are common in art therapy when one is reinforcing the patient's creative behavior or art product.

But none of these are "interpretations," which in insight-oriented therapy usually include explanation, not simply translation. In well-conducted analytic psychotherapy or psychoanalysis, such interpretations are not made until one is fairly sure that the patient is ready to accept them. Most clinicians offer interpretive statements as possibilities, sometimes as probabilities, but rarely as certainties. They usually invite the patient to consider the connections suggested, but never insist that they are correct without some confirmation from the patient. Unfortunately, defenses being what they are, confirmation is rarely a simple, calm affirmation; but negation is not necessarily an indication that the interpretation was incorrect. The only valid index, which makes as much sense in art therapy as in psychoanalysis, is to be found in the subsequent material—in that session and in later ones. If it reveals a clarifying of the conflict or a loosening of defenses, as suggested in the interpretation, then one can be pretty sure that one is moving in the right direction, no matter what the patient says. Of course, in art therapy, the subsequent material includes the art as well as the verbal behavior, which is often less disguised and more rapidly revealing of the patient's unconscious response to what has been suggested.

Therapist interventions during the discussion of art products and processes are perhaps more loaded than many that occur during the evoking and facilitating phases of the work. Words, after all, are still the common currency of real-life communication, and patients tend to respond strongly to them. This is especially true when one is talking about a patient's creation, which is felt as an extension and often a part of himself. Because of this narcissistic aspect of everyone's art, it is especially important to be acutely tuned in to potential sensitivities when discussing patient products. So, in addition to being creative and persistent in the pursuit of associations, and being clear about how and when to help a patient discover the meaning for him of his own art, one also needs to be very tactful.

Such tact is essential in all facets of art therapy, but the lack of it is more visible and perhaps more toxic during the discussion phase of a session. Getting anyone to receive any kind of message requires putting it into a form that is both comprehensible and acceptable to the other person. If it is also relatively more appealing and relatively less threatening, then it is much more likely to be heard and considered. It is a little like extracting a splinter. It is best done carefully and gently, thereby

causing minimal pain and maximizing the likelihood that the wound will heal safely and well. Whether one considers this to be "sugarcoating the pill," or overcoming resistance (which is inevitable), or simply doing one's therapist job as artistically as one's artist job, I should like to put in a strong plea for artistry in art therapy, the subject of the next chapter.

REFERENCES

Jones, E. The theory of symbolism (1916). In *Papers on psycho-analysis* (5th ed.). Baltimore: Williams & Wilkins, 1948.
Reik, T. *Listening with the third ear*. New York: Farrar, Straus, 1948.

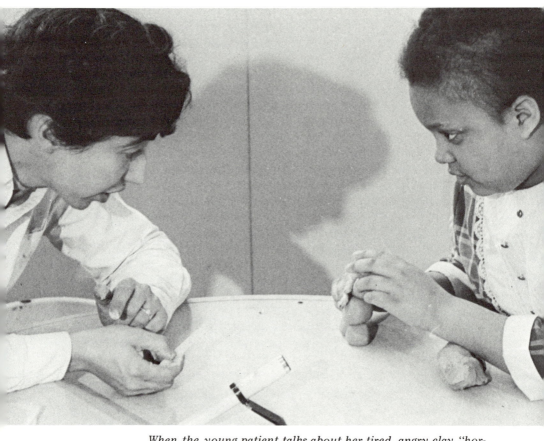

When the young patient talks about her tired, angry clay "hor-sie," the art therapist understands that she is also talking about herself.

Working together without talking enables people to experience a visual-gesture-image language directly and artistically.

Chapter 12

Working Artistically

Although I thought of this book originally as describing the art of art therapy, what also became apparent during the writing was the need for artistry in doing one's work. While this may seem to be a fine distinction, it is an important one. For it is possible to master the art of many things, such as piano playing, gourmet cooking, crewel embroidery, and to do them well, i.e., skillfully or competently. But to do them in such a way that people sigh when they hear one's sonatas, or eat one's mousse, or view one's wall hangings requires something above and beyond mastery of the art form itself—something best identified as artistry.

One might argue that outstanding performance in any area is usually attributed to the possession of special gifts or talents. It may well be true that there are natural clinicians, individuals who already have so many of the personal prerequisites for successful work as therapists that they seem to develop the necessary skills effortlessly. However, such natural capacities (like warmth, empathy, sensitivity, and intelligence) are limited in value, if they are not harnessed to therapeutic work which is also well understood. That is, such personal qualities are worth less than they might be if the person does not also possess the necessary understandings about both art and therapy outlined so far. When such knowledge is integrated and used by someone who takes to the work with comfort and pleasure, then there is the possibility of true artistry.

There can never be a good reason to be careless or sloppy in one's work as an art therapist. There is no excuse for being heavy-handed in

art therapy, with the possible exception of lack of experience. What is impressive about art therapy is that, even when it is done in an awkward, clumsy fashion, it is still a potent diagnostic and therapeutic modality. This is most apparent when students in training begin their supervised work. One can only think of what is ultimately possible when the powerful tool of art in therapy is handled with the most exquisite and knowledgeable care!

Perhaps even more important, as an artist turned therapist, I find that I get great pleasure out of doing my work creatively, even though it is now people who are my concern rather than products. Whatever satisfactions accompany the creative process in other realms must also attend doing creative work in human services. I derive satisfaction not only from seeing people get better, but also from the aesthetic pleasure of trying to help them to do that in an artistic and inventive way. Maybe it is the artist in me, after all, that prompted this book. Perhaps the question ought not to be, as one of my favorite colleagues posed it years ago, "Are you an artist *or* a therapist?" (Ault, 1977). Rather, it should be, "Are you an artist *and* a therapist?" Or, better yet, "Are you an artist *as* a therapist?"

It seems to me increasingly clear that good therapy, especially through art, is always a creative adventure. That is probably why, though I sometimes get bored with teaching or lecturing or even supervision (which is also a change/growth process), I never get bored with art therapy—and I have been doing it full-time for over two decades. The creative challenge of the work, the puzzle of each new patient, and the delicate task of figuring out how to help each person move toward better adjustment—all of these are unpredictable, stimulating, and endlessly fascinating. In all, through the people, their problems, and the therapeutic process, I am continually learning and discovering something new. Despite the universality of certain human problems and of some artistic symbols, the variety in people and their imagery is endless. The particular twists and turns of any therapeutic journey are sufficiently unpredictable and unique that it is almost always fascinating, whether one ends up feeling successful or frustrated.

Of course, I know that I also get satisfaction for a variety of personal reasons from many aspects of the work, from "rescuing" others, to "peeking" at their secrets, to the occasional feelings of heightened aliveness which can occur in art therapy. Needless to say, there are also the less attractive aspects of the work, like carrying heavy supplies, cleaning up sloppy messes, or being on the receiving end of a violently negative transference which expresses itself in a particularly irritating way. As

I get older, I find that the high energy level and occasional destructive-
ness of younger children is more often distressing and less often delightful; and that someone who refuses to engage with media or me can
strain my patience, especially if I am fatigued or upset. But, despite the
many intrinsic frustrations of doing art therapy with disturbed people,
it is generally such fascinating fun that I actually look forward to each
day of work and frequently feel a sense of excitement while I am with
a patient, usually in response to an aesthetic achievement or some other
long-awaited sign of progress.

I hope that is true for every art therapist. I suspect that it must be so,
since the work is so physically and psychologically demanding that one
would need to derive some ongoing satisfactions in order to stay with
it. This is especially true since the financial rewards are rarely substantial,
and most art therapists get much more significant reinforcement from
their work than from their paychecks. I have suggested here that one
reason it can be so gratifying is that doing art therapy can be experienced
as a creative venture, one which can be carried out more or less artistically.

I submit, though without any hope of ever being able to control the
variables involved sufficiently to prove it, that the patient's ability to
grow through art therapy is directly proportional to the artistry of the
therapist. And, whatever the limits on the patient's potential development, the more knowledgeable one is, the more artistic one can be. In
work with patients of all ages and in all settings, art therapists use what
they know about art and therapy to help people to prevent or to overcome mental pain. If they can use that knowledge in a well-synthesized
way, then they have mastered the interface—the area where art and
therapy meet. If that well synthesized and fully integrated knowledge
is then utilized in an *artistic* way, they are much more likely to be effective
than if they are heavy-handed or careless in style or manner of work.

The difficult question of how and when to intervene requires a kind
of continuous tracking, a constant alertness on the part of the art therapist, who tries to stay tuned in to the patient, family, or group as
empathically as possible. On the basis of such observations, one sometimes gets the feeling that it would be good to intervene in some way,
verbally or nonverbally, but deciding exactly when and precisely how
is not easy. The decision about whether or not to move in is probably
made largely on the basis of cognitive awareness, i.e., some understanding of the vicissitudes of the therapeutic/creative process in relation to
the patient's needs. But the how (the form the intervention takes), the
when (the precise timing and tempo), and the style (the specific manner

of action or words involved), these are as much artistic decisions as clinical ones. Unless they fit comfortably or aesthetically into the patient's space at that moment, they will not be effective. Even if inherently uncomfortable, as is true with most confrontations, how and when they are made have a great deal to do with the nature of the patient's response.

It may help, for a moment, to think of the relevance of other art forms to the issues involved in the questions of timing and mode of a therapist-initiated intervention. The tracking referred to is largely visual; it requires looking at not only details (e.g., facial expressions or hand movements), but also the larger picture, continually shifting lenses like a photographer from close-up to telephoto, especially with a group. It is something like being present at the performance of a symphony, an opera, a play, or a dance recital. One's gaze constantly shifts from particular parts to the whole, just as one's overall sensory consciousness includes not only the visual input, but also the sounds, the words, and the movements of bodies in space. What is different about a therapy group is that it is more like a chamber music concert in one's living room, because of one's closeness to what is observed. It can also feel sometimes as if the therapist is the conductor of such a performance, constantly alert to each player's music as well as to the sound of the ensemble, offering leadership, guidance, and support for the efforts of both individuals and the group.

One mustn't stretch these analogies too far. A therapist does not, except in the most structured kind of clinical work or necessary limit-setting, need to use the kind of authoritarian control possessed by a conductor. But a listening/watching/feeling art therapist *is* aware of the music between herself and an individual, as well as the vibrations between members of a family or a group. She can sense whether things are synchronous or dissynchronous and might even try to help people to harmonize at times, especially with those who need to learn socialization. She might wish at times to echo a patient, at others to blend, and at others to work together in a related but more differentiated way, as in counterpoint. She might even see it as useful to the patient to present herself as very different, in a dissonant way, as in some modern music. Similarly, she might want to get into the patient's rhythm, to respond to it, or to change to a different one which challenges and confronts.

More often, the therapist is the interpreter of the patient's music (often as yet unwritten)—his internal strivings toward actualization, and the tensions and dissonances which must be lived through in order to reach

a harmonious finale. The process of therapy can also be seen as similar to a symphony, with a series of fairly separate movements or phases, yet a common underlying set of themes, often repeated in various guises, and a central unifying motif or key. As with symphonic movements, it is best if each aspect of the patient or stage of the process can be permitted its full development, possible only when there is no time limit on the treatment. With ample time, the full range of each musical idea (conflict or part of the personality) can be explored, developed, and allowed to come to a natural dénouement in the course of the overall work. The finale, of course, may include a replay of earlier themes and may be stormy as well as calm; endings in music usually involve both crescendos and decrescendos, just like terminations in art therapy.

The treatment process is largely one of improvisation, as opposed to a scripted or fully composed score or drama. As in all improvisational work—in music (jazz), drama (street theater), or art (free painting)—the artist/therapist's job is, as that of a director, to help people give form to whatever emerges. With an individual, one's energy can go into facilitating the form-finding and refining processes. With a group, some energy is also needed to help people to stay in some coherent aesthetic relationship to one another. Whether this seems geometrically organized like a Mondrian or fluidly ordered like a Pollock is not important. What does matter is that the participant(s) experience the organizing principle involved as something present, constant, and integrating for them individually as well.

Since the art should be the patient's own, the therapist needs to be the kind of coach or teacher who helps a musician to fully develop his own personal style of interpretation, even though the composition may come from another. Similarly, a group or family art therapist often feels like the choreographer of those in the room, though in a much more subtle and responsive way than is usually thought of in regard to that role. She responds to the hints of movement in the patients; she helps each one to carry them further, and to shape them in whatever direction seems artistically and psychologically right for each person at that moment. When the therapist puts connections into words through interpretations, they are meant to clarify and to explain, much as a ballet master might do with a dancer. As with any art form, such thoughtful connection-making is also a way of giving relevant emphasis to important components and creating an overall sense of order out of something that was previously confusing.

The ideas of aesthetician Suzanne Langer (1953) are most congenial to art therapists. She proposed that the arts are tangible forms of human

feeling, which is often inexpressible in words. The art therapist helps the patient to not only capture and express feeling through art, but also feel in touch and in charge through nonverbal behavior (smiling, crying, frowning) as well as words. Words that name significant ideas are like artistic forms—they relieve tension because they provide an externalization that is concrete and discrete. And, like more complex verbal constructions or visual creations, words provide containers for all of the complex feelings, thoughts, and images they are trying to convey. When one can use *both words and art* to help patients with the task of expressing and containing their feelings, one is then better able to assist them in channeling their life energy into a coherent existence.

Drama is an art form that involves words much more than art, music, or dance. I often find myself thinking of a therapy session itself as a dramatic event, or of a course of psychotherapy through art as a kind of drama. However, the visual arts, which are static, cannot in and of themselves capture (except in a series of sequential images) the feeling of development over time which is so well represented in drama. Thus the unfolding of any person's or group's therapeutic drama is like what happens in a play, beginning when areas of conflict and concern are laid out, followed by the heightening of tension and working through of conflict, ending with the dénouement and resolution of the plot. In the process the tension builds up, often leading to one or more climactic moments. In art, the focus is on what is central in the visual product, its meaning as well as its appearance. In any art form and in any therapy, it may take some time to express, to clarify, and to focus on those major themes. Only after that has been done is it possible to work toward either elaboration or development, and only after those have been accomplished is it possible to work toward climax and resolution.

In the moment-to-moment interchange of a therapeutic encounter, one is also engaged in a kind of dance with the patient. This is especially visible in individual therapy, but is also present in groups at a more complex level. In the therapeutic dance, the challenge is to engage with the person when necessary and appropriate, for instance, when it is clear to the therapist, though not always to the patient, that he could use some help with the art process, or when the clinician wants the client to see or consider a way of thinking about his symbolism. On the other hand, one also needs to know when it is best to disengage, to give a patient the kind of space and freedom necessary for him to truly develop his own step, rhythm, and form (work of art). The necessary total disengagement at the end of each session is difficult for many patients, especially as the transference develops. Some need more help

to connect, and others require more assistance to disconnect. But in either case, one thing that facilitates the differentiation (separation) process is the art therapist's role as critic.

Like the person who writes art, drama, film, and music reviews for the local newspaper, the clinician uses her expertise with art therapy to help people learn what to look *for* and what to look *at*. She also helps them to gain a sense of perspective, to step back and look at the painting or performance in a larger context, just as she helps each person to look at his art and himself in therapy, in the matrix of his entire life space. Just as a good critic educates the public by showing connections between the art of the past and that of the present, so a good art therapist helps patients to see relationships between the immediate past and the present, e.g., what they have been drawing or painting over the course of the preceding days or months of treatment. Perhaps even more important, she helps them to see connections between their art in the present and what happened in their personal/social/cultural past, since their art and associations so often refer to issues or memories from earlier periods in their lives.

This chronological, historical, genetic framework is as useful to patients as psychodynamic or learning constructs. All three perspectives are important, and synthesizing them is ultimately necessary for the fullest understanding by both therapist and patient. I am, however, skeptical about the value of insight for many patients, especially when conceived of in too limited a fashion, as a linear, verbal, explanatory "knowing." I am quite convinced that therapeutic change has a strong experiential component that also involves a kind of learning, which does not get verbalized or explained but which is most powerful when felt genuinely and strongly. If the patient is able to further comprehend the art therapy experience through language that explains (e.g., insight), he achieves an even greater sense of control.

But insight is not possible or essential for many patients, and, if it is overemphasized as a goal in treatment, can detract from the power of direct experience. Insight alone is too intellectual; like *knowing* about art and therapy without *believing* or *being*, it is flat and one-dimensional. This is another reason why I think art therapy is so potent: It combines a powerful, deeply involving experience with a distancing, organizing perspective. Through both vision and words, the looking at, considering, capturing, and comprehending of the experience become possible . . . a true "in-sight" ("seeing in").

Rudolf Arnheim (1982) has recently suggested that man and art view the world either from the center (like a bull's eye) or from a distance

(like a grid). In the doing part of art therapy, patients do not talk about feelings or relationships from a distance (the grid), but they get into them, and feel them, as if at the center of a target or a whirlpool. In the reflecting part, there is the possibility of both distance and perspective. The availability of both kinds of experience in art therapy, as part of the total composition or script, provides a multidimensional kind of "knowing" for a patient. When the distant view of cognition can be integrated with the close-up of affect, the person is able to gain a genuine and full understanding of what goes on inside himself and in relation to others.

I believe that it is the presence of both components, the involvement and the reflection, that makes for maximally useful art therapy. Thus, it is not the catharsis alone that is valuable, but the experience of strong affect in a controlled context that makes it safe, bearable, acceptable, and knowable. And it is not insight alone that is curative, but "seeing-in" after "being-in," understanding and grasping (feeling, owning, controlling) previously feared impulses, ideas, fantasies. There are times when such a perspective can be attained with few or no words, but with the kind of reflective distance and consideration of process and product described earlier.

When sublimation is successful, it must partake of intense involvement, as well as the taming and forming required to make the product attractive to self and others. The act of containing forbidden impulses and ideas in an aesthetic form may provide a sense of mastery, similar to the more intellectual act of understanding what is hidden in the art. Sublimation is a most useful defensive/adaptive mechanism for otherwise unacceptable impulses, permitting as it does both gratification and disguise in symbolic form. I am uncertain whether the capture of such wishes on paper or canvas is as clinically useful as knowing about and accepting them in full consciousness. Some studies suggest that neurosis interferes with the creative process, which requires conflict-free energy for its work, while others insist that it is conflict or tension which must fuel creative activity. As with most observations about man and the arts, there is probably truth in both positions.

What does seem true is that some people improve in their mental health following involvement in creative activity with minimal reflection, so that the healing element probably is sublimation, or some other aspect of the creative act itself. On the other hand, it is also true that for many people genuine creative involvement seems impossible to achieve. And for others, despite such involvement, the art process provides only a temporary respite from crippling tensions and feelings of despair. Yet many of these people can achieve significant psychological growth,

through an art therapy in which as much attention is given to the reflective as to the productive components of making art. Their reflection is not always on the level of awareness that many would call insight; yet there is usually some degree of understanding more, and of getting a better perspective on themselves through looking. It is my impression that, if linked closely in time with the doing and feeling part, this component of art therapy is a richly fruitful area, requiring knowledge and artistry to reach its fullest potential.

I believe this to be true for all aspects and phases of art therapy with any patient, in any setting, and at any time. The more artistic one is about the way one applies what one knows about art and therapy, the more effective one is likely to be. One sign of such artistry is in one's ability to really follow the patient, whether it be "feeling with" his creative activity, or staying with the "red thread" of his expressed themes. There is a constant tension throughout any session between following the lead of the patient and deciding whether, when, and how to intervene. In truth, there are always multiple leads, verbal and non-verbal, symbolic and direct; and the challenge of selecting which to follow is best met through being deeply knowledgeable about both art and therapy. To intervene in a way that is most effective is to do so artistically, as if one were an experienced conductor or director.

In choosing which of the many possible directions to follow, a therapist needs to select one that seems both critical to the patient's problems *and* most accessible at that moment in time. Any artwork, for example, contains imagery with both manifest and latent meanings. While the manifest content may be a disguise, it is but a partial one, so there is always something to be learned from its consideration. And, in terms of accessibility, one can always be sure that it is more acceptable to the patient's ego, since it was actually represented. One cannot intervene effectively if a patient is not ready to deal with an issue. Even if he seems ready, critical areas are likely to be tender or sore; the more delicately and artistically one works, the more likely the patient is to be able to see and hear what the therapist has to convey. The skill (the *art* of art therapy) lies primarily in knowing enough about one's work (art *and* therapy) to be able to make clinically appropriate decisions most of the time. The *artistry*, which goes beyond mere competence, lies in being able to implement those decisions in a way which works clinically, just as a brilliant interpretation of a sonata works musically.

So, I should like to put in an invitation—no, a plea—for greater attention to *artistry* in art therapy. While some of the human talents involved may seem natural and inborn, they are latent in most people and

capable of development in a facilitating supervisory relationship. I also think that many clinicians who are vaguely aware may improve by simply monitoring themselves in regard to the artistry of their work. As the artistry in one's art therapy grows, one will experience increasing reinforcement in one's clinical work—from patients, from their families, and from one's colleagues. As someone once said, "Nothing succeeds like success." The reinforcement derived from doing artistic clinical work is itself highly motivating, serving as intrinsic gratification, as well as a stimulus for external rewards. As with creating a lovely painting, doing effective therapy can be gratifying in and of itself. Like painting, the work is often slow, frustrating, difficult, painful, and boring; and it is also at times stimulating, pleasurable, and exciting. Both experiences can be immensely rewarding in an infinite variety of ways, and in both it is always true that the more artistic the better.

REFERENCES

Arnheim, R. *The power of the center: A theory of visual composition.* Berkeley: University of California Press, 1982.
Ault, R. Are you an artist or a therapist? A professional dilemma of art therapists. In R. H. Shoemaker & S.E. Gonick-Barris (Eds.), *Creativity and the art therapist's identity.* Baltimore: American Art Therapy Association, 1977, pp. 53-56.
Langer, S.K. *Feeling and form.* New York: Scribner's, 1953.

PART IV

Indirect Service

The first three parts of this book were concerned with the basics underlying the art of art therapy: the art part, the therapy part, and the interface where the two come together in the actual clinical work. There are other areas that are not essential but are useful to know, especially if one is to fully develop one's talents in the service of the profession. In order for any discipline to continue, some way must be found to impart the essentials of the field to those who wish to learn. Some are trainees, who need more than models of good clinical work in order to develop their own skills. Specifically, they need to be taught and they need to be supervised, so that knowing both teaching and supervision is essential for any art therapist who finds herself in the position of training others.

Then there are those who may not wish to become art therapists, but who do need to understand the field well enough to make appropriate referrals of patients for diagnosis or treatment through art. Sometimes these people work in the same institution, in which case the intervention is usually called inservice training. At other times they work elsewhere, in which case the intervention is more often called consultation. Whatever the nomenclature, the important thing to remember is that these are all an *indirect* use of the art therapist's skills, as opposed to the *direct* use of those skills in work with patients. Both indirect and direct service involve helping relationships, but there are differences between therapy and supervision or therapy and consultation. An art therapist

needs to have a clear understanding of what is meant by each of these roles, to know the areas of overlap as well as those of differentiation.

So, after some internal debate, I have decided to add several chapters to those about the basics, which are extras for beginners, but are probably essential for experienced art therapists who are often asked to give in-direct service. The three chapters about such work deal with teaching, supervision, and consultation. There is yet another important "extra" which could even be considered "basic" if viewed broadly, but is usually thought of in a more narrow and specialized fashion: research. I believe this to be one of the more seriously neglected areas in some training programs and in the field at large, though it is also probably one of the more critical for ultimate acceptance of our work. In a chapter on re-search, I shall note some of the issues especially relevant to art therapy research, as well as what any art therapist needs to know in order to be able to understand research findings in related disciplines.

Although refining the artistry of art therapy in our direct work with patients is related to the growth and development of our field, these other areas are also vital to our survival in the mental health world, since they often influence those who decide whether or not to hire or to refer patients to art therapists. Less political and more enduring, the development of artistry in teaching, supervision, consultation, and re-search in art therapy is necessary in order to better understand and to utilize the powerful creative modality we offer. These "extras," while not essential for each individual practitioner, do become more significant as one assumes a broader perspective and a more generative role in the profession.

There is one last "extra," of interest to only a minority of art therapists, but also important for the further development of the discipline: theory. In the section on *The Therapy Part*, the importance of knowing and un-derstanding the different theoretical models of personality and psycho-therapy in current use was often noted. The development of a valid theory about art therapy is a more demanding task, yet perhaps the most important "extra" of all. For, if we are unable to account for our effectiveness in a logical and communicable way, we will continue to be viewed as either charming romantics or hopeless airheads, depending on the bias of the perceiver. In the chapter on theory, I shall describe the kind of theorizing that seems appropriate to art therapy, and some of what people need to know in order to develop in that direction.

I am not suggesting that most clinicians are interested in becoming theorists any more than I would expect most therapists to like doing research. But I do think that art therapists, once they have learned to

do their work artistically, have a responsibility to those they may train, advise, supervise, or inform to be able to understand theory in their own field and in related disciplines, just as they have a responsibility to be able to read and grasp relevant research studies. Another reason for including this section on "extras" is that, while many art therapists are not formally designated as teachers, supervisors, consultants, researchers, or theorists, *all* art therapists *in*formally assume each of those roles, often without even being aware that they are doing so. If nothing else, this section of the book will serve to raise the issues involved in each chapter to a more conscious level, so that individuals can decide whether or not they wish to pursue further training and greater sophistication in any of these "extra," indirect dimensions of art therapy.

Students in an art therapy class take turns showing and discussing their individual creations with the group.

Chapter 13

Knowing Teaching

Although the principles of good pedagogy probably apply to the teaching of any subject matter, it is my impression that many art therapists find themselves in the position of teaching about the field with little or no preparation. Like myself, many have never taken a course in art therapy, since the time when they were learning the discipline was before the availability of formal training opportunities. Although I happen to have studied in schools of education, and have taught art to children and art education to college students, many art therapists now teaching others have not had access to any formal training in education or any relevant prior experience at the post-secondary level. This, by the way, is true for most clinician-teachers in other therapies, who find themselves offering courses or leading seminars without any background or experience in higher education. And, like art therapists who know little about teaching, they are often unable to convey what they know about their discipline, because they are uninformed about how best to help people to learn.

As with the areas noted as basic to art therapy, this book is not the place for a detailed treatise on principles of pedagogy or teaching methodology. As with other fields, such information is available elsewhere, in books, in courses, and through the guidance of experienced instructors. But it seems appropriate to briefly alert those art therapists who find themselves teaching without formal preparation for that role to some of the issues especially pertinent to learning in our discipline. Most apply to any teaching situation, whether the students are one-time work-

shop attendees or two-year master's degree candidates. As with the difference between short- and long-term therapy, the goals in diverse situations are necessarily different, but the keys to effective learning are the same.

The first issue in any kind of teaching situation is knowing clearly what it is one wishes to convey. While one might think that is simple, already defined by the title of the course, workshop, or lecture, there are always choices to be made among the many facets of any topic in art therapy. One criterion, of course, is one's own sense of what is most important for these people to learn about the topic involved. In order to make that decision intelligently, however, one must find out just what it is the students or audience *already know*—"where they are" in any specific subject. One may be able to find out by checking just what learning experiences they have already had (previously required courses, for example), though it is likely, even in a sequentially designed curriculum, that people will be at different levels of awareness, knowledge, and sophistication on any topic. The decision one must then make is just where to "pitch" the course, lecture, or workshop, given the fact that there is probably a range of preparedness among those attending. My own preference is to try to communicate to a level around the middle, between the most sophisticated and the least informed, and then to provide in some way for those at the extremes.

In addition to one's own ideas about the key learnings in any area and the preparation level of one's students, one should also gear what is taught to the needs and interests of the learners. Given the broad range of subject matter within any area in art therapy, another variable governing selection of topics should be the students' greatest concerns. What this means in practice is that some time at the beginning of any learning experience, short- or long-term, is well spent in finding out where people are in regard to their areas of special interest. It is analogous to beginning diagnostically when dealing with patients in therapy, since what the therapist has to offer, in either case, can only be received if given at their level and in accord with their motivation.

All of this might seem self-evident, but I have been surprised at the number of times I have assessed learner level and interest and have heard from the students that they were not used to being asked such questions. Like patients in art therapy, students often prefer to be spoon-fed, even force-fed, to have the academic "diet" preselected for them, and to be told with no ambiguity what to do, what to read, and what to write (or draw). The type of "food" offered may well need to be decided on by someone who knows more than they do about art therapy

nutrition. I am reminded of the classic study by a child psychologist in which infants, offered nothing but healthy foods from which to choose, ended up selecting balanced diets when given independence, although they did go on periodic binges in the course of the study (Davis, 1928). Similarly, the academic food made available to weekend workshop or semester course participants needs to be "good" stuff, any and all of which is relevant to the topic and nutritious for the learning art therapist. But the sequence in which they partake and the shifts from breadth to depth in approach can be determined by the interests of the learners.

The reason for recommending such an approach to teaching, within the structure of any curriculum or goal, is that self-motivated learning always seems to take hold faster and with more lasting effects than that which is dictated primarily or solely by others. Even if the students' freedom is limited to helping in decisions about the sequence of subjects or the relative time spent on different facets of a topic, I am convinced that such involvement pays off handsomely in a high level of interest in the learning activity and subsequent retention of material. If, for some reason, one feels that the flexibility in course subjects or sequence must be limited, one can always make it possible for students to choose such things as term paper or project topics according to their own special interests. I am not suggesting that *all* the decisions come from the learners, but that within the structure provided by the teacher's definition of the essential and optional facets of any topic, there should be enough freedom for people to go in directions especially fascinating to them as individuals.

Well, one might say, that is all very fine if one has a whole semester of a three-credit course within which to shift topics and priorities; but what if one is limited to a three-hour seminar or a one-day workshop? Isn't it the teacher's responsibility to decide what is most important for people to learn in such a tight time frame? Yes, of course. The instructor has that same responsibility in any time span and the shorter it is, the less flexibility one will probably have. But the importance of trying to reach the level and meet the needs of the learners remains. Much of the information-gathering about both will probably have to be done in advance, by inquiring of the person inviting the art therapist about the level of sophistication and particular needs/interests of the group. I usually suggest that the liaison person ask, at a gathering close in time to the one I will be leading (like a scheduled staff meeting), just what aspects of art therapy individuals most want to learn about. Even in a brief encounter, one can be prepared to go in one direction or another, which can sometimes be assessed at the time. I often decide exactly

which exercise I will use or which film I will show after meeting the participants, even in a short presentation. Needless to say, one must have available either film or a variety of supplies in order to be able to shift gears on any specific activity at short notice.

Level of sophistication is important, whatever the nature of the group being addressed. It is also important, whether the audience is composed of laymen or professionals from other disciplines, to use language and ideas that make sense and are familiar to the group. I might use the same set of slides with parents, teachers, or psychiatrists; but I would say very different kinds of things about them with each population, since I would try always to speak in terms both meaningful and comprehensible to the audience. Similarly, I might ask a group of child care workers or of psychologists to engage in the same art activity (like a scribble drawing or a nonverbal dyadic drawing), but the terms in which I would discuss it with each would probably be slightly different. The rationale given each group for the experience might well differ too, depending again on the nature of the members. And the discussion afterward would, of course, be based upon what the participants had to say about the experience, following their lead as one would with a patient group.

In teaching situations, one needs to decide not only on the content of what will be offered, but also on the form in which it will be conveyed. I am quite convinced that direct involvement in art activities, along with a chance to look at them reflectively and relate them to theories and techniques in the literature, is the best combination. While I am not always successful in making such direct experience possible, I usually attempt to do so, even if the involvement is simply drawing with pencil on a piece of paper on the arm of a classroom chair, or manipulating a small piece of plasticine while sitting in an auditorium seat. Art therapy, by its very nature, involves both doing and reflecting. It makes sense, then, that any time one wants to teach others about it, whether at a deep or a superficial level, they will understand best if they themselves can be directly involved in creating something which is then looked at. The emotional impact of discovering something about oneself is of a far different order from the intellectual discovery of the power of art therapy, even through seeing dramatic case studies.

As noted earlier, however, the very best situation for learning about art therapy involves both direct involvement with subsequent reflection, and a more distant perspective, usually by hearing from the presenter about work done in some kind of setting. To present such work only in words is also to lose one of art therapy's most central and valuable

elements: visual imagery. Although most art therapists do use either original artwork or slide reproductions in their presentations, surprisingly this is not always the case. The reason given is usually the unavailability of a projector or of particular artwork. However, if an art therapist is convinced of the necessity to illustrate any descriptions of her work with visual images, she will make sure in planning and preparing that proper equipment or relevant art products will be available, even if she has to bring the paintings or the projector herself.

Another problem many teaching art therapists seem to have is that, even when they have put slides together to illustrate a talk, the slides (or the actual art products) are shown in a bunch after the main presentation, with descriptive commentary that is sometimes not related to what has been said earlier. It takes time and careful planning but is infinitely more useful to the audience if the slides literally illustrate the verbal presentation and are shown at those points in either the prepared or extemporaneous talk where they best fit. The simultaneous hearing of description and seeing of illustration facilitate the ability of the audience to fully integrate the message from the art therapist.

In addition, it seems that while many art therapists show products, relatively few presenters show pictures of people at work. Yet for the naive listener, what is impossible to imagine is how the room looked, how the patients behaved, and just how those creative products became realities in time and space. Occasional slides, videotapes, or films of the art therapy situation in action can help to give concrete form to what might otherwise look quite different in the audience's imagination. One might object that pictures of patients violate rights of privacy, but people are quite agreeable to having their pictures taken, in both inpatient and outpatient settings, if they are assured that these will be used only for educational purposes. Of course, it is essential for both legal and ethical reasons to obtain written consent from the patient or guardian. Another safeguard I utilize is never to show pictures of people who might be recognizable to groups in the same city. Another is to take shots from an angle so that faces cannot easily be seen, in order to reduce the likelihood of people being recognized.

A final important element in the ideal art therapy learning situation is the relating of what has been experienced and seen to a larger picture. The larger scene might be the field in general—locally, statewide, or nationally—at that moment in time. Or it might be a historical perspective, perhaps about the role of art therapy in the particular area being discussed. Just as it is best to include some direct involvement and reflection and to present some vivid clinical material that illustrates what

can be done, so it is ideal if whatever has been experienced (directly and indirectly) can be put into a broader context. This might involve, in addition to lecturing, the assigning of readings or projects, especially in an ongoing teaching situation.

One might argue that the three approaches just advocated as the ideal elements in the *form* of a presentation are relevant for any subject matter and are not unique to art therapy. However, the integration of doing and reflecting and of imagery with words, which I have recommended in a teaching situation, is also the essence of art therapy itself. The last element, putting the learning into a larger perspective, is also part of good art therapy, where the patient is helped to use the experience in a way that enables him to understand and to enrich his life in general, not just the moments he spends with the art therapist. If teaching, like therapy, is to have any kind of lasting impact, it must be internalized and eventually generalized by the learner.

This leads to yet another recommendation about the teaching of art therapy, especially to students training in the field. Any didactic learning should always be complemented by something more direct, either in the form of observation (on site or videotape) or, as soon as possible, doing something oneself. Anyone who has conducted an individual art interview with another human being, even outside a treatment setting, has an understanding of that kind of event which is much fuller than is possible from reading or observing alone. If such "practice" activities can then be examined in some detail, either individually or in a group, the potential for learning is further extended. Even in an introductory course, students can be required to conduct art evaluations with individuals or families (excluding people they know) and can learn a great deal by discussing these in the group. A related approach is to use role play, more practical for short-term learning situations (like weekend workshops), where students pretend to be therapists or patients (individuals, groups, or families) and can get at least a feel for the kinds of tensions and dilemmas involved in art therapy, as well as the pleasures and joys.

Just as people are known to learn more when they are interested in a topic, so they are known to learn more when they are emotionally involved as well as intellectually fascinated. Doing one's own art, role playing with other students, and practicing on willing nonpatient helpers, these are all excellent ways to involve trainees in the learning process at a feeling level. What is critical, however, is that the doing always be integrated with the didactic learning of the moment. Just as the slides are best shown along with the words of the talk, so the activity com-

ponents of the learning process are best if connected by the instructor with the theoretical, technical, and historical information being learned.

Not only is action plus cognition a good formula for learning technique, it is also the only possible way of making theory come alive. No one has ever seen an id, an ego, or a superego; and no one can specify the color of transference or the texture of a working alliance. But only when these abstract concepts come alive in one's own direct experience do they start to have meaning which can be comprehended and generalized. One inventive instructor had the marvellous idea of asking students to create visual representations of such abstract theoretical concepts using art media (Allen & Wadeson, 1982). I am sure they understood them better after doing so; just as I am sure that drawing a feeling or a life line gives anyone a new perspective on the particular topic, even though the person might have thought he knew it already.

I stressed earlier the importance of gauging the level of sophistication of the audience, as well as their areas of greatest interest. In regard to the kind of learning which involves doing, it is also essential to be extremely cautious and to monitor throughout the activity the group's level of comfort or anxiety about the task and the ensuing discussion. This is most critical when people are doing their own artwork and looking at it reflectively. One must then use one's clinical judgment about the appropriateness of the task and how far to go in the discussion in regard to potentially touchy areas. It is always safer to err on the side of caution and restraint.

One way to protect individuals against exposure and to insure that everyone gets a chance to talk as much or as little as he wishes about what he has made is to ask people in a group to pair up for the discussion time. Each partner first presents what he has created to the other member of the pair who then interviews him about it, having been given guidance in advance about asking mostly open-ended questions. They then switch roles, so that by the end of the time available, everyone has had a chance to see what it feels like to talk about his own creation, as well as to interview another person about his artwork. Then, time permitting, the leader may wish to invite anyone who so desires to talk to the whole group about the experience. This discussion might have any of a number of possible foci, depending on the nature of the group and the learning situation.

Just as it is useful to promote direct involvement in any learning situation, so it always helps to convey something that the learners can take with them and use. This is one reason why building a presentation on learner interests makes so much sense, since they will be not only

more involved at the time, but are also more likely to use what they have learned in the future. It might help to think of that goal in planning as well. Given choices among areas of learner interest that can be conveyed in a given time, which are they most likely to be able to utilize in their own lives or work in the near future?

Another way of thinking of the future is to see as a relevant goal of any learning situation not only taking in something new and valuable, but also discovering what more one needs to learn about a particular topic, and perhaps defining some avenues for development. With some groups, simply getting across the idea that art therapy is very complicated and requires a great deal of skill and supervised learning might be a major goal. Many laymen and some professionals still think that all one needs is "a paintbrush and a patient" and one can call oneself an art therapist, to quote one of our pioneers (Howard, 1964). In such instances, I work hard to convince the audience of the complexity and sophistication of the work, so that they will neither conduct nor sanction irresponsible art therapy with patient populations.

Of course, there is much more that could be written about the teaching of art therapy to others, whether one is giving a single talk or designing a two-year master's degree program. Certainly, the latter involves issues of sequencing in training experiences and selection of subject areas which are, at least in part, a matter of opinion on the part of the art therapist in charge. But whatever one's theoretical or technical priorities, any organized plan of training ought to build gradually both knowledge and competencies, always linking the doing with understanding, as in art therapy itself.

Finally, any kind of teaching situation needs to be evaluated by the learners. It may be difficult or awkward to do this in a short talk or at a conference, but it can be quite useful to the presenter. Inviting some kind of evaluation by students is a responsibility of every art therapist involved in any substantial amount of teaching. I often suggest that such evaluations be typed and anonymous in order to encourage people to be honest about their criticisms. I have also stressed, when presenting evaluation forms or questions, that I, like anyone, enjoy praise and pats on the back; but that what I need in order to grow is critical feedback, especially if there are specific suggestions for improvement. Having taught at the college level for twenty years, I have received many such written evaluations and have learned a good deal from them over that time span. Of course, it is sometimes shocking or painful to see in black and white how negatively someone regarded one's teaching. But a good

art therapist should be constantly evaluating her work, and so should a responsible teacher.

One of the most interesting kinds of evaluation of any type of learning is when one is able to follow up one's input at some point later in time, to find out not what people can write or say at the end of the workshop or course, but whether and how they are using what they were taught. I have sometimes had that opportunity, and it has been fascinating. I have often felt that those who retained the most and showed the most growth were the individuals who already had the potential and maybe even the knowledge, but who needed permission to use their own creativity in their work and felt as if I gave them that permission. I do not mean to imply that they would not have moved at all without the learning experience, but I do sometimes wonder whether it is possible to teach people who, for reasons of personality more than intellect, are not able to fully use what one has to offer. This dilemma becomes even more acute in clinical supervision, the subject of the next chapter, where one sometimes feels challenged to make gold out of straw.

REFERENCES

Allen, P., & Wadeson, H. Art making for conceptualization, integration, and self-awareness in art therapy training. In A.E. DiMaria, et al. (Eds.), *Art therapy: A bridge between worlds*. Falls Church, VA: American Art Therapy Association, 1982, pp. 83-85.

Davis, C.M. Self-selection of diet by newly-weaned infants. *American Journal of Diseases of Children*, 1928, *36*, 651-679.

Howard, M. An art therapist looks at her professional identity. *Bulletin of Art Therapy*, 1964, *4*, 153-156.

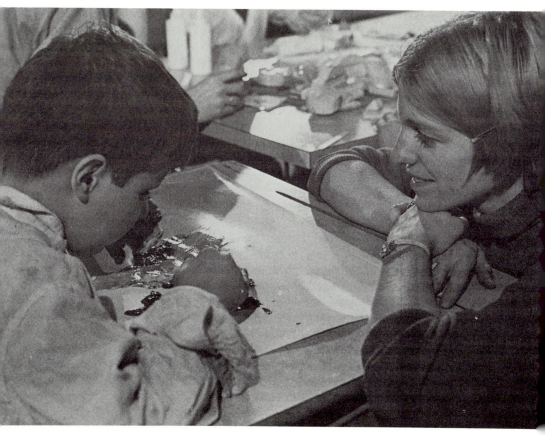

An art therapy student under supervision demonstrates her increasing skills in watching, listening, and writing down what the child has to say.

Chapter 14

Knowing Supervision

Most art therapists who find themselves supervising others have not been trained in supervision per se any more than most who find themselves educating others have been trained in teaching. There does exist a relevant literature, including some very fine writings which attempt to conceptualize the issues and the processes of clinical supervision. It becomes clear very quickly that supervising someone's clinical work is quite different from administrative supervision. Unfortunately, the same art therapist often has to play both roles, though it is much simpler to do either one without the encumbrance of the other. Since the roles are most often combined rather than separated, it is important to keep the two areas distinct in one's own mind, as administrative supervision usually involves many more clear-cut, either-or issues than does the supervision of clinical work. Although the answers might be generally clearer on administrative matters, however, the role of the supervisor is in certain ways consistent.

What is most critical is to be clear at all times that a supervisor's primary job is to develop the skills of the supervisee. Just as it might be easier to do something for or to tell a patient than to help him find the answer for himself, so it is often simpler to give the answer to a supervisee or even to undertake some difficult task for her, than to help her to do it herself. But, as with a patient, it is the growth of the other individual that is the supervisor's goal; and if one is to promote that, one must help that person to think and do for himself. Although one might think one would naturally promote autonomy, since one doesn't

157

want any supervisee to be overly dependent, the fact remains that there are some gratifications for a supervisor in being seen as omnipotent, omniscient, or essential to the supervisee, just as there are for a therapist with a needy, insecure patient. We all have a little of that infant grandiosity in us, and we probably enter a helping profession partly in order to be the heroic rescuer of the weak and helpless. It is a good feeling to be needed by anyone, whether a supervisee or a patient, and it is therefore vital not to abuse the supervision situation in order to obtain such gratifications at the learner's expense.

On the other hand, the supervisor is responsible for the actions of a supervisee in a way that one is not for a patient, at least not legally. This means that, although it is necessary to promote increasing independence on the part of the supervisee, care should be taken that she does not take advantage of the situation and act without permission or support in a way for which the supervisor may have to answer. Ironically, while there are supervisees who beg for a dependent relationship and who are eager to be "fed" and led, there are also supervisees who have difficulty taking whatever one has to offer; they come for supervision, but seem either not to digest or to "spit out" whatever is given to them, and show no evidence over time of having integrated any learning.

Since there are clearly emotional as well as intellectual issues involved in any kind of supervision, knowledge about development, dynamics, and therapy will stand the supervisor in good stead. What one understands about the transference and the working alliance are especially relevant. Although, strictly speaking, one would not use such terms to characterize the supervisor-supervisee relationship, there are important analogies in supervision to what goes on between therapist and patient. There is a "real" relationship, and there should be a "learning alliance," where both partners work conscientiously toward the goal of growth for one of them. There are also transference reactions, as in everyday life, which are distorted responses on the part of each individual to the other. Because one is dependent upon the other for evaluation, and because one is responsible for the other's performance to others in the institution, there are necessarily strains and tensions in this unique learning situation. It is not therapy, but it is also not teaching, except as it resembles a tutorial, and it is best if it is not strictly didactic.

So what is it? Supervision is a peculiar kind of relationship, where one individual agrees to help another to develop clinical skills, but without leading by the hand, or showing how (as in an apprenticeship), or even telling in so many words. Yet, in truth, all of these modes of helping

do become part of any effective supervision—showing, supporting, and even telling—at times when each seems appropriate. Deciding on the best supervision intervention is as difficult as the clinical decisions with patients about what to do at any moment in time. Even though there are no art media on the table, one must still decide whether to listen, to interrupt, to tell about, to ask about, and if intervening, just how to do so. And, as with a patient, one must assess from moment to moment the supervisee's readiness for any given intervention.

In order to keep the learning curve and growth goals clear in one's mind with any supervisee, one needs to remain constantly aware of the not-so-rational elements in the transaction: the transference reactions of either person to the other at any moment in time. Since the supervisor has more distance than the supervisee does, it may be a little easier for the supervisor to keep track of the supervisee's countertransference responses to patients, as well as her transferences to other staff members. These are so powerful, and so easily rationalized, that one must keep an ever-watchful eye on them, so that they do not distort one's understanding of what the supervisee is actually facing in her work.

Since such irrational responses are so influential, one might wonder whether doing effective supervision isn't really the same as conducting good therapy. While there are some similarities, as noted earlier, the two are also quite distinct. The help one has agreed to give to the art therapy supervisee is in relation to developing her clinical skills and understandings, not improving her mental health. I have no sympathy for the position of those who feel one can do both simultaneously. This seems a rather grandiose notion, and I have yet to meet the individual who can remain neutral enough to be a good therapist and yet explicit enough to be a good supervisor. The role requirements are simply not compatible. An even more serious complication is that it places unfair pressures on the supervisee, who cannot use the supervisor without conflict as either teacher or therapist, and whose growth in both areas may be gravely compromised.

What a good supervisor can do, however, is to help the supervisee to pinpoint what may be happening in the way of distorted perceptions, reactions, or behaviors, and to suggest or support the individual's obtaining therapy for herself. A not uncommon phenomenon, for example, is the replaying in the supervisory situation of what is going on between patient and supervisee. Reflecting on this interaction can often help both of them to understand what is going on between the supervisee and the patient. If, however, the supervisee has trouble seeing or accepting any distortions on her part, then it is the responsibility of the supervisor to

introduce the idea of therapy. I not only see personal therapy as essential for any art therapist, but I also feel that it may be necessary to do some work on oneself more than once or twice in a lifetime. Of course, if one knows it will be threatening to the individual, one will want to prepare her for it gently and to introduce the idea with compassion and concern. But it is important to remember that, if psychological problems are interfering with the supervisee's work, the answer is not becoming her therapist/supervisor; rather, it is helping her to decide on and to find a competent clinician for herself.

The issues noted so far have been rather general ones, having to do with the supervisor-supervisee relationship, its goals and its potential complications. More specific issues include the question of the best way of structuring the supervision session itself, as well as the advisability of adjunctive modes of training, such as observing, being observed, or working as a cotherapist with the supervisee. As with patients, it is important to remember that each supervisee is a unique individual and that what works best with one may be quite inappropriate for another. But there are some guidelines which are applicable to clinical supervision of either trainees or staff members in art therapy.

As with therapy, it makes sense to begin by assessing where the individual is in her clinical skills, which includes not only how she behaves, but also how she understands what is going on with patients and herself. In this regard, it is probably best to begin as in an initial art interview, in an open-ended fashion, to see just how this individual approaches the supervision situation. Does she come in with a list of questions, with a process record of a single session, with the artwork done by one or more patients, or does she sit back and wait for the supervisor to structure the time? Does she seem to want to prove her competence, or does she seem overly self-critical or fearful of criticism? In other words, in addition to finding out where someone is in regard to clinical skills, it is also helpful to get a sense of how she regards herself as a clinician. In addition, the initial unstructured supervisory sessions are most helpful in giving a feel for what and how much the individual wants and expects from the supervisor.

In order to assess clinical skills more systematically, one might suggest that the supervisee list any questions occurring to her during the time between meetings. Eventually, I usually request detailed reports of single sessions, preferring a depth to a breadth approach in learning clinical skills. I always ask that any patient artwork be brought along, if at all possible, and that the supervisee note the date and number in sequence of each item. Eventually, when the supervisee seems comfortable, I may

ask to observe a session—if possible, through a one-way vision window or, if necessary, in the same room (more feasible with groups than individuals). If live observation is not possible or seems too threatening to either the therapist or the patients, I will then ask that the clinician videotape a session, and if that is not possible, to tape the audio portion of an interview. Although direct observation is sometimes not feasible, I find that doing so as early as possible in supervision is extremely helpful, since no clinician can report to a supervisor on areas that are probably blind spots, and are therefore all the more important to be aware of.

In giving feedback after an observation or report, the supervisor needs to be especially sensitive to the clinician's narcissism and should try hard to find positive as well as negative things to say. Though it sounds rather simplistic, I always try to begin with positive comments, after which I believe negative ones can be more comfortably heard by anyone, no matter how secure the individual may seem to be. Conscientious reinforcement of a supervisee's strengths and successes is at least as important in helping her to grow as sharply accurate criticism of her work. The way in which comments or questions are worded, the tone of voice in which they are said, and the expression on the supervisor's face are as powerful in their impact as in communications with patients. Ironically, many supervisors seem able to be exquisitely sensitive with patients, yet astonishingly callous with supervisees, as if they are working out some hidden agenda of their own in this particular transaction.

Because of the nature of my own training experiences, both as an art therapist and a psychoanalyst, I have had many different supervisors, each of whom had his or her own style and approach. Some have been rather casual and passive, allowing me to structure the session according to my own felt needs; others have been quite insistent on a particular way of reporting and examining work with patients. Some have been very task-oriented, using the time to discuss only clinical work; others have been looser about boundaries and have brought up other areas where our paths have crossed, often in ways which seemed relevant to the supervision. As with art therapy, supervision is an activity in which each individual needs to develop her own style of work, a way of relating which is syntonic for her. But, as is also true with art therapy with particular patients, it is important that the supervisor adapt her characteristic style to the specific needs of the individual supervisee.

As I am currently supervising more staff members and graduate students than ever before, I have become especially alert to the different "flavor" of each supervisory hour, despite the fact that I think I am

relatively consistent throughout. After years of experimentation with a variety of ways of structuring the time, I have come to feel that it is best to give some guidance to those who do not spontaneously utilize the opportunity in thoughtful ways that indicate prior preparation. Some supervisees are able to sort out their priorities very well and can usually be trusted to use the supervision session in the fashion they most need at any moment in time. Others, however, need to be taught how to use supervision efficiently and well, especially if what was called supervision in prior learning situations was more administrative or superficial.

When staff members are delivering many hours of direct service and are able to reflect on it with a supervisor for only one or two hours a week, it hardly makes sense to use that precious time for a literal reporting of all that has happened, a communication that can occur more efficiently in brief written descriptions of each art therapy session. Nor does it make much sense to use supervision to talk mainly about what went well, since one is hardly likely to grow through praise alone. So for those who do not spontaneously utilize their supervision time productively, I have found it helpful to spend some time pinpointing with them their areas of discomfort or inadequacy and planning together ways of helping them to grow in those domains. This would include specific ways of preparing for the supervision session, as well as other possibilities for professional development.

Although the primary work of clinical supervision takes place in the supervisory session, for the best training in art therapy the supervisor should be flexible about other kinds of recommended activities or uses of herself. Actions one might recommend to a supervisee include reading specific papers or books on a topic needing to be better understood, as well as observing other therapists at work. One problem with most clinical training programs, including those in art therapy, is that the learner is provided with few live models. She reads a great deal about what people say they do (which is often different from what they actually do), and she hears a lot in classes and case seminars about what others report they have done. But, except for required observations or an art therapist with whom she may work as assistant or cotherapist, she rarely if ever gets to observe other art therapists at work. To date, there are few teaching films and tapes that show art therapists working with patients, and because of the editing involved, they inevitably present a distorted picture.

As is true for many clinicians, one's own therapist often becomes a model; but this person is rarely an art therapist, so that the usefulness of identification here is somewhat limited. Yet in many domains, such

as parenting and teaching, the way in which a person behaves in a role is based largely on experiences with others who had that relationship to the person in the past. For a brief period, I experimented with having supervisees create and discuss their own art for half of each session, but found that the role conflicts between therapist and supervisor were, as noted earlier, irreconcilable, even in this admittedly "as if" learning situation. Perhaps because the intensity of the transference is diluted among all members, a teaching group in art therapy has been more successful, where students learn by doing, discussing, and then relating what has occurred among them to what is known about group art therapy.

But for the purpose of exploring and developing one's own style as a therapist, I believe that self-knowledge is best supplemented by as many observations of other art therapists at work as is feasible. Needless to say, this can also include observations of the supervisor as well, though in such cases one must be especially alert to the possible transference meaning of such an event for both parties. Just as grandiose rescue fantasies are probably ubiquitous, so are exhibitionistic ones part of every artist's unconscious power source. It is inevitable that anyone entering the field of art therapy will have a special interest in the voyeurism that can also be sublimated in this kind of work. So, to "show off" and to "peek" have especially loaded meanings in a tilted relationship like the supervisory one, and need to be well understood before the supervisee is invited to observe the supervisor.

The reverse situation, while also loaded, is a little less risky and considerably more defensible. As noted earlier, no one's report of what goes on can fully convey the actuality of an art therapy situation; therefore, it is very helpful to get a direct look when possible at the supervisee's way of working with patients. Despite prior preparation, the supervisee is likely to be self-conscious, so it is especially important to do one's observing in a way which is minimally anxiety-provoking. If no observation room is available, for example, it is important for the supervisor to find out just where in the room and at what level of participation her presence will be least disruptive to the supervisee. Since this may be difficult to establish in advance, the supervisor may need to explore through trial and error where it is best to sit, and whether or not her participation in either doing or discussing will be comfortable or awkward for patients or therapist. If it seems that some kind of participation on the supervisor's part is most comfortable, then she can also use herself in a casual and natural way as a model of how to interact with, help, and interview the patient(s).

Since supervision is primarily a learning situation (although the curriculum is more flexible than in most teaching), it makes sense to periodically step back and evaluate with the supervisee where she is and where she now wants/needs to go, and to think together how best to help her to get there. Sometimes the work together is limited by time (a semester's internship) or some other variable (the patient's termination). When it occurs, a separation from a supervisor has many of the same elements as a termination in therapy and needs to be handled with care and tact, taking account of all of the feelings involved. Where there is no arbitrary time limitation (as in the supervision of regular staff members), it is especially important to regularly reassess goals and ways of reaching them with the supervisee.

In some situations, with both students and staff there is much to be gained through group kinds of supervisory experiences. These should never be used instead of individual supervision, for which there is no adequate substitute; but they can supplement and complement it in a growth-enhancing way. For example, in organizing the creative and expressive arts therapy program in our hospital, we planned for individual supervision for each staff member, the length and frequency to be determined as much as possible by individual needs. We also planned for weekly clinical conferences, in which a group of staff members in related disciplines would take turns presenting case material for several weeks at a time, allowing others to react and discuss, in order to get a broader perspective on treatment.

Given sufficient flexibility, these group learning sessions have also been used to review diagnostic interviews with both individuals and families, sometimes using videotape, and have occasionally been more didactic, as in reading an article written or recommended by one of the members and of interest to the group. There are clearly values in sharing ideas within a small group about what a painting or a behavior might mean, or discussing possible implications for understanding or action, which are qualitatively different from considering the same material in a one-to-one supervisory situation. Most obvious is the expansion of each individual's experience through sharing that of others. Equally valuable is the stimulation provided by the competitive/cooperative brainstorming within the group.

But what about the supervisor? Is growth to occur only in the supervisee? As with therapy or education, while the primary change is in the other person, it is possible for the caregiver to grow as well, especially if she takes the time to think about and reflect on her work. Since there

are some things that are unique to supervision, it is good to read some
of the relevant literature, to discuss the different theories and techniques
of supervision, and the pros and cons of each. It is also helpful, if at all
possible, to get a critique (or a consultation) of one's own work as a
supervisor. One of the most helpful experiences I ever had was in a
course required for my doctoral program: group supervision of supervision, where we were each required to supervise a master's candidate
in the counseling program and to tape our sessions. These tapes were
then listened to carefully by another group member, who would then
replay the tape with the supervisor, raising questions, offering criticisms,
and giving suggestions. This feedback was later discussed in the small
group in relation to theories of supervision, a course that had been
required the preceding term.

Currently, I try to meet such needs in twice-weekly collaboration sessions with my colleague who co-directs the creative arts therapy program. Each of us consults with the other regarding any questions or
problems we are having in work with our respective supervisees. I
imagine that if I did not have easy access to someone on the staff with
whom I could be so frank, I would probably deal with problems as a
supervisor in the same way that I now deal with problems as a therapist—by scheduling a consultation with one or another respected colleague. It is naive to think that one can ever reach a point at which one's
own transference reactions, biases, or blind spots could not potentially
interfere with one's effectiveness in any clinical role. What is most important is being alert to such problems and being comfortable with the
idea that, no matter how experienced one is, a more objective person
can always help one to do one's therapeutic or supervisory job better.
The clinicians for whom I have the most respect are also those who are
the quickest to ask for help when they sense they might need it. This
may be true for one's work as a supervisor at least as often as it is for
one's work as a therapist.

In art therapy, there are some other ways in which we can help ourselves and our supervisees, through using our modality. One way is to
draw a picture of the supervisee or her patient, which one may or may
not choose to share with the therapist; but which will usually help the
supervisor to identify more clearly any confused feelings she has been
having about the clinician or the case. Another is to have the supervisee
represent the patient(s) or staff member(s) with whom she deals, offering
another way for joint reflection on what is happening in the treatment
situation. Yet another, more loaded, but potentially fruitful approach is

without talking to draw on the same sheet of paper as the supervisee, to be followed by a discussion of what is happening in the supervisory relationship, as reflected in the drawing and the process of making it.

In a supervision group, asking each member to represent her image of the patient(s) being described may be helpful in gaining a fuller understanding of the situation under consideration. If tensions seem to be disrupting the learning orientation of this group, representations of the group itself are one way to begin to look at what is going on within, and to learn about group dynamics as well. There are probably many other possible uses of art in supervision, limited only by the imagination of the supervisor, parallel to what is true about the infinite number of potential art activities in the therapeutic situation. As with the latter, it is critical to utilize such approaches only when the need is strongly felt and the relevance of the activity seems clear. In such cases, art can be as powerful a tool in supervision as it is in diagnosis or therapy.

Two workshop participants examine their jointly-created draw-ing in order to learn from the experience.

As consultant to a school, an art therapist finds that observing a boy at work and discussing his art experience with him helps in advising the institution about a therapeutic art program.

Chapter 15

Knowing Consultation

Consultation, like teaching and supervision, is rarely something for which art therapists have formal educational preparation. Yet it is not an uncommon role for an art therapist, who is often asked by an institution or an individual to serve as a consultant. Consultation, however, is not the same as therapy, nor is it identical to either education or supervision, though it contains elements of all three. There is a literature on consultation in general, as well as more specialized writing in the area of mental health consultation. In the latter, a distinction is usually made between program consultation and case consultation. Traditional mental health professionals are more likely to be asked to consult with staff groups or individuals on specific case management questions, a role frequently filled by a consulting psychiatrist or psychologist. Art therapists seem to be asked more often to help with program development, although the work may at times involve guiding others in the understanding or treatment of specific cases.

One of the most critical areas in institutional consultation is the system itself. Just as one needs to understand an individual's dynamics or a family's interaction patterns, so one needs to get as full a picture as possible of the way in which any larger system functions. This includes a historical as well as a current perspective, which requires looking at the history of the institution and especially at the role of art and therapy within it. Assessing a system also includes an understanding of present-day dynamics, which means primarily identifying sources of power, their functioning, and the values expressed in how the organization

169

operates. What is publicly presented as the value structure may or may not reflect the latent attitudes of the system.

The reader may be feeling by now that these ideas sound fine but seem difficult to implement in real life, especially when an institution is asking the consultant for a specific kind of service, and is not asking to be assessed or understood in any larger sense. It is true that the position of a consultant is somewhat more ambiguous in this regard than that of either a therapist, a teacher, or a supervisor. With all of the latter, while there may be anxiety and resistance to one's diagnostic curiosity, there will also be some logical understanding of why one needs to know about the past and wants to understand the larger picture. The challenge, when invited into a system as a consultant, is to find ways to glean the information required that will be minimally threatening and will make the most sense to those asking for assistance. Actually, if one is convinced of the utility of getting a larger picture in order to help, one will probably be able to find some way to do the kind of observation, record reading, and interviewing necessary for such a systems analysis.

Just as people often ask for something from therapy that is not what they most need (of which they are not yet aware), so institutions often request something from an art therapy consultant that is somewhat peripheral, or at best the tip of the iceberg. However, as with therapy, one must always begin where the institution is, and, through the kind of assessment described above, gradually define larger needs and long-term goals. In the beginning, it is important to listen very carefully to what it is people think they want of the consultant. One may be able to give them just that, or one may, after learning more about the situation, feel that it would be best to offer something a little different from the original request.

Perhaps as important as the gradual building of a mental picture of the system's inner workings is the gradual building of alliances with significant individuals and groups within it. In order to do so, it is necessary for the consultant to behave in a way analogous to that which leads to trusting alliances with patients, students, and supervisees. One needs, first and foremost, to listen empathically, to try to understand just what it is that the individuals are feeling, thinking, and wishing —especially what it is that they seem to be wanting. Rarely, by the way, do they simply want what they say they want. More often, as in other relationships where one person asks for and pays another for help, they are wanting many things, some appropriate and some not, with few of them in their awareness. However, listening with a clinician's "third ear," one can begin to hear and see what is between the lines, which

may never be made explicit, but will be a great help in figuring out how best to enable the people in this institution to achieve what they are after.

Asking to observe and to meet with relevant individuals is usually seen as an indication of one's interest, and, if requested with confidence, of one's expertise in knowing what it is one needs to know in order to help. If done tactfully and over time, along with the careful building of alliances and trust, it will help one to have an impact on the institution which usually reaches much further and deeper than simply meeting the initial request. As I think back over the consulting situations in which I have been involved over the past twenty years, I am astonished at how extensive the ultimate input and impact was in some. As with treatment, I probably could not have predicted at the beginning just how art therapy would develop in any of these settings. Being open to possibilities, being flexible, and allowing institutional growth to be as organic as individual flowering can help to permit and promote exciting change.

Almost inevitably, the initial request made of any art therapy consultant is fairly narrow and specific. And equally inevitably, as the situation develops over time, other needs become apparent with which one may be able to help. If the consultant has built good relationships with individuals who have some degree of power and influence in the system, and if she is deliberate and selective about her timing, she will be able to stimulate movement in directions which may become apparent to her before they are visible to others. Her first step may simply be to find ways to sensitize others to such needs and then to work within the system's existing structure to implement change.

One important element in my thinking when I am a consultant is that of economy, and the long-term potential of any investment of my time, which is usually limited as specified by some contractual agreement. Given a choice between influencing many people temporarily and making a structural change in the system which could last beyond my tenure, I always opt for the latter. For example, the art program still exists at the institution for handicapped children where I helped it to get started in 1967. The individuals I supervised in their jobs there are long since gone; but the program has stayed and expanded, and so have the bulletin boards and display cases, which required many meetings with anxious staff members before they were permitted. Similarly, the preschool for retarded children still uses many creative play materials that were not available until I worked with the director and staff to introduce them, along with a less structured way of helping children to play. Although many faces have changed over the years, there is still an art teacher and

a creative arts therapist at the school for blind children, as well as a social worker in both upper and lower schools—none of these positions existed prior to their gradual implementation during a decade of consultation.

The attitudes towards children's emotional needs and problems are very different now in all of these settings, as they are at a school for the deaf where I currently consult. I do not mean to imply that I, single-handedly, was responsible for all of these changes. I do mean to suggest that, when deciding how best to use my consulting time, I almost always prefer a way which could lead to potentially permanent structural changes in the institution. Of course, most of my consultation time at all of these places was spent in meeting with various individuals and groups of staff members around a variety of agreed-upon tasks, ranging from individual art therapy supervision to the planning and writing of grant applications.

Art therapy consultation activities are often very concrete and practical, like ordering supplies, helping to plan and organize art rooms, doing inservice training, and conducting demonstration interviews. The latter reflects another approach I have found useful in consultation. Although normally consultation (like supervision) should involve helping others to change things rather than doing it for them, the idea of using art therapeutically can be so unfamiliar that I have often chosen to begin by doing some kind of pilot program to find out just what the population was capable of, in order to be able to plan for appropriate program development.

Expectations, especially of those who are deviant, are so often beneath the capacities of the people involved, that to accept the consultee's judgment of who can benefit from art therapy is rarely indicated. In almost every instance, from crippled children to retarded preschoolers to multiply-handicapped blind children and many adult psychiatric classifications, the expectations of those requesting a program were far below what the patients or students could actually accomplish. Doing pilot work is therefore more than a useful way of becoming familiar with the particular population. It can also be helpful in the modification of attitudes and expectations, especially if staff members are invited to observe such art therapy sessions.

Although I have suggested that art therapists are more often asked to consult on program development than on individual cases, the latter does sometimes occur. As with supervision, it is essential to remember that the goal is to increase the understanding and skill of others in coping with the particular individual. How one chooses to do that, however,

can vary considerably. In art therapy, it may well require an actual observation of the patient, looking through a series of his drawings, or even having an art interview with him. As the expressive therapy program in the psychiatric hospital has so far developed, the art therapists are often asked to work with individuals who are nonverbal or highly resistant and to share their findings with other staff members. Sometimes they are put into a kind of consulting role and asked to clarify for others just what is "wrong" with this person, whether this patient is ready to be discharged, or is suicidal, etc. Although they are members of the treatment team like the other clinicians, the presence of the art product, which may be the patient's only clear communication, requires that they not only present it but also explain it to the others, thereby putting them into a kind of consulting role.

One of the most hazardous kinds of case consultation for an art therapist lies in the seductive invitation to discourse on a patient via his products alone. Often other staff members, who may or may not be psychologically sophisticated, will bring to an art therapist one or more examples of work by a patient, asking for help in understanding their meaning and sometimes requesting assistance in getting the patient to produce more. As with a supervisee, one needs to ask many questions about the context in which the work was produced and about any associative comments or actions that might give valid clues to its meaning. If there are too few such clues, it is best to decline the invitation to interpret the art, except when one is very explicit about the purely speculative nature of any comments one might offer.

The reader may not think this sounds so seductive, but it is a big temptation for anyone to be able to decipher what others cannot—to have a key which unlocks a code. And, the more artwork one has seen, the more ideas will be generated as potentially useful hypotheses when one sees and hears about patient products. I am not suggesting that one refuse to share one's thoughts, but that if one does so, it is essential to be very explicit about the amount of guesswork involved, the lack of validity, and the possibility that what one says may not be just slightly, but completely off base. There is nothing I find quite as upsetting as an art therapist who makes a practice of doing blind analysis of people's artwork—an exciting, titillating, but very risky exercise.

What one can do, which is very helpful to most consultees, is to ask how they think one might go about understanding the meaning of art products. Using the example(s) they have brought with them, one can do a good deal of teaching—perhaps through role play—of the ways in which a person can observe and question that lead to a potentially valid

comprehension of symbolic meaning. Even though art therapists are probably less likely than other clinicians to project their own ideas onto patient work, having been trained not to do so (and hopefully knowing themselves through personal therapy), they are still subject to moments of wishful grandiosity, magic, and voyeuristic powers. And, knowing all they have learned about symbolism and development in art expression, they can have very good educated hunches about anyone's art product, especially when also provided with some information about the artist and the context in which the work was produced. My plea is for caution, modesty, and an unyielding position in relation to this particularly titillating temptation; for it does our field much more harm than good in the long run, and may even do harm to the individual(s) involved, if hunches are taken as certainties by the person asking the art therapist's opinion.

In a recent situation where I was asked by a police department to consult on a suspected case of child abuse, I was first presented with some drawings done by the youngster and asked to translate their meaning. I refused to do so but offered instead to have an art interview with the child. The girl revealed, through her drawings, doll play, and talk with me, that her stepfather had indeed abused her sexually, but that she had been fearful of saying this in court since she also loved him and didn't want him to have to leave home. The expressive nature of the one-hour interview probably did help this child to say first symbolically and then directly what was on her mind. The drawings by themselves simply reflected her confusion and were not sufficient "evidence" for any courtroom or for me as a clinician.

I do not in any way wish to minimize the tremendous value of the art product in consultation. Just as it is often true that "a picture is worth a thousand words," the advantage of artwork in convincing others of the worth of such activities is probably not quantifiable. Although a direct personal experience with creative media is even more persuasive, one can only introduce that in the context of consultation when asked to do some inservice training. As indicated in the chapter on teaching, I usually try to arrange for some direct staff involvement with materials, even if it is minimal. But if that is not possible, it is also true that art produced by an individual or group, especially if it is done over a period of time and shows some modification visible to the observer, can have a powerful impact on those in decision-making positions. This is especially true if they know the artist(s), but find that they now "know" or "see" something quite new as a result of seeing the art itself. This kind of perceptual drama has occurred so often with individuals of all

diagnostic classifications in so many settings that I am deeply impressed with the power of art to evoke and to reveal hidden aspects of human beings. This seems to be true even when the patients are under intensive scrutiny by numerous sophisticated professionals, as in the psychiatric teaching hospital in which I now work.

So I do not wish to throw out the art/baby with the blind analysis/bathwater. I simply want to remind art therapists that we have access to a powerful educative tool, if only we do not abuse it. Some of the many abuses of the past have led professionals, as well as patients, to be appropriately anxious or skeptical about what we can tell about people on the basis of their art. It is my wish that we would not contribute to any further confusion but that in a responsible and restrained consideration of patient art as serious and worthwhile data, we might help to regain some of the lost status of projective approaches in general. In order to do so, I believe that we must respect the limitations as well as the riches of "reading" people from their products.

A similar kind of restraint is perhaps more necessary when doing consultation than in any other role discussed so far, except for that of therapist. The grandiose rescue fantasies that often interfere with clinical work can also interfere with consultation. While there is a similar risk in both teaching and supervision, the temptation to accept the consultee's wishes for massive change is of a magnitude similar to the lure of a patient's dreams of carefree recovery. In both instances, someone has deliberately asked and is paying for the art therapist's help—rarely true in teaching and only occasionally in supervision, which is usually required. Of all the possible roles for an art therapist, consultation is probably the one which is most freely chosen by the person asking for assistance, so that the level of motivation and the desire to use what one has to offer are generally quite high. What is important to remember is that institutional change is no less complex or slow-going than individual or family modification. It is also true that, despite a sincere wish to make changes, there is always resistance and anxiety involved.

I am not suggesting that an art therapy consultant be either pessimistic or suspicious, but that she be realistic in her assessment of the situation and as gradual as possible in developing a plan of how best to help. This is true even if she agrees immediately to meet for so many hours a week with one or more staff members for teaching or supervision in art therapy. Her diagnosis of the system should continue throughout the time she is involved, just as, in really good therapy, one is constantly modifying one's assessment of the nature of the patient's illness and its etiology. As with a patient or a supervisee, the consultant will probably

know about interventions she wishes to make long before she actually makes them, and will be looking for the right moment, when she senses that the person or group is ready to hear what she has to say or to see what she wants to show. So it is probably necessary in consultation, as in supervision, to use many clinical skills appropriate to therapy, especially in the timing and wording of interventions.

If one is open-minded about the direction and possibilities for growth in the institution, participating in indirect change as a consultant can be highly stimulating and very rewarding. Like teaching and supervision, it is probably done best if it is done artistically. Yet it is important, in all of these indirect roles, to remember which role one is playing and to respect the boundaries of each. Of course, there are times when one might feel like a supportive therapist, while listening to a consultee or student bemoaning a difficult situation. And of course, there are educative components in both consultation and supervision, varying according to the needs and readiness of the learner, as well as the extent of the intervention.

But in some ways these are analogous to the therapist/supervisor role issues discussed in the previous chapter. If one feels that a consultee really needs to do in-depth learning in a particular area, one would probably refer him to a book or a class, rather than attempt to incorporate that much teaching into the rest of one's job. It would seem, therefore, that there is a quantitative as well as a qualitative component influencing one's recommendation of something else from somebody else, whether it be therapy, teaching, supervision, or consultation. There may be a small component of each of these in any of the others, but to let it grow any larger would be to blur boundaries and do any of these jobs less well than if one were clear about one's course and stuck to it.

I am spending much time and space on issues of role blurring and possible conflict, since I have seen these happen so often with intelligent and well-meaning art therapists. I decided to include these "extras" in the book partly because of my distress at the common confusion about these different roles, each of which has validity and can be a small part of the others, but each of which ultimately has to have its own clear boundaries. I hope that what I have written here will help to clarify rather than further blur this admittedly confusing area.

A blind girl and her teacher working with pipe cleaners help the therapist understand their school and the best kind of art program to recommend as a consultant.

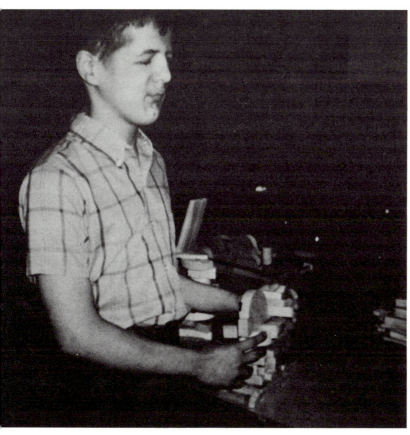

In an experimental investigation of "tactile aesthetic" perception, a blind "judge" responds to wood scrap constructions made by other blind or partially-sighted children.

Chapter 16

Knowing Research

Sometimes I wonder if it is possible for a really good art therapist to be genuinely interested in research. It seems to me that many of the interpersonal satisfactions available in clinical work are also present in those indirect service areas discussed so far in this section: in teaching, in supervision, and in consultation. But research, even if it involves working with subjects in order to collect data, is less likely to be as rewarding clinically. It is also rarely as flexible as any of the other roles, because of the necessary control of important variables. Research allows creativity primarily in its design and analysis, but hardly ever in the actual implementation of the study. Yet there are a few art therapists who are good clinicians and who also enjoy designing and conducting research.

One probable motivator is curiosity, which is also satisfied to some extent in solving patient puzzles, as well as in helping patients to reveal and to deal with their secrets. Certainly the sublimated voyeurism, which is utilized in the work of understanding patient art, can be an energizing force behind many kinds of empirical studies. It is likely that at least some of those art therapists drawn to research are also drawn to thinking in theoretical terms, though not always. Both, however, are a way of stepping back and trying to look at the issues in art therapy from a broader and deeper perspective than is possible when looking only at technique. For myself the three are closely related, perhaps inextricably so. I cannot imagine knowing what to do technically if I were not operating in terms of some theoretical premises about art and

therapy. Nor can I imagine ever being able to make significant progress in technique, without at some point validating impressions through well-designed empirical studies.

One serious problem inhibiting the development of more research in and about art therapy is the paucity of individuals who understand both areas in a thorough fashion. Only when someone really comprehends both art therapy and research methodology is one in a position to design a relevant study. One also needs to have some degree of perspective, as well as a clear sense of priorities. For one of the first questions anyone ought to ask before doing any kind of research is whether it is of value, and if so, in what way? It is foolish to take research time, energy, and often money to investigate the number of angels on the head of a pin, when there are much more potentially fruitful and important questions to be asked. This is not to suggest that one never do basic or exploratory research studies—those without any immediate obvious application. On the contrary, that is probably what our field needs more than anything else—a mapping of many territories which we now move in without sure guidelines, where we could travel so much better if we but knew the terrain.

For example, there is a need to study in detail the development of art expression in areas other than drawing and in nonrepresentational as well as representational modes. There is also a need to define norms for adult artwork in order to be able to make meaningful comparisons and inferences from patient products. The whole area of mental imagery is being mapped primarily by cognitive psychologists, with hardly any utilization of expressive visual modes in its study and definition. Similarly, the question of which parts of the brain mediate thought in images as well as in other systems is also being investigated by largely nonvisual types, who may test responses to visual stimuli but hardly ever utilize productive creative acts. I could go on and on with the kinds of descriptive studies that need to be done in order for our work to be based more on fact and less on fancy.

There are also many studies crying for implementation in regard to the influence of the modality—paint vs. clay or art vs. drama—on the form and content of what an individual creates, as well as on self-concept or the ability to gain insight. Sequences of tasks, degree of specificity, nature of therapist involvement—all of these are methodological issues which are debated in terms of opinion alone, with hardly any attempts to investigate them systematically. Even in the area of diagnosis through art products, there has been a mere trickle of investigations. And when it comes to most issues of technique, such as how much to help edu-

cationally and how much to discuss analytically, hot air predominates over hard findings (including most of this book!). Are such studies inhibited only by the lack of individuals trained in both art therapy and research methodology? Are there perhaps other less rational constraints, such as loyalty to a particular school of thought which might not fare well if tested more objectively?

Whatever the cause, much of the research being done in art therapy is of mediocre quality, and is generally inadequate in both quantity and scope. Having been so outspokenly critical, I now wish to suggest an alternative course of action, one which I have used even at the undergraduate level in training art teachers, and have also tried successfully with graduate students in art therapy and other disciplines. It is a teaching/learning model similar to that proposed for art therapy itself, where doing always occurs along with any kind of didactic instruction. If it is possible as a first step, it is best to incorporate something like observation, e.g., acting as a research assistant/observer on someone else's project. But to study research methodology or statistics without applying them at the same time is much too intellectual, and is very difficult for most inexperienced researchers to integrate—especially most art therapists, who tend to be uncomfortable with mathematics and abstract conceptualizations.

The only way I have found that enables people to genuinely grasp the thinking behind empirical research is to actually design and conduct a study in art therapy with the consultation and guidance of someone who is more experienced in both areas. Going through the process of selecting, defining, and refining the question or hypothesis; living through, with guidance and associated reading/observing, the process of deciding on subject population, methodology, etc.; actually gathering the data, experiencing the complexity of controlling variables; and finally, dealing with what has been collected in a statistically sound and meaningful way—that is the only way I have ever found for students to really learn about research. It is ideal, because if the study is in or about art therapy, the problems that arise can be dealt with in vivo, and the complexities of such work can be genuinely understood.

The reader may be wondering how many years or lifetimes this program would require, since it may sound a bit too ambitious. Actually, depending on the amount of learning time available, it can be more or less elaborate and more or less formal. It can be as limited as a single assignment for a semester course, or it can be as extensive as a master's thesis or doctoral dissertation. The extent would be a function of the learner's goals and the requirements or expectations of those doing the

teaching. If more art therapists had even a mini-experience of this nature, their attitude toward empirical research would probably be very different.

They might be much more interested than at present in collaborating with others on studies of small or large scope, and could grow considerably in their own research/statistical skills through working with individuals versed in those fields. Perhaps I am overly biased by my own positive experiences in this regard. It occurs to me that much of what I have learned over the years has come about through collaboration with someone else who had a skill or understanding that I lacked, but who was interested in working together on a study related to art therapy. This has happened with special frequency in research, where I have worked with a number of different collaborators, always including one or more who knew statistics and methodology much better than I. The books I had read and courses I had taken actually came alive through these experiences, and not before then.

I include these anecdotal thoughts, since many art therapists may not be taking courses or degrees but may well be able to work with statistically knowledgeable colleagues on studies of mutual interest. Needless to say, the art therapist may have to modify her own research interests to some extent, in order to agree on something that excites the collaborator from whom she wishes to learn. However, given a reasonably broad range of questions which intrigue her about art therapy, there will surely be one or a derivative thereof that will spark her colleague's interest as well. Doing collaborative work in research has many of the same pros and cons, stresses and pleasures, as doing cotherapy or coteaching; however, if the work is carefully planned, the advantages far outweigh the possible disadvantages. Needless to say, agreeing to conduct a study which is of no particular interest to the therapist just in order to get some sophisticated consultation, might prove to be a bargain better not made.

In addition to direct experience with conceptualizing and doing research, art therapists would also do well to think of it in less esoteric terms. Research, after all, is simply the systematic asking of questions in a way that enables those that are posed appropriately to be answered. Identifying the questions one has and deciding if they are worth the time and effort of serious study is only the first step. Deciding exactly how best to answer them is the creative and challenging part of doing research, as exciting in some ways as the development of relevant tasks or activities in doing or teaching art therapy. For example, one might decide, as I did some years ago, to study intraindividual variability

within people's art products. The issue arose (as do most research questions) after noticing a repeated phenomenon. In this case, it was the fact that people are often highly variable, yet so much of the diagnostic use of art seems not to take this variability into account. What was unknown, however, was what relationship such variability might have to either chronological age or to sex.

It was finally decided, after much brainstorming with a multidisciplinary research study group, to undertake a normative study and to use a series of human figure drawings as the task (four drawings within eight days). A minimum of twenty subjects at each age level, half male and half female, all drawn from nonpatient school populations, was also recommended by the group. The reason for the numbers was statistical; the reason for the choice of task was that it was so frequently used to evaluate both intellectual level (Harris, 1963) and personality (Machover, 1949), and that there were reliable scoring methods which could be used to compare at least one kind of variability (in score). Another activity undertaken prior to doing the actual study was to write to experts in the use of human figure drawings—Kellogg (1969), Koppitz (1968), and Harris (1963)—in order to ask if any comparable study already existed. This was a purely practical move, since it would have made little sense to spend the time, energy, and money involved if a similar investigation had already been completed. At the very least, we would need to know of such a study so that we might be able to replicate any relevant aspects. As it happened, there was no such study known to any of our expert consultants, each of whom encouraged us to pursue the research.

After gathering the drawings (collected by teachers in their classrooms) and having them scored by trained judges, it was then necessary to decide how to deal with the numerical data that emerged. We considered treating the four scores obtained for each child by one statistical technique (a repeated measures analysis of variance), but eventually decided on another (a standard deviation among the four scores) as an even more appropriate measure of score variability, certainly more refined than the range of lowest to highest score. We were then faced with yet another creative challenge: how to measure the variability among drawings that was visually apparent but not necessarily related to the score (which reflects primarily the number of details). After experimentation with several sets of measures, we finally developed a four-point scale of visual variability which allowed us to give each set of four drawings a single global rating. The same scale also proved to be useful for rating content variability as well (man, woman, boy, girl), another way in which the four drawings by each individual were potentially different

from one another. This rather detailed description of some of the issues faced in the initiation and implementation of this research project will hopefully not deter the interested art therapist, but will rather whet her appetite for the imaginative challenges involved in the systematic asking and answering of questions through research. (Rubin et al., 1983)

It is, of course, quite common for research in art therapy to focus on the art product, whether one is measuring or scoring some aspect of it, judging its normality/pathology, or evaluating it in some other way. Unfortunately, while the products of art therapy are eminently concrete and permanent, reliable and/or valid ways of scoring them are not. For example, while the area of self-esteem is one which many expect will improve as a result of art therapy, those few scales that have been developed for scoring drawings on that dimension are limited to figure drawings in pencil, seem quite unrelated to other indices, and have proved insensitive (if not invalid) in the few studies where I have used them. The problem here is similar to that identified in the area of theory: that those who have developed most existing judging scales for drawings or paintings are not artists or art therapists, but are more likely to be psychologists with an experimental bent. Perhaps quantification is not the way to get at the qualities meaningful to art therapists in patient art. I am not suggesting that I have an answer; however, if art therapists with an understanding of validity and reliability were to concentrate on such problems, more valid and dependable methods of objectively describing patient art might be developed. If nothing else, it seems important to move once and for all beyond the realm of the pencil drawing of a human figure into the world of color, shape, nuance, and form which is art.

Similar problems attend any attempt to measure or describe the creative process. Here, too, we may have gotten caught in the empiricist's numerical web, refusing to recognize the phenomenologically subjective nature of the creative experience. Yes, it is possible to develop observation guides and even relatively objective rating scales of behavior during the art process. As an example of an objective index, the number of times a child asked for help from the art therapist in pre- vs. post-program interviews was used in one study and was something that changed to a statistically significant extent following the art program. What could not be measured, however, was the look in the child's eyes, the pleading in his voice, or the anxiety in the request, all of which were also important aspects of his Independence/Dependence, the variable supposedly being measured.

Inferential indices such as the intensity of a person's involvement in

the creative task are what we need to find ways of describing—qualitatively if possible, quantitatively if feasible. How often someone steps away from the easel and reconsiders his painting may be as valid a measure of his observing ego as his ability to discuss the painting later in the group. Understanding and evaluating the art process are complex challenges, which need to be tackled with a more phenomenological and less quantitative methodology, as has been suggested by art education researcher Kenneth Beittel (1973).

But the hardest thing to measure, and the one most desired, is the effectiveness of art therapy. Whether the indices are intrinsic (like paintings from the first and last session) or extrinsic (like scores on a written test of self-esteem), it is always difficult to isolate influences in this, as in other outcome research. Nevertheless, it is in this area that we should concentrate our efforts, in order to document the changes that all art therapists feel sure take place but cannot easily communicate without less biased evidence. A second area needing study is the effectiveness of different methodologies, such as more vs. less structure in tasks, or the optimal amount of therapist-initiated intervention with a particular population. While it is difficult to conceptualize, let alone control, all of the relevant variables involved in answering such questions, we will be on much sounder ground and will gain significant respect if we attempt to look more objectively at ourselves.

One of the really exciting things about research in and through art therapy is that it *is* so very undeveloped, that the possibilities are endless and stretch in multiple directions. Hopefully, future clinicians will be helped to be less uncomfortable with the idea of empirical research and will be able to initiate as well as respond to interest on the part of others. Collaborating with other mental health professionals on questions of common interest is surely much more than a way for an individual art therapist to grow in understanding research. It is also a way to build bridges, based primarily on intellectual excitement. If we can view ourselves as capable of learning how to do meaningful research and can be viewed by others as potentially valuable collaborators, our stature will grow and we will begin to make contributions in yet other realms of mental health, beyond bringing the arts directly to those who are troubled. For, as noted earlier, there is a great deal to be understood about the mind and its functions through a more detailed, in-depth understanding of how it works when making art.

In addition to the challenge and importance of conducting well-designed research in and about art therapy, it is important for any art therapist in a position of responsibility to be able to understand and

evaluate relevant research in related fields. Without some comprehension of what is involved in experimental design or in the handling of emergent data, it is really impossible to make sense of the reports of research by others. This is significant for several reasons. First, there is much that is of value to us and related to our work in studies from allied disciplines, but we need to be able to evaluate its quality and comprehend its implications in order to make use of it. In a recent issue of *Studies in Art Education*, for example, there was a report of an investigation of "the effects of students' sense of agency or self-determination as a motivational force in art learning" (King, 1983). All of the outcome measures, including both achievement and attitude, revealed differences favoring the student-choice condition. What this means is that, at least for the subjects in this study (208 sixth graders involved in different art-learning situations for three months), the condition in which they could select their own activities resulted in greater progress in art achievement, in self-concept, and in attitudes toward art. The relevance of this study for issues of methodology in art therapy is quite clear. What makes it so important is that it was also very carefully designed, so that the independent variable of choice was isolated and controlled much more precisely than is usually the case, making the findings all the more significant.

In the same issue of the same journal, a review of the literature on cognitive style and its implications for research in art production (and art criticism) also has relevance for our field (Lovano-Kerr, 1983). While the paper is primarily a discussion of the literature and the implications for research, it is also a well-considered reminder of the importance of cognitive style as it affects different methods of working with different people in art. It is clearly useful to be able to read and evaluate research in related fields—especially in all of those disciplines that overlap in some way with the field of art therapy. Since there are many areas of similarity and even congruence with such fields, it seems ostrichlike not to be aware of developments that may be relevant to our own work. Just as it would enrich art therapy to conduct research in collaboration with those whose expertise is in statistics, so it would also broaden our discipline to design studies, in depth, with sophisticated colleagues from fields such as special education and clinical psychology.

Some of this polemic is a response to what appears to be an excessively narrow perspective on the part of many art therapists, even those involved in training others and publishing in art therapy journals. This is a danger for any professional group, especially a young one which is carefully defining and jealously guarding its relatively new identity.

Hopefully, we will not be so insular that we have to reinvent the wheel too many times in the process, and we will be able to harness our strengths to those of others for all of that needed and exciting research in the future. Hopefully, too, many of us can learn to enjoy doing such work, so that there will be more and better studies designed by those who really understand the discipline.

REFERENCES

Beittel, K.E. *Alternatives for art education research*. Dubuque, IA: William C Brown, 1973.

Harris, D.B. *Children's drawings as measures of intellectual maturity*. New York: Harcourt, Brace, & World, 1963.

Kellogg, R. *Analyzing children's art*. Palo Alto: National Press Books, 1969.

King, A. Agency, achievement, and self-concept of young adolescent art students. *Studies in Art Education*, 1983, 24, 187-194.

Koppitz, E.M. *Psychological evaluation of children's human figure drawings*. New York: Grune & Stratton, 1968.

Lovano-Kerr, J. Cognitive style revisited: Implications for research in art production and art criticism. *Studies in Art Education*, 1983, 24, 195-205.

Machover, K. *Personality projection in the drawing of the human figure*. Springfield, IL: Charles C Thomas, 1949.

Rubin, J.A., Schachter, J., & Ragins, N. Intraindividual variability in human figure drawings: A developmental study. *American Journal of Orthopsychiatry*, 1983, 53, 654-667.

Any viable theory of art therapy has to be able to account for this rare example of self-therapy through art. A rural laborer told how much it had helped him to carve this larger-than-life-size figure from a tree trunk following the untimely death of his young wife.

Chapter 17

Knowing Theory

Having made a strong pitch for collaboration with those from other disciplines in developing sound research in art therapy, I shall now make what will probably appear to be a 180-degree turn and argue for greater independence in our thinking in the area of theory. It is significant, I think, that a number of art therapists have had to obtain advanced training in some other discipline, largely because such training has not been available in our own. While it is exciting to enrich our field with the well-digested perspectives of others, it is also depressing. It is sad that we so often seem to borrow theories in order to explain what happens when people create, just as we attach to ourselves the identities of others when we obtain doctorates in other disciplines.

It is important to realize that those who have theorized about the creative process and its relationship to mental health have rarely been artists, though they may have done creative thinking in other realms. Mental health professionals, like Freud (1900), Arieti (1976), and Maslow (1968), have done much to further our understanding of what motivates creative behavior and what it may accomplish for the individual. While it is important to be literate and knowledgeable about existing theories, it is also vital to remember that they tend to be rather intellectualized, based as they are on observation, interview, or speculation about the direct experiences of others. Although there have also been some artists who have written thoughtfully about their work, most have not been trained in psychology or psychopathology. Their notions, therefore,

while often pregnant with intuitive truths, are as one-sided as those of the nonartist psychologists.

In art therapy itself, there is a discipline that (ideally) combines a sophisticated understanding of the art process with an equally sophisticated understanding of psychology. There is now the possibility that a theory about the therapeutic aspects of art will be developed by those who understand both art and therapy. Our "pioneers," incidentally, are not by any means the first people who worked with patients using art. But they are the people who wrote thoughtfully about their work. They did not just write descriptively, but analytically as well, always trying to understand why what they were doing was having the effects they observed. In other words, they developed theories about the use of art in therapy, in which they tried to synthesize their knowledge of both art and psychology. The writings of Naumburg, Kramer, Ulman (1961, 1971), and Rhyne are distinguished by this attempt to not only describe but also understand. They have given us good models, which have been followed by a few other art therapists (e.g., Betensky, Robbins) to whom theorizing has an appeal (cf. *Suggested Readings*, Part III, for specific references).

All of these individuals have done considerable borrowing from the theories of others, whether it is the appealing aesthetic constructs of Suzanne Langer (1953), or the ego psychology of Ernst Kris (1952). What is needed now is the development of meaningful theoretical constructs from the matrix of art therapy itself. But art is art and people are people, the reader will say, and so it makes sense that we have much to learn and to legitimately borrow from those who have studied either creativity or human beings in some depth. While I do not for a moment deny the possible relevance of theories from other disciplines and their application to our own, I feel some uneasiness about the possibility that we may be forcing art therapy into theoretical molds that do not quite "fit."

Although this may sound inconsistent with my plea not to reinvent the wheel or to isolate ourselves in our research endeavors, I believe that theory is qualitatively different. Of course, in order to be able to converse and to communicate with students and other professionals, it is necessary to know and understand the similarities and differences between things like gestalt psychology and gestalt therapy, or classical psychoanalytic drive theory and the recent developments in object relations. Being familiar with different theories of how and why people function in general, and particularly in art, cannot but deepen our understanding of the phenomena with which we deal. It is especially useful, where possible, to read the original (not just someone else's

translation of meaning) in order to fully grasp something like Freud's theory of dream formation and its technical implications (e.g., Altman, 1975; Freud, 1900). But that should be only the beginning.

The goal is to study and think about what goes on in art therapy as we do, advise, and supervise such work, as well as to try to explain the effects of a full art experience in ways which truly fit the facts of actual practice. Now, one may object that, insofar as technique is derived from theory, the way in which different individuals practice art therapy will vary according to their underlying models of mental and creative functioning. That is probably true, but it is also very likely that in most cases the art therapist herself has never really thought consciously or clearly about the constructs that inevitably lie behind her work. I am simply suggesting that art therapists try to do just that.

I am also suggesting that, if we are to enable people to truly understand the theories of others or, if possible, to develop their own, they will need some help and some practice with guidance in order to feel comfortable in this realm. In this respect, theoretical thinking is similar to research—something often seen by the average art therapist as alien, esoteric, and much too difficult. While it is even more abstract than most empirical research studies, such thinking is not beyond the grasp of the average practitioner. Unfortunately, our educational system, with its neglect of philosophy, has done little to train or encourage this capacity, but it is as latent in most people as the ability to work creatively with art media. One way to encourage its development would be to initiate projects in training and supervision similar to those suggested for the promotion of research abilities. This means asking art therapists at all stages of development to sit back and think about how it is they conceptualize an individual's or group's creative functioning at any moment in time, and then to think as reflectively about their own behavior and what they expect will come from it, i.e., their underlying theoretical constructs about the mechanisms involved in promoting change and growth.

Alternating such reflective exercises (in writing as well as orally) with those in which art experience is looked at in terms of one or another existing theory will certainly help art therapists to become more comfortable with such thinking. Theory is only meaningful and worthwhile if it helps to explain the phenomena with which it deals in a way that enables us to work better with them. To learn or to develop theories of personality, psychotherapy, or creativity without actually applying them to real life situations is to grasp neither their meaning nor their significance. Theory and technique should go hand in hand: the one based

on and growing out of the other, each constantly modifying the other over time.

Although this may sound too intellectual for most art therapists, it may be as important to the continued development of our field as defining the basics. Thinking theoretically is a kind of creative problem-solving which is more abstract than art. But art itself is an abstraction of reality, whether representational or nonfigurative in its manifest form. Theories are usually expressed in words, although that does not mean that they must be or that they are always best conceptualized in that modality. It is significant that several major theoretical constructs in the natural sciences were stimulated by intuitive apprehensions of visual imagery—the visual thinking about which Arnheim (1969) writes so persuasively and which lay behind Kekulé's discovery of the benzene ring or Einstein's awareness of relativity. It is quite probable that the use of visual imagery, both two- and three-dimensional, would extend our power to theorize, to conceptualize, and to hypothesize the invisible forces with which we deal and which we hope to influence. One of my frequent thoughts as I went through classical psychoanalytic training was that I could imagine the id, ego, and superego much more easily as sounds, shapes, textures, or movements than as abstract concepts or agencies of the mind. Or, when thinking of conflict theory, of the dynamics of impulse, prohibition, and compromise involved in defense mechanisms and symptom formation, I often found myself imagining something three-dimensional and in motion. This idea could best be represented in an animated film, which would capture more fully than any words or linear diagrams the actuality of internalized conflict and the psyche's attempts at resolution.

In an informal study, I explored with various individuals the creation of one image after another in various media in order to get an idea of what the mind would do with free association in art imagery (rather than in words). Although it is a territory barely defined and hardly charted, it is one full of implications for thinking in general, including theoretical kinds of thinking about the work we do. I do not yet have a formed theory to propose, but hope that all art therapists will work toward such a goal, and will do so as much as possible within the context of our work itself and what it involves. I do not wish to suggest that we throw out all those other theories as useless, but that we be careful not to see in them what we want and need to see, in a way that distorts either their original meaning or our own experience with art in therapy.

This danger is especially acute with those constructs which best seem to "fit" our field, like Langer's notion of art as forms of human feeling

(1953), the psychoanalysts' ideas about symbolization (Jones, 1916) or sublimation (Hartmann, 1955), Maslow's concept of peak experience (1968), Arieti's concept of the tertiary process (1976), and so on. These notions are indeed relevant and related but not quite as syntonic as we seem to wish. Langer, for example, seems to be using "feeling" in a much broader way than it is usually understood or meant by art therapists, who would not find some of her associated ideas so congenial.

Sublimation, still a hotly debated concept in psychoanalysis, seems a rather limited and perhaps overly sociological way of referring to what is involved in creating art. While the containment of drive energies in an aesthetic form is indeed pleasing and does relieve tension for the moment, it rarely seems to achieve any kind of lasting problem-resolution for the individual. Perhaps more important, while it seems to be a component of many a creative process, it is not always definably present nor is it ever the totality of the event. In other words, without nit-picking, we seem to have grabbed hold of partially digested and appealing ideas in our eager efforts to make sense of what we do. This may have been a necessary first step and has certainly enabled us to communicate meaningfully with those from other disciplines. But the time has come to take yet another step, this time toward a theory of art therapy itself which grows out of its own essence, nature, and being.

Having been so critical of others, I now feel obliged to expose some of my own partly formed notions, which may someday lead to a useful theory of art therapy. I hope that in so doing I will encourage others to share their thoughts as well, so that we ourselves can engage in the kind of collaborative theory-building which people have done for so long in philosophy, psychology, and other scholarly domains. I shall start with the *Art Part*, as in the organization of this book, for I believe, despite my fondness for reflection and awareness, that art is and must be at the core of art therapy.

The art process has its own internal rhythm and essence, which involve a human being not only in mastery of media, but also in a kind of temporary fusion with the work itself. Art-making also involves a person in an externalization of the self in concrete form, a new way of saying "me" or "I," and perhaps more important, a new way of saying "I *do*" or "I *can* do." In a fashion that reminds one of looking in a mirror, a creation in any medium becomes a new kind of self-reflection for the artist. In this way, it provides human beings at all developmental levels with an important experience of self and nonself, yet where the nonself has paradoxically been created by the self. In this sense, I am talking about something related to Winnicott's (1953) notion of the "transitional

object," but not quite the same. (That, by the way, is one of the many constructs I believe we have wisely apprehended as relevant, but may have swallowed whole too quickly, without selecting the parts that we really can incorporate as art therapists.)

In this peculiar experiential duality, the art process provides an individual with temporary fusion and loss of boundaries, along with an experience of heightened separateness from another object, which is yet, paradoxically, of and from the self. Such experiences, perhaps unique to the visual arts, are extremely important in the internal construction of what some have called a self-representation. This is not a clearly defined or always stable visual image, any more than the body image is literally a mental picture. But there is a set of feelings about the self in regard to the environment, human and nonhuman, which are intimately related to the experience of creating in art. The art object can, of course, also be related to as if it were totally nonself. It can be attacked, admired, and dealt with in any way which is needed by the individual at that moment in time to maintain his psychic equilibrium. No such freedom is present when dealing with other concrete objects or with other human beings.

Indeed, the absolute and complete freedom the creator enjoys in relation to his art is probably unique in human experience. If this seems extensive in regard to a finished product (which can ultimately be preserved or destroyed by the creator), just think how infinite it is when dealing with media in their unstructured form. Despite the fact that each medium has its own built-in limitations and constraints, it is possible within these boundaries for the creator to do anything he can imagine and accomplish. The value of such an experience of near-total freedom in a world that cannot permit or tolerate it in other realms is something of which most practicing artists are well aware. It is also of significant value in art therapy. Needless to say, the patient's freedom is limited by the extent to which the art therapist tells him what to do with the medium; however, it is also true that his ability to use it creatively may be enhanced by the lending of idea or ego by the clinician.

Most people who have psychological problems do not feel free to use their resources in the way that they could or should. If they are not overly constricted, they may be unable to control or channel their energies in a way that is constructive. In either case, art provides a place where both not only *can* happen, but also *must* inevitably happen if art is to occur. That is, a creative situation in art therapy provides for an experience of freedom (within a safe and securely bound framework), which can be liberating to the human spirit in a way that may never be

measurable. Yet creating in art, because it requires discipline, control, decision making, and forming, also provides people with an experience of channeling energies in a constructive and potentially coherent fashion.

The creative art experience also draws on all parts of the mind. Whatever we call the part that creates our dreams or our waking fantasies, we know that in sleep and in periods of altered consciousness our images are more frequent and our thoughts more playful, less logical. In a complete art experience, the creator is able to get in touch with and draw upon this kind of largely visual thinking, sometimes called primary process. Although this used to be thought of as primitive (developmentally earlier and less sophisticated), recent work in hemispheric specialization and psychoanalysis suggests that this is not an inferior mode of thought, but simply a different mode of thought. There is even a good deal of evidence for the possibility that such thinking has its own developmental line, that it is not simply something prior to or less than secondary process (logical) thought. This new way of viewing wholistic, imagic, fantastic thinking is quite synchronous with the experience of artists over the ages, as well as with those cultures which for one or another reason have valued the mystical and the nonrational.

In any case, no one will deny that art, if it is to have energy and derive from the inner world of the creator, must draw upon the storehouse of imagery buried deep in that part of the mind not conscious during waking hours. But—and this is also undeniable—in order for such unconscious or preconscious ideas to become art, they must be given form. A dream may be the stuff which art is made of, but by itself it is no more art than ramblings are poetry. This raw material must be shaped, selections made, parts omitted, and other parts added or extended. The creation of art, therefore, also involves the other part of the mind, whatever we call it, which organizes and gives form. Perhaps it is true, as Arieti (1976) suggests, that it is a third part, intermediary between the fantasy of the one and the logic of the other, which creates artistic form ("tertiary process").

It probably doesn't matter how many components we theorize exist in the human mind. As with stages of artistic development, it is probably possible (or will be some day) to make increasingly finer discriminations. What is important is that there is clearly more than one distinct mode of thought, and that art creation is one of the very few human activities available to all age levels in which all modes must be operative. And, if they are to be successful as art, these modes must also be integrated or synthesized. This may be the greatest reason of all for art's value in

therapy—that it requires the integration of so many usually separated, isolated parts of the mind and aspects of human experience. I believe this to be true, whether we see art as an integration of inner and outer worlds, of self and nonself, of good and bad, of primary and secondary processes, of matter and mind, or of any other such polarities.

I have focused so far on those values in the art experience that seem to be inherently therapeutic and growth-enhancing. But art in therapy is art in the presence of someone else, and there, I believe, derives an additional aspect of its healing power. Not only does the therapist create a situation where others are supported in creative art-making; she also functions in a variety of significant ways in relationship to those other human beings. This peculiar combination of supporter/teacher/helper, reflector/looker/analyzer, and symbolic object of positive/negative transference feelings gives immense power to the art therapist role. If she were simply an art teacher, she might be moderately helpful, but nowhere near as much as she potentially is in the artist/teacher/therapist combination.

It is in the very nature of art therapy that the clinician is required to be all three—an artist, a teacher, and a therapist. It is also true that therapist is the primary role, to which the others are subservient. But to experience another human being in this rare combination of roles is probably as unique for most patients as having a genuinely creative encounter with art. In addition to being useful to the patient as an object of transference with whom unresolved issues and conflicted longings can be experienced, understood, and worked through, the art therapist is simultaneously a guide and helper, not only in the journey through the mind provided in every psychotherapy, but also in the realm of creative art—a new, exciting, and potentially frightening world. The adventure undergone with the art therapist is therefore twofold: into the self, but also out of the self and, in a very concrete way, into the world.

Most patients have great difficulty comfortably accepting either themselves or the world. Since an art therapist deals with all aspects of the self (for example, destructive as well as constructive), she makes available a wide range of shared experience through which the patient can make visible, and eventually accept, unwanted aspects of the self. Because the work involves acting on and sometimes representing the physical world, it requires a real encounter with real things as part of the difficult task of coming to grips with reality. The art therapist helps in the task of translating the patient's often distorted psychic reality into a better approximation of what is "really" out there, which he must eventually accept with comfort if he is to live successfully within it.

These latter arguments sound a bit forced, but we often minimize the importance of integrating physical, concrete, motoric-kinesthetic expressions of the self with more verbal, intellectual images of the self. Art therapy necessarily involves the body, more with certain media than others, but always present and active in some way. The additional components of visual thinking, plus verbalizing about the experience and the product, may enable an acceptance of the self's experience or perceptions in a much more integrated way than is possible through any single modality alone. Art activity, especially with young children, is at least as much a motor activity as it is a cognitive or affective one. Watching a tape of an art therapy session without sound is one good way of tuning in more clearly to this dimension, which often escapes us in our usual focus on the visual/verbal axis. In any case, it may well be this truly multimodal aspect of any art process that makes it so helpful as an integrating experience.

We cannot overemphasize the usefulness of the concrete product, which enables one to sit back and look at what has been made, reflect on and experience the process and the external object in a way that is not possible while immersed in the doing of it. We are thereby engaging not only the experiencing, doing, active self, but also the observing, reflective, passive self in relation to the same art object. These two modes of being are related but not identical to the two modes of thinking discussed above. In this regard, as in the utilization of both linear and wholistic mentation, art therapy also helps human beings to integrate different aspects of themselves.

To be immersed in creating is very different from looking at one's creation and allowing oneself to become involved in it as a stimulus for thought. The associations can be either logical or illogical; the state of the viewer is more physically relaxed but more mentally active than that of the creator during the doing part of the process. Both ways of being are essential to healthy living and growing. To be able to engage fully in an activity, whether it is painting or dancing or playing tennis or making love, requires that the individual let go of certain controls and inhibitions, and allow the motor-rhythmic parts of the self to be in charge. To be able to reflect upon the outcome of that activity, as when one looks at the art product one has created, requires that the individual adopt a more consciously thoughtful state, one in which the loosening of logical controls can also facilitate a freer associative process. Eventually, however, even when the associations have been relatively unfettered by logic, it is necessary in art therapy to adopt yet another state of mind—a thoughtful one—which attempts to find and to express some meaning and order in what has been perceived and thought. This or-

dering of one's thoughts in response to the art product is analogous to the ordering of elements in the creative work itself; yet now both the free play of ideas and the attempt to find form take place entirely in the realm of thoughts expressed in words, quite different from the two similar components in the active, making phase.

While it is possible and sometimes necessary to focus more on one component than the other in doing art therapy, for the fullest use of the modality, it is important to try to enable both involved doing and relaxed reflection. Of course, there are patients for whom one or the other may not be possible at some moments and perhaps not ever, or only to a minimal degree. But we give people the most integrated and integrating experience when we try to provide for both. Others differ with this position, but hopefully, along with the refinement of theory in the field, there will come increasingly sophisticated research studies, wherein we can test out the validity of the sometimes incompatible assumptions which we now debate.

REFERENCES

Altman, L.L. *The dream in psychoanalysis.* (2nd ed.). New York: International Universities Press, 1975.

Arieti, S. *Creativity: The magic synthesis.* New York: Basic Books, 1976.

Arnheim, R. *Visual thinking.* Berkeley: University of California Press, 1969.

Freud, S. *The interpretation of dreams* (1900). *Standard Edition*, Vols. 4-5, London: Hogarth, 1955.

Hartmann, H. Notes on the theory of sublimation. *Psychoanalytic Study of the Child*, 1955, 10, 9-29.

Jones, E. The theory of symbolism (1916). In *Papers on psycho-analysis* (5th ed.). Baltimore: Williams & Wilkins, 1948, pp. 87-144.

Kris, E. *Psychoanalytic explorations in art.* New York: Schocken, 1952.

Langer, S.K. *Feeling and form.* New York: Scribner's, 1953.

Maslow, A.H. *Toward a psychology of being* (2nd ed.). New York: Van Nostrand, 1968.

Ulman, E. Art therapy: Problems of definition. *Bulletin of Art Therapy.* 1961, *1*(2), 10-20.

Ulman, E. The power of art in therapy. In I. Jakab (Ed.). *Psychiatry and art*, Vol. 3. New York: S. Karger, 1971, pp. 93-102.

Winnicott, D.W. Transitional objects and transitional phenomena. *International Journal of Psycho-Analysis*, 1953, *34*, 89-97.

PART V

Applications

Although this book is not the place for detailed examples of work in art therapy, either direct or indirect, it seems important to include some of the key issues involved when using art therapy with different populations, in different settings, and in different modes. Happily, art therapy can be used with almost all populations needing help, although its potential and direction will differ with diverse groups. Issues to consider when dealing with people at different levels of development, with different types of psychopathology, and with different kinds of handicaps will be noted, as well as particular problems related to art therapy.

Settings, the subject matter of the second chapter in this section, include all kinds, for there, too, art therapy is quite adaptable. It is now used in almost every sort of human service institution imaginable, but most often in hospitals, clinics, rehabilitation centers, and schools. There are also other settings where it has also been found useful, from community centers and art schools to prisons and hospices. The chapter, however, deals with some of the key issues an art therapist needs to be aware of in regard to the setting, the general type as well as the particular place. Most central are the development and definition of the role of the art therapist, and the place of art therapy within the institution.

By "mode" I refer here to the different possible configurations used in art therapy today, of which the main ones are: individual, group, and family art therapy. There are also other possibilities, such as working with couples or multiple family groups; and there are many potential variations, like using works of art as stimuli for discussion, rather than

asking for art production per se. Considerations relevant for each of the major modes of treatment will be discussed, such as the frequency and length of sessions and the particular goals that seem appropriate, which will determine the choice of mode when feasible. Another way of working is in collaboration with another clinician, whether parallel with individuals or as cotherapists with a family or group. This person might be an art therapist or someone from another discipline, which could be a traditional mental health field or another one of the creative arts therapies. Some of the special issues involved in collaboration and cotherapy will be noted, with particular attention to ways of combining skills in different expressive modalities.

In order to best apply what one knows about art and therapy—the basics as well as the extras—one must really understand each of the subjects discussed in this section: the population(s), the setting(s), and the mode(s) in which one works. Without some awareness in all of these areas, even an art therapist who knows a great deal may be unable to apply it successfully, because she does not know enough about the particular soil in which she hopes to plant her art therapy seeds. I suppose that, if she is as "artistic" as I would wish, she would be creative and sensitive in the way she deals with institutions, other professionals, and patients of any age or diagnosis, using any form of art therapy. But, as was noted earlier, in order for artistry to be possible, it must be based on knowledge, and there are some things one needs to learn if one is to work with any particular population in any particular setting and in any particular mode.

Being aware that such learning is needed is just the initial step; finding out where to get it is, of course, the necessary next move. Rarely is it handed to anyone on a platter, and never is all of it available "by the seat of one's pants." So finding out where and how one can learn what one needs to know in order to function most effectively in any particular situation becomes a continuing part of professional growth. One's search must be within the constraints of reality for the best kind of learning that is available and accessible. But with a will, there is usually a way, especially if one can think and act with flexibility.

I have also included an addendum on "Knowing What you Don't Know." Perhaps this is the highest level of professional development in art therapy as elsewhere: a sense not only of wonder but also of openness, a conviction that people and art and therapy are complex, and that simple answers are simply inadequate. Along with humility, a healthy dose of skepticism is very useful, though both need to exist

in a matrix of overall confidence in oneself and in one's discipline. While I sometimes have doubts about me, I never have doubts about the value, the potential, and the power of art therapy.

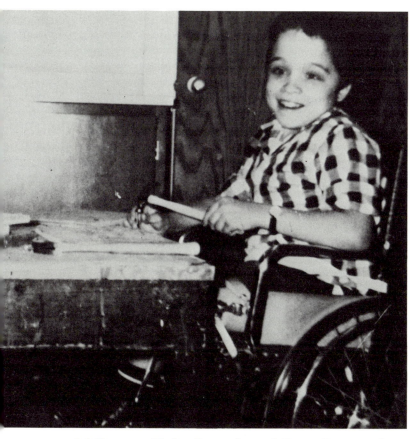

Art therapy with handicapped populations often necessitates adaptations like lower work tables to make creative activity possible.

Chapter 18

Different Populations

The first and most important thing to remember about different populations is that all human beings, whatever their age or disability, can do something creative with art materials. One of the most distressing and most common attitudes one encounters is a negative or skeptical one in regard to a particular group's ability to use art media constructively. I can hardly think of an age level or disability where at one time or another someone—usually a knowledgeable professional, sometimes an art therapist—has not expressed the opinion that people in that group were incapable of doing anything meaningful in art. The reasons given always sound rational, and the experiences or literature on which such negative expectations are based usually seem legitimate. But the effect of expectations on people's ability to perform is so powerful that even documentation of failure with one or another type of patient is not sufficient reason for giving up in advance.

Almost anyone is capable of creative expression, with very few (if any) exceptions; the critical variables are the art therapist's optimism and creativity. Both are important, since positive expectations alone will not solve all of the problems some people will have in using art media. Whether those problems are primarily sensory, physical, mental, or behavioral, an inventive approach to solving them is usually successful, especially when it is combined with an optimistic attitude about the outcome. Frequently the negative expectation is not applied to the group as a whole, but rather to subgroups or individuals; the principle, however, is the same. The challenge for the art therapist is to find a way,

given the physical and mental condition of the individual patient, for that person to be able to create. Whether one needs to devise a mechanical contraption or to use one's own ego in an auxiliary fashion, whether one needs to design the least distracting setting or the most stimulating motivation, the challenge can be met if approached with optimism and creativity.

Having delivered the polemic that no one should be denied the opportunity to have art therapy because it seems to some that an individual is incapable of creative behavior, let us look more closely at the most significant variables in regard to different populations. The first and most obvious is age, since art therapists can work successfully with toddlers through geriatrics, but the approach naturally needs to vary for different developmental levels. Both chronological and mental age are important, the former because of the likely physical maturation and interests, the latter because of the probable emotional maturity and developmental capacities. When there is a significant discrepancy between the two, as in retardation, one must pay attention to both. Knowing normal development well is clearly one major key to understanding and dealing in a meaningful way with people at different stages of life.

In addition to the expanded range of skills and understandings that become possible during the years from early childhood to adolescence, there is also a corresponding change in the life or growth tasks that are primary at each developmental stage. The therapist becomes less and less of a caretaker over this period, while needing throughout to maintain both support and the setting of limits. Of course, one must talk differently to a three-year-old than to a ten-year-old, and differently to a teenager than to an adult. It seems that knowing about development is only part of what is needed if one is to do successful art therapy with different age levels.

It is also necessary to be able to relate with comfort and pleasure to people at varying stages of life, and not everyone can do so with equal ease. I have elsewhere (Rubin, 1982) stressed some of the special qualities needed for work with children which, while desirable, are less essential for success with adults: for example, a sincere enjoyment of the young, playfulness, or the ability to set limits on destructive behavior in a calm and confident manner. People at different life stages can evoke different kinds of responses in clinicians depending in part on the therapist s own stage of development, as well as on her past experiences at different stages and with individuals in each age group. Someone who has had a close relationship with a grandparent, for example, will probably be able to relate more effectively and more comfortably to elderly patients

than someone whose only contact was distant or aversive. Someone who has been a parent can empathize with a mother and father's problems with their children in a way that an unmarried clinician cannot.

What matters most is that the art therapist be as honest as possible about the developmental levels which are most appealing and that she try, if at all possible, to obtain work with the ages with which she is most comfortable. When that is not feasible, and she finds herself working with an age range that makes her feel uneasy, she has a responsibility not only to obtain fuller information about that developmental level, but also to do some therapeutic work on herself, in order to try to overcome the aversion which is more often based on emotional than intellectual factors.

The implicit as well as the explicit demands made by individuals at different developmental levels vary tremendously; and the dependency of a young child or a retarded adult may be quite threatening to an insecure art therapist and quite rewarding to a nurturant one. Similarly, the distancing and sparring so common with adolescents, who are necessarily ambivalent about developing intimate relationships with adults (working as they are on separation from their parents), may be great fun for some clinicians and quite distressing for others. Active children can be experienced as a joy or a nuisance, depending as much on the emotional response of the art therapist as on any qualities inherent in the youngsters.

While examining the sources of any response in oneself should be part of supervision (and therapy, when necessary), learning more about the particular developmental level involved can sometimes make a big difference in how one reacts to patients. Such learning, like any other, is always best when it can be tested and confirmed in real life, so that recommending books or articles on different developmental levels being encountered often seems appropriate in supervision. In addition to being relevant for people who are working with patients of that age range, such knowledge may also help those whose patients may be older, but are stuck on difficulties related to earlier developmental tasks. Readings on separation-individuation, for example, can be useful to art therapists seeing adult borderlines, as well as to those working with preschoolers (e.g., Mahler et al., 1975).

There are some implications here for training in art therapy: that any trainee at the master's level should have experienced, either as observer or worker, art therapy with people of all age levels—from early childhood through old age. Of course, an in-depth experience with each stage is not possible, but a look or a brief practicum is and can be one goal of

any serious training program. The same recommendation makes sense regarding different types of disability: from mental (retardation, brain damage) to physical (palsy, blindness, deafness) to psychological (neurosis and psychosis), each in as many forms as possible. Exposure via observation is a minimum requirement. No amount of reading about diagnostic classifications or exceptionalities can compare with even a brief but live interaction with a person who fits the description.

I have been stressing the art therapist's comfort or distress with different age levels, as well as the need to know about normal developmental tasks and capacities. The same is true of disabilities: It is important to know about and to have at least some experience with all of the major kinds, and it is equally important to be aware of one's own subjective response to patients in different diagnostic categories. A combination of learning about the group and examining the emotional roots of one's own reactions is probably ideal. Both can be most helpful in overcoming the common feelings of disgust, helplessness, and aversion, as well as overwhelming pity or excessive attraction.

The reader may be wondering when I am going to tell him or her what to *do* with different age levels or with different diagnostic groups. It would be nice if there were a way to classify approaches in art therapy according to either developmental levels or disorders. It is, of course, possible to attempt to build a treatment program on what people normally do sequentially with art media, as in the developmental therapy approach (Williams & Wood, 1977). It is also possible to generalize, at least statistically, about the frequency of one or another formal or thematic characteristic in the art of patients with different diagnostic classifications or degrees or types of pathology.

However, while behavior and art creations do reflect development, dynamics, and deviations, this does not mean that there are significantly distinct and predictable *approaches* which can be generalized either for different age levels, specific disabilities, or types of pathology. There is so much inter- as well as intraindividual variability in art behaviors that I have yet to find a generalization which works for any population. The only one which makes sense is that it is always a trial-and-error process, and that an open choice along with active support is probably the best way to find out just where anyone "is" in art, no matter what information one may already have about age, IQ, or diagnosis.

Almost as toxic as negative expectations about particular populations are rigid attitudes and expectations about what one *ought* to do with specific groups, however that is defined. As with overly simplistic generalizations about symbolic meaning, there is probably some validity in

all of the more commonly accepted maxims. It does make sense, for example, to focus on the developmental tasks of any age level when using a theme-centered approach, so that life review for the aged is appropriate, as is identity for the adolescent. Of course, it would be frustrating to invite anyone to use a tool or medium which he could not possibly manage physically, despite adaptational efforts. But it is more common to underestimate than to overestimate patients' abilities in that regard, as well as in the degree of cooperation, concentration, or reflection of which they are capable. My recent experience with acutely ill schizophrenics is a case in point, where no one would have predicted either their ability to become focused and absorbed in the creative process for up to two hours at a time, or their ability to carry on a group discussion, demanding distance and reflection, for an hour or more regarding their productions. Yet it has been happening for months now—art therapy groups of over three hours in length. While I have yet to be able to explain it (except as a reflection of the charisma and skill of the particular clinician), I cannot deny the facts, nor how this amazing finding contradicts well accepted and logical assumptions.

I confess other surprises as well (despite my avowed open-mindedness and optimism), like the ability of children with conduct disorders to function much more cooperatively than I had anticipated, in small art groups with minimal structure; or the capacity of some geriatric patients to write poetry about their paintings largely out of their own creative wellsprings, and led by a woman with no special training or facility in that art form; or the refusal of those with major affective disorders to paint or draw in the way that diagnosed depressed patients are supposed to, and so on. And I often have such surprises about therapists as well, like the capacity of a rather shy, white, middle-aged woman to evoke impressive artwork from angry black males, who are of a socioeconomic group that would normally not relate positively to such a proper, middle-class lady. Yet she can, in her art therapy groups, find hidden talents and release some of their most poignant, sensitive images and thoughts, flying in the face of all of my expectations of both patients and therapist.

Am I saying, then, that there are no guidelines at all about what to offer or how to deal with patients from different populations? Not at all. What I have found is that many art therapists accept the secondhand literature from other art therapists about what to do with group A, or what the art of group B means. What is needed, as with theory, is to go to the more primary literature and to learn about the characteristics and needs of people at different developmental levels, of different socioeconomic or cultural groups, and in different diagnostic classifica-

tions. The more one understands the psychobiological nature of adolescence, the better one will be able to work in art therapy with teenagers. The more one comprehends about the nature of schizophrenia, the better one will be able to work in art therapy with schizophrenics. Then one will also be in a better position to evaluate the clinical material available, such as another art therapist's report of a particular methodology or finding with that population.

The classifications currently in vogue in psychiatry (APA, 1980; Levy, 1982) are largely descriptive, as are contemporary ways of identifying types of exceptionality. An art therapist who is to work in a meaningful way with any population needs to go beyond a description of how that group functions or looks to some coherent way of understanding why those people are as they appear. Even if the condition itself is unmodifiable, the subjective attitude and experience of it may well be altered. This is not to suggest that we eliminate or disregard classification or categorizing, for communication without them would be at a terribly primitive and concrete level. More simply, knowing at a descriptive level is only a first step for a therapist; understanding at a deeper (dynamic) level is essential for meaningful work with any population.

My own reluctance to think in terms of labels sometimes backfires, however. I recently sat on the doctoral committee of an individual who has studied extensively with me and knows my writings quite well. In her competency paper she described the paucity of reports on art therapy with retarded individuals. I was surprised and mildly offended that she did not think of quite a few children discussed in my book. But then I realized that in many, if not all, cases I had either omitted or minimized the fact of their retardation, so that no one would be likely to think of them as belonging to that category. In stressing their capacities and their ability to use art therapeutically like children of average intelligence, I had denied the actuality of their mental retardation. This was a useful learning experience, for I have always had a tendency to focus (perhaps defensively) on capacities rather than deficits. While it may be a useful attitude in helping people to create, it is not helpful to students to deny the existence of such disorders as retardation, brain damage, or psychosis when they are present.

Labeling can, in many ways, be quite useful in thinking about patients. It can also get in the way. It is done, in most psychiatric and special education settings, partly because it is necessary in order to receive funds. The more I have learned about diagnostic labels, even with the careful decision-making system used in DSM-III, the more skeptical I have become. Like statistics, they can be used by the sophisticated cli-

nician in a variety of "legal" ways, which can give manifestly different impressions. One needs to become knowledgeable enough to understand the kind of reasoning behind primary vs. secondary diagnosis, or personality vs. developmental disorder, in order to translate current diagnostic jargon in a sensible way. Despite the many sincere efforts at objective tests, there is ultimately a good deal of subjectivity in any kind of assessment. At this stage of the art of one human being understanding another, that seems inevitable. One just needs to know that it exists.

On the other side of the coin, when labels help the therapist to better understand the nature of the patient's disorder, they also help to indicate appropriate forms and methods of treatment. Art therapy, as indicated in earlier sections, can be more or less structured, more or less intense, and can be aimed primarily at building psychic structures or at undoing defenses. A clear understanding, not so much of the name, but certainly of the nature of a patient's problem, can be immensely helpful in decisions about the appropriateness of art therapy and the general as well as specific approach that is likely to help. Assessment is a most important part of treatment; and developmental and dynamic evaluation (as well as analysis of the family system) seem to have at least as much relevance as specific nosological labels. If both can be done thoughtfully, however, with attention to etiology and underlying dynamic mechanisms, then both can be of great assistance in the always murky work of psychotherapy through art. (Parenthetically, art products can be very useful in the difficult task of differential diagnosis.)

One rather important aspect of understanding populations was alluded to earlier in relation to one's responses to different age groups, and impacts significantly on one's ability to empathize. This is the simple fact that, while we all have been children once and some of us have been parents, very few art therapists have been schizophrenic or blind or retarded. While all of us are "normal neurotics" and should be able to empathize with most feeling-states stemming from anxiety, the majority of disabilities and disorders are quite foreign to our personal experience and must remain so. It is useful, therefore, to read books by individuals who have lived with a serious mental illness or a physical disability in order to get some sense of what life is like for someone so afflicted (Beers, 1908; Cutsforth, 1951; DeLoach, 1981; Greenberg, 1964; Hunt, 1967; Sechehaye, 1951).

There is probably resistance in all of us to the thought of actually experiencing life from the perspective of a deaf or a paranoid individual. It is frightening even to think about, and the normal human reaction is one of relief at being free of the burden, whatever it is. Yet this resistance

needs to be overcome if one is to be an effective therapist. For in order to have real empathy for another person, one needs to not only connect mentally with the human experiences one has in common with a patient, but also imagine what it is like to see or feel or think like that person, with full recognition that one may never be able to fully put oneself in the shoes of another. It is an exercise primarily of the imagination, one at which art therapists, usually comfortable with fantasy, ought to do well. Sometimes one can learn from a concrete exercise, such as blindfolding oneself for a period of time in a familiar locale and trying to do all one's usual activities without sight.

Such attempts to "feel with" and "into," while difficult and sometimes painful, are probably more important in the long run in understanding and relating to different populations than any amount of book or classroom learning. It is especially important to try to imagine what the art therapy experience is like for a particular individual or member of any group—how the space looks and feels, how such a person might react to the other people and/or the therapist, how he might understand and feel about the request to create, and how the creative task itself might appear to him. This seems self-evident, yet art therapists, like many other clinicians, often distance themselves in a defensive fashion from too close an involvement with the disabled or "crazy" patient(s) with whom they find themselves working.

The phenomenon of burnout in work with difficult patient populations is very real. It is my impression, however, that it may be less common among art therapists than among other mental health professionals. Perhaps that is a result of our schedules, which tend to require periodic rather than continuous contact with any single patient or group. It may also be related to our capacity to tap the strengths and creativity in people, which can be exciting to us as well as to them. Perhaps it is also an index of an ease with empathy, due to our comfort with imagination and fantasy, an ability to flow with patients in all their craziness and confusion. I am quite convinced that art therapists are much more comfortable with primary process thinking than are most clinicians, that we often find the free-flowing fantastic aspects of psychotic thought rather appealing, even fascinating. And, most important for work with different populations, we may not be as afraid as some to feel with people who think strangely, since that is such a familiar state from our own creative activity in art. Similarly, the lack of logic of a retarded or braindamaged individual is relatively congenial for us because we are comfortable with an alogical, primary process mode of thought.

I hope that I am not being naive about art therapists in my optimism

about our capacity for entering alien mental/perceptual worlds. We are often successful with groups who do not usually respond well to treatment, in part because of this enhanced capacity for empathy. It is usually thought and said that we succeed because we offer a modality which resistant or nonverbal patients can use in order to express themselves. While that is quite true, it is also true that we offer ourselves to both support and understand the individual's struggles with self-expression. In this aspect of our task, as well as in reflecting upon what has been expressed, we must call on our empathy, which must also be felt by the other person if we are to be really effective. It probably doesn't matter how many books or courses one has under one's professional belt about any particular population; if one can imagine what it feels like to be that way, one is well on the road to an art therapy that works.

REFERENCES

American Psychiatric Association. *Diagnostic and Statistical Manual of Mental Disorders* (3rd ed.). Washington: American Psychiatric Association, 1980.

Beers, C.W. *A mind that found itself: An autobiography* (1908) (5th ed.). Pittsburgh: University of Pittsburgh Press, 1981.

Cutsforth, T.D. *The blind in school and society: A psychological study* (Rev. ed.). New York: American Foundation for the Blind, 1951.

DeLoach, C. *A metamorphosis: Adjustment to severe disability*. New York: McGraw-Hill, 1981.

Green, H. *I never promised you a rose garden*. New York: Holt, Rinehart & Winston, 1964.

Hunt, N. *The world of Nigel Hunt: The diary of a mongoloid*. New York: Garrett, 1967.

Levy, R. *The new language of psychiatry: Learning and using DSM-III*. Boston: Little, Brown, 1982.

Mahler, M.S., et al. *The psychological birth of the human infant*. New York: Basic Books, 1975.

Rubin, J.A. Special personality traits of child therapists. In I. Jakab (Ed.), *The personality of the therapist*. Pittsburgh: American Society of Psychopathology of Expression, 1982, pp. 111-116.

Sechehaye, M., & Renee (pseud.). *Autobiography of a schizophrenic girl*. New York: Grune & Stratton, 1951.

Williams, G.H., & Wood, M.M. *Developmental art therapy*. Baltimore: University Park Press, 1977.

Residents become involved with their drawing during an art therapy group session in a nursing home.

Chapter 19

Different Settings

Working in diverse settings can be as different as working with diverse populations. Like the latter, it requires getting to know about and to understand the setting(s) in which one finds oneself. And, as is also true for populations, one needs to understand the type of setting in general as well as the particular one involved. One might think that knowing different kinds of settings is simpler and more straightforward than getting to know different populations, a complex task with many subjective components in both the definition of the group and the response of the art therapist. However, settings and institutions have personalities too, and they also can look one way on the surface and another if one probes more deeply. As noted in the chapter on consultation, analyzing a system is as complicated and demanding as analyzing the dynamics of a family—perhaps more so because of the many subsystems and the larger number of people usually involved.

In any case, the art therapist who works in a school is in a very different kind of situation from the one who works in a clinic, and both of them are in settings vastly different from an inpatient ward or a residential treatment center. It is still common for an art therapist to be the first and only one of a kind in many places, which means that, in addition to getting to know the setting itself, she must also define her role within it from scratch. That task, of course, is greatly affected by the institution's expectations of art therapy, which are rarely consistent from person to person. The art therapist's perception of how best she

213

can be used is also a significant variable, which depends very much on her getting to know and understand the needs of the particular setting.

As with therapy, supervision, and consultation, there is usually no choice but to start "where they are"—where the institution wants one to begin. Even in a setting that has already found ways of using the skills of one or more art therapists (as students or staff), it is always best to work with those in charge toward flexibility in role definition. Although it may take a good deal of time before an institution and an art therapist learn how best to use the skills of the one in the service of the other, such an organic kind of program development is less likely to occur if the art therapist herself is not thinking imaginatively from the beginning. As with the other roles one plays, one needs to be patient and to assess strengths, weaknesses, and dynamics in addition to needs, all the time developing ideas about how art therapy can be utilized in the particular setting. When and with whom these ideas are shared depend, as in therapy, supervision, or consultation, on the art therapist's judgment of the readiness and receptivity on the part of the other(s), as well as on an assessment of who is likely to be helpful in effecting the modifications seen as appropriate.

The need to understand the covert as well as the overt values and power structure of an institution cannot be overstressed. Many a good idea about using art therapy in a particular setting has never been implemented, not because no one thought of it, but because the art therapist went about trying to sell it in an inappropriate way. Perhaps she went to the wrong person, or perhaps it was the wrong time, or perhaps the time and the person were all right but the method of presenting the idea was poorly conceived. Sometimes the art therapist goes to the right person (as defined by charts of administration) but fails to inform or to obtain the support of significant others, who may be offended and who might have been critical allies.

In order to use oneself in an optimal way in any setting, one must be constantly alert to possibilities for service or research or some other role. In order to take advantage of opportunities as they present themselves, the art therapist needs to have a fairly clear hidden agenda of relevant ways to develop the role of art in the institution. Then she is much more likely to see opportunities when they arise and to utilize a change of administration, a new program, or any other perceived opening in a creative way. Without ideas that have been germinating and becoming clear for some time, it is unlikely that the opportunity for development will even be perceived, let alone utilized.

It may seem strange to begin a chapter on work in different settings

by emphasizing role and program development. It is my conviction, however, that if art therapists do not participate actively and creatively in this aspect of their work in most settings, they are likely to be placed in pigeon-holes which make sense to some administrator, but are often not the best use of their skills. In attempting to get those in charge to permit program development, it is useful to be able to point to relevant models—reputable places of the same sort, where the kind of program one is suggesting has been implemented with success. Of course, the more one knows about art therapy programs in other institutions similar to one's own, the more ideas one will be introduced to vicariously about possible directions for development. Some of this information is available in the published literature, primarily in journals. Much more is available through professional organizations, both national and local, in their newsletters and at their conferences. Knowing about art therapy in any particular kind of setting is as important for healthy program development as knowing about the population(s) one serves.

Knowing about the type of facility is, of course, necessary if one is to understand its mission and its goals. As in other attempts at understanding, knowing the history of the kind of facility is almost as helpful as knowing the history of the particular place. While not absolutely essential, I have found such knowledge to be more helpful than one would imagine in conceptualizing the possible role of an art therapist in any institution. Each of the kinds of settings where an art therapist is likely to work has its own fascinating history, as a type and as a specific example. If one is to become a well-integrated part of the institution, it does help to become familiar with the "family background" as a way of getting oriented.

Of course, the real challenge in becoming integrated is finding ways to become an accepted and respected part of the particular institutional family. As with entering any existing group, this requires the careful avoidance of stepping on anyone's toes or territory, as well as becoming useful to others. Working together collaboratively is one good way to begin personal alliances, whether the work is in research or service, inservice training or public relations. It is best if such collaboration involves art therapy, though serving on staff committees or joining other groups can also help one to become part of the family. As one begins to develop ideas about further uses of one's talents as an art therapist in this place, one will be able to use the connections one has formed for advice and assistance in accomplishing specific goals.

It is not always so easy for an art therapist to be integrated into a setting, especially one that has never before employed such a person.

Many individuals will be skeptical, some may be fearful, and others may be critical of spending always scarce resources in this particular way. "Arty" people are always a little threatening to nonartists, so that dressing in a normal way and behaving according to the rules and regulations of the institution may help to allay any anxieties that the art therapist will be strange or flaky. Certain concerns—that an art therapist might overstimulate patients, create unbearable messes, or fool around without accomplishing anything substantial—are inevitable and are sure to be present in almost any institution, whether a school, a hospital, or a clinic.

As with defenses and resistances, such expectations and anxieties need to be identified and ways found to modify them, if one is to be accepted. One technique I found quite useful in my early days in a child guidance center was to invite other clinicians to observe individual art evaluation or therapy, as well as offering to work alongside others with families or groups. In this way, many staff members got a look at what this strange new thing was like, had a chance to discuss it following the session, and were able to modify any distorted notions they may have had about art therapy. In encouraging them to ask questions, I was able to become aware of some misunderstandings and concerns that might not have occurred to me.

Another useful approach is to offer inservice training or consultation to anyone who is interested, either short- or long-term. Presentations to discipline groups about art therapy and consultations with clinicians on drawings from their own patients were also helpful ice-breakers in those early days. At the psychiatric hospital where I currently supervise three art therapists, we have used many similar approaches to introduce the program and to allay staff anxieties, differing as needed from one unit to another. Even though no one in the administration of the hospital or the units, for example, required the art therapists to attend team or unit meetings, I suggested that they do so as much as possible, from the beginning.

I also suggested that they bring along the artwork of those patients who might be discussed, and offer to show and to explain it to the others. This has paid off handsomely, with an increase from half-time to full-time employment in less than a year, as well as requests for additional services like diagnostic evaluations of individuals or families, leadership of low-functioning groups, and individual work with nonverbal patients. While all of these were offered at the initiation of the new program, none were requested until the people in decision-making

positions on each unit came to recognize and respect the individual art therapists, through their work with groups. Since the program in this hospital is still in a state of dynamic development, seeds are constantly being planted by myself as supervisor and the art therapists as well for many possibilities in growth. Although it often takes months for ideas to germinate, planting them in the right place(s) can bear surprising fruit, sometimes more rapidly than one would anticipate.

One of the most difficult aspects of role definition and development involves those close relatives in other disciplines, mentioned in the chapter on developing one's identity as an art therapist. When someone already in the system is doing something even superficially similar to what an art therapist might do, then issues of competition and territory become critical and the risks of tension great. One way to minimize such problems is to be aware of their likelihood and to try to develop links from the beginning, informally if not formally, with those in related fields doing similar work with patients or students. If both can work together to refine and define respective roles, so that neither is felt as a threat to the other, things can work out very well. If they do not work collaboratively, they may collide head-on at some point in time, with possible injury to one or both.

When I first came to the child guidance center, clinical psychologists requested drawings in diagnostic evaluations, most clinicians used some art supplies in play therapy with children, and social group workers included many crafts in their activity groups. I worked with some of the psychologists on drawing analysis studies and offered to consult with anyone on how to use art with children, the possible meanings of a child's products, or how to help a child to talk about what he has made. Both activities seemed to allay anxiety and to reassure everyone that we could share the territory quite comfortably. With the group workers, I offered any help they might want in ordering or using supplies, which eventuated in a year-long series of meetings where they used a variety of materials with my guidance and discussed how to use them with children's groups.

When a psychologist and I developed a family art evaluation, others were curious and some were a bit jealous, making remarks which indicated that they felt left out, as if we two now owned that particular territory. We invited the whole staff to a showing of a videotape of a family art evaluation, after which many indicated a desire to learn more. We offered a family art study group, in which individuals conducted family art evaluations observed by other group members, and then dis-

cussed these live sessions the following week. The group met for almost a year, and the members (from all disciplines) went on to use art with families in both evaluation and therapy.

In general, then, it is always best to be open and not exclusive about what one does, especially when others have very legitimate reasons for using art or craft materials with patients or students. On the geriatric unit of the psychiatric hospital, for example, the nurses teach crafts to patients several afternoons a week. Although they have yet to take us up on our offer, I hope that by the time these words see print, the art therapist will be involved either in working alongside the nurses in these groups, consulting to them about materials, supplies, and activities, or leading creative crafts groups herself. Had the Occupational Therapy Department not been eliminated, I am sure that the art therapists in the hospital would be facing possible conflicts with that group, which used lots of art and craft materials. It would have been vital to establish an ongoing communication mechanism, as well as a way of defining for other staff (those who refer patients) how these two kinds of activities which look so similar are really so different.

A common instance of potential conflict occurs when both an art therapist and an art teacher work in a school or rehabilitation center with exceptional (handicapped) children. It is then necessary to differentiate the two, not on the basis of population or setting (which are identical), or activity (which can also look identical), but in terms of primary goal. If the goal is primarily educational (e.g., learning about art), then the art educator is the art-giver of choice. If, however, the goal is primarily psychological (e.g., assessing the child's problems or treating a neurotic inhibition), then the art therapist is the art-giver of choice. Most handicapped children probably need both, and choices should not be made as if it were an either/or situation, just as most psychiatric patients probably can benefit from both art and occupational therapy.

Sometimes, because of a child's or a patient's extreme deficiencies, he is not able to use the usual approach to art or therapy; then, too, the art therapist becomes the caregiver of choice. For example, if a child is severely and profoundly retarded, it may be hard (or even impossible) for a regular art teacher to reach and teach him, while the special training and experience of the art therapist with deviant populations make it more likely that she will be successful. Moreover, the goals, even in art, will probably be at a pre-art or sensory level, having much more to do with differentiating self from nonself than with learning about art techniques. The patient who is unreachable by the nurse or psychiatrist because he refuses or is unable to talk is a similar kind of case where

the art therapist is called in to do the psychotherapy, because she uses a modality to which such a patient can respond. It is not that the goals are necessarily different in either case from what an art teacher or another kind of therapist might normally have; it is just that the means to reach them are less available to either of them than to an art therapist.

Different kinds of institutions present different kinds of problems in role definition and relationship with staff members in related fields. But whether it is the art teacher in the school, the occupational therapist in the hospital, or the activities worker in the rehabilitation center, a major task for the art therapist is to define the differences between her expertise and theirs, between her role(s) and theirs. Because of the similarities (which cause the inevitable confusion and possible competition), there also exist many possibilities for cooperation, collaboration, and mutual growth. Such alliances, as in study groups or other peer situations, are very helpful in avoiding problems (building trust and minimizing suspiciousness).

If the setting happens to include specialists in one or more arts therapies, the potential there, too, is for either destructive competition and envy or constructive collaboration and mutual growth. Although not always in the same department (as in our hospital), it is probably a good idea for art therapists to attempt to work collaboratively with music, dance, or drama therapists in the same institution, even if only occasionally. The collaborative work can be in assessment, therapy, inservice training, or research, and can involve healthy, stimulating competition, rather than the more toxic sort. Individuals may be nervous, self-conscious, or shy about initiating such partnerships, and may need to be encouraged by those in charge. Of course, there is a great deal to be learned as a therapist through any kind of work with another professional. In addition, such collaborative activities lessen the likelihood of too much envy or competition, which could potentially drain staff energies.

One problem that has become quite apparent in our own program is the relatively easier "salability" of art therapy, as compared with dance, drama, and music. In general, hospital staff members were more anxious about the other art forms, even before the program started, and have been less eager to ask for increased time from the other creative disciplines, though the clinicians are as skilled as the art therapists. Not only is art less threatening than dance or drama, which requires moving around and performing in front of others, but it can even be less scary than music, which seems to some patients and staff to require more technical skill or talent. In addition, the visibility of art therapy seems

to be a major factor in its relatively faster acceptance and utilization. The often dramatic patient products, which do speak so much more eloquently than words, vivify concretely the potential of art to enhance communication. Sometimes they also help the staff to clarify the diagnosis, as well as the source(s) of a particular patient's distress.

In any case, the concreteness of the art product seems to play a large part in the growth of art therapy programs in institutions, and should be conscientiously utilized by the art therapist. We requested, for example, very large bulletin boards for each floor, the size of which alarmed both the purchasing department and the head nurses who had to decide where to put them. But the large size has made it possible to display more patient artwork and commentary, and to frame pictures more clearly and dramatically. The work on the boards is used not only with patients in the art groups, but also as an ever-present way of educating staff and visiting families about the values of art therapy. An art therapist in any institution who does not use patient artwork in communications with other professionals, or who does not, when possible, exhibit those products that the artists agree may be shown, is not fully using one of the major assets of art therapy. It is one of the best ways to move art therapy both physically and psychologically into any setting.

So far I have written at a general level, about things one needs to know and to think about and to do in all kinds of settings. The reader may be wondering whether there are any specifics about inpatient vs. outpatient, school vs. hospital, or clinic vs. rehabilitation center which an art therapist ought to know. Of course there are, just as there are differences between manic depressives and obsessional neurotics, or conduct-disordered and autistic children. But this book is not the place to go into detail about specific settings, any more than it is the place to write in detail about specific diagnostic or handicapped groups. Settings, like populations, differ widely. There are types just as there are groups, and there are particular places, just as there are individual patients. In both areas, it is useful to know both the general (about the type of person or setting) and the particular (about the individual person or place).

In both cases, it also helps to know how art therapy has been found useful by others. With populations, one needs to know what the literature has to say about art by a particular group (diagnostically), as well as what kinds of approaches have been found to be effective (therapeutically). With settings, one needs to know what other professionals have to say about the place and role of an art therapist in such an institution, what has been found to be possible as well as useful. In neither instance should one stop at such findings, or consider them either sufficiently

or necessarily applicable to the particular person or place. But they are useful as reference points, stimuli, guidelines, possibilities to know about and perhaps to convey to others, in an effort to develop a program of art therapy for any population in any setting.

In addition to these generally applicable ways of thinking about settings and what an art therapist needs to know, there are a few others which also seem similar to what needs to be understood about populations. These relate to empathy—how it is important to try to imagine what it is like to be someone so different from oneself, especially how it would feel to be that person confronted with an invitation to create art. In regard to setting, one needs to develop such a perspective about one's coworkers, to respect the strain they are under and the tensions of their jobs, from responsibility as well as wear and tear.

One needs to be sensitive to how the institution is viewed by others, as when working with a handicapped or psychotic individual. As sometimes happens with a person who may stimulate discomfort in others, an institution can become a little paranoid, can feel unappreciated or undervalued by its board or by the community. Conversely, it can feel grandiose and omnipotent, especially if there have been many recent successes. Whatever the institution's image in the community, it is helpful to try to get a sense of how it sees itself, especially as that impacts on those employees with whom one must work and whose support one needs for program development. If one can in some way connect what one has to offer with what individuals in power see as a primary (perhaps even neglected) role in the community, this may be yet another way to accomplish more and better art therapy.

While I don't mean to anthropomorphize institutions or settings, it can sometimes be helpful to think of them as having personalities, priorities, and an image of themselves which may be different from those held by others. In any case, it is important at a much deeper level to empathize with the pressures that affect any institution, just as one needs to do in regard to individual workers. Without such empathy, one's attempts to function and grow in any setting are likely to fizzle. Being sensitive to pressures on people in decision-making positions is part of what is involved in knowing when to take action on any personal or programmatic goal.

Being sensitive to how it feels to be a patient or pupil in an inpatient setting or a special school may be as difficult as imagining what it is like to be a schizophrenic, since the art therapist probably never had to be in such a place. It may also be hard to imagine what it feels like to be in a rehabilitation center, whether long-term or short-term, whether

inpatient, outpatient, or partial. Similarly, it may not be easy to know how it feels for the nurses, who work eight-hour shifts with the same patients, compared to the art therapist's more common one- or two-hour groups.

Outpatient settings are yet another matter, from the clinic waiting room to the offices, conference rooms, and group rooms where the action occurs. It feels different to both patients and staff to work in this kind of setting being in one where people are literally separated from the outside world for days, weeks, or months at a time. Perhaps this is mainly a reflection of my own reaction to a recent change from outpatient to inpatient work. But I find there is a dramatic difference in the flavor of the place, the attitudes of both staff and patients, and in my internal responses to both settings. While neither may be typical of their genres, many of the differences between them do seem to depend on factors related to the type of setting, and, of course, the type of patient and patient care appropriate to each. Although the personnel in the two buildings also differ, many individuals work on "both sides of the street," as both are part of the department of psychiatry at the same university. But, in spite of the fact that the faces in the elevator are often the same, the mood and the atmosphere are not, and I have come more and more to feel that such differences are due, at least in part, to intrinsic distinctions between the two kinds of settings.

As with different patient groups, one may find oneself reacting with considerable discomfort to some settings and not to others. It is then vital to try to understand just what it is one is responding to, and how one can modify one's reaction in order to work with relative comfort in that particular place. While understanding the source of one's reaction may not wipe it out, it can sometimes help one to feel very differently about a setting.

Although I have stressed the development of art therapy services and programs, such growth should ideally be consonant with the personal development of the art therapist. So many of the same events promote both, such as collaborative work in research, service, or training. Also, in a more general way, an institution which feels well served by an art therapist is much more likely to be permissive and flexible in regard to requests that are primarily for the personal professional growth of the clinician. Any time an art therapist invests in further training will probably benefit the setting she is in, especially if it is clearly relevant to her work there. It seems considerate to arrange any such personal development activities in ways that least impinge on one's job responsibilities and to be sure that neither the quantity nor the quality of one's work

suffers. If, therefore, one is sensitive to one's employer in the selection and timing of further training, it is likely that he will be supportive, flexible about arrangements, and maybe even willing to pay some of the costs, if that is possible.

In any case, it is not just the setting that grows with the development of an art therapy program; it is also the individual clinician. If there is no space or time for personal development as an artist and a therapist, then one's work is bound to be affected, not to mention one's morale. The art therapist may find that some settings are more congenial, just as she may find that she prefers some age and/or type of patient. But "knowing about" and "feeling with" seem as important in creating a secure place for art therapy in any setting as they do in working effectively in art therapy with any kind of patient.

Working together on a large flat surface, with or without discussion, is one possible approach to group art therapy.

Chapter 20

Different Modes

As noted in the preface to this section of the book, there are many possible ways of working in art therapy, whether the emphasis is diagnostic or therapeutic. Individual art therapy may be the most common mode, though for economic reasons, group treatment is becoming increasingly popular. Nevertheless, it is likely that most of the art therapy being practiced in countless settings and with diverse populations still involves one person who is a therapist and another who is a patient. Frequency and length of sessions will depend on many factors, including the level of motivation and the ability of the patient to participate. In outpatient treatment, weekly hour-long sessions are the norm, though that does not necessarily mean that they are optimal.

Since I have begun to see all of my outpatients privately, I have experimented with different frequencies and patterns of meeting. Ironically, it seems that once a week hardly ever seems to be optimal, unless there are external reasons which impose some constraint, such as the distance the patient needs to travel, parental or patient resistance to increased frequency, or the involvement of the patient in other forms of treatment. If individual art therapy is the sole form of treatment, as is most often the case in my own practice, then twice a week has come to seem a much more reasonable minimum for intervention. The more frequent contact seems to accelerate the patient's involvement in the creative as well as the therapeutic process, to promote continuity between sessions, and to intensify both the alliance and the transference. It is my impression, though untested (and perhaps untestable), that

seeing people twice a week may enable them to work through their problems in fewer sessions than is possible in the more usual weekly contact.

I have been influenced in this regard by my psychoanalytic training, which required me to participate and to see my adult patients five times a week. With child analytic patients, the minimum was four times a week, so that I soon got accustomed to seeing people on a much more frequent basis than had been possible following the usual outpatient pattern of a child guidance center. Then, the only time I changed a child's meetings to twice a week was in response to a worsening of the child's symptoms and a feeling that the therapeutic dosage needed to be increased. My more recent experience with inpatient treatment has also served to modify my sense of what is best in regard to frequency, since the hospital we serve is one in which patients stay for a relatively short time (from less than a week to three or four months). In order to accomplish even limited goals with individuals referred for art therapy, it has been essential to see them at least twice a week, sometimes more often. The latter has frequently occurred because the patient was not able to tolerate long sessions at first, needing to start perhaps at 15 minutes and to gradually lengthen meetings to a half or a whole hour.

I have also become more flexible about the length of separate sessions in individual work, though it is best for the patient, once one has decided on a length of time, to keep it consistent (with the possible exception of some low-functioning patients, with whom the explicit goal is to increase their ability to work longer in art therapy). In any case, some very young children do quite well with 30- or 45-minute sessions, while some older ones can tolerate a full hour or even more. To go beyond an hour in individual work, with rare exceptions, is probably not possible for most clinicians, bound as we usually are to fixed schedules.

Art therapists should try, whenever it is feasible, to be as flexible in their thinking about length as about frequency of sessions. There is no magic to the 50-minute hour; what may be magical about it is how important the time frame (whatever it is) becomes to the patient and how one can work on so many issues in relation to it. While it might be fun to experiment with an open-ended time span for individual appointments (scheduling a full morning, for example, for one person), it would probably only make therapeutic sense if the patient were engaged in work with a medium that necessarily demanded more time, like stone-carving or animated-film making. Given the immense power and usefulness of the time limit in therapy, however, the minutes gained would probably not be worth the treatment lost. As with frequency of

appointment, I am not supporting the notion that one should be change-able from week to week or from session to session, but rather that one be open-minded in deciding upon the best format for any individual and acknowledge the ever-present possibility that some modification might be indicated.

As an illustration of my own rigidity in this regard, I once was working with a boy who used to come twice a week—once during school and once after school. As a fifth grader, he was anxious about missing school too often, and the Tuesday morning time had been chosen by him because it was during a nonacademic class. Because of a schedule con-flict, I could no longer see him on the Thursday afternoon when we had met, which had seemed fairly well related in time to the Tuesday morn-ing appointment. He chose Wednesday afternoon in preference to the Friday time I offered, but insisted that Tuesday morning would still work best. I was skeptical about meeting only twice a week for two days in a row, but agreed to try it out at his insistence. Much to my surprise, the new schedule helped immensely in his treatment, in which there had been a good deal of resistance. He was much more able to continue on the following day with what he had begun on a Tuesday than he had been before with two-and-a-half days in between. As has happened so often, I learned that I had been operating on an assumption that might well be false, at least in certain cases.

Individual work is more than a matter of scheduling, of course. What goes on between patient and therapist in a one-to-one situation is nec-essarily more focused and often more intense than in work with groups and families. The alliance and the transference both develop rapidly, so that the management of potential transference resistance becomes a more common concern than in group work. In terms of the art modality, individual therapy is the mode I find the most fascinating in a depth sense, and the one I feel is most useful for training others in the fine points of technique. It can be conducted in a variety of ways (like work with families or groups), with more or less support, and with more or less of an attempt to uncover and promote insight. My personal pref-erence is to shift my approach flexibly, according to the needs of the individual patient at any particular moment in time.

To assist in the development of any person as an artist and a more comfortable human being is deeply rewarding. It can also be frustrating and distressing, especially at moments of confusion or impasse in the therapy. Depending on one's goals and those of the patient, individual art therapy can be quite brief (four to six sessions) or quite lengthy (four to six years). Sometimes a youngster will terminate at one stage of de-

velopment (like latency) and return for further work at another (like
adolescence or young adulthood). The same is true for adults, of course,
who may feel satisfied or unable to further invest themselves at termination, but may later decide that there is more self-development that
they would like to pursue through art therapy.

One of the difficult decisions in art therapy, especially with individuals, is where to position oneself physically. It is important to do so
thoughtfully, so that the patient does not experience the therapist as
either an intrusive, or a disinterested presence. Some art therapists sit
quite far away from the patient (who may be at an easel or a table), so
as not to interfere with his involvement in the creative process. Others
sit quite close, either at the side of the work table (catty-corner) or
opposite the patient (my own preference). Of course, if I get the feeling
that looking at the person working is having an inhibiting effect, I might
start working with media myself or even move to my desk chair, which
is still fairly close. I like being across from the patient, since I can easily
observe facial expressions and subtle body movements, as well as hear
softly spoken or mumbled comments. It also makes it very easy and
natural for the patient to talk while he works, if that is appealing to him.

Saving the artwork of individual patients seems important to me and
is easily implemented by a very tall set of deep, wide, open shelves, on
which each person has his own space. Most children put their names
or a code on a piece of tape on their shelves; most adults prefer the
privacy of a set of cardboard drawers, which are also in my office. In
this way, the patient's work is always accessible to him and is often
looked at spontaneously after the session in which it was created. In a
more formal way, if that does not come up as an idea from the patient
during the termination phase, I usually suggest that it would be interesting to go through the art on the shelf, perhaps in order, as a way of
reviewing the therapy.

In addition, after many years of debate on the pros and cons (in which
the cons had always won), I finally decided to use a bulletin board on
one office wall for display. It is large enough so that all of the individuals
I might see at any point in time can have a space on it, if they wish.
Each is told that he may choose to pin one (small size) picture up there
if he likes at any point in time. Whether or not people choose to display,
what they choose to show others, and how they respond to the work
of other patients have turned out to be a most useful kind of "grist for
the mill." Patients often feel competitive, superior to, or envious of
others' work; I don't think I have ever had a patient who did not at
some point think he was entitled to more space on the board, wishing

to be special. Some patients of course, children as well as adults, choose not to display. This decision, too, is useful to explore and to understand as part of the therapy. In any case, having overcome my own resistance to the idea, it turns out to be rather fascinating, quite useful clinically, and definitely enhances the appearance of my office.

Before leaving the subject of individual art therapy, it is important to note that the responsibility and role of the art therapist and probably the nature of the art therapy are both heavily influenced by whether she is the only person treating the patient, or whether there are others involved. When one is working adjunctively, especially with individuals, one can freely concentrate on the creative process itself, since the primary psychotherapeutic responsibility is being handled by one or more others. When one is working alone, then all aspects of the patient's problems become one's concern, which usually necessitates broadening the art therapy to include connections with the patient's real life and may also involve contacts with others involved with the person (schools, hospitals, doctors).* When treating a child who has behavioral difficulties in school, for example, an art therapist—like any other clinician—may need to make school visits and perhaps consult with the teacher. When treating an adult who is a drug addict, an art therapist—like any other clinician—may need to be in contact with the patient's physician, as well as with any agencies involved in detoxification or rehabilitation.

Such responsibility also rests on the shoulders of any art therapist who is the sole clinician involved with members of a group or family who have come for help. In such instances, the fact that one is a therapist first and foremost, albeit of a particular type (art), becomes quite apparent. There are differences, however, between individual and group or family art therapy, which exist regardless of whether the work is independent or adjunctive. Some of the issues discussed in regard to individuals also need to be considered, but the parameters become more complex because of the need to accommodate more individuals. The superiority of greater frequency, while probably true for group and family art therapy, is often not worth the effort and resistance involved in trying to schedule more than one weekly meeting, at least in outpatient work.

Inpatient or partial hospitalization work is quite different, since the group is closer to being "captive," available to meet more than once a

---

*An art therapist in private practice, no matter how experienced, has an ethical responsibility to secure medical or other professional consultation whenever it seems indicated.

week, even daily if deemed appropriate. In short-term care settings, a greater frequency of group meetings seems to be more effective, especially in overcoming the initial resistance of many adults to art therapy. In our psychiatric hospital, the substance abuse patients have two hours of creative arts therapy every day: one in art, the other in dance, music, or drama. Other patients, who are functioning at a very low level, get their regular daily psychotherapy in an art or movement group, rather than a verbal one. Other groups, open to any interested patient, meet less frequently (usually two or three times a week) and are often of a longer duration, allowing for more complex work with materials.

Groups in art therapy, like groups in any kind of therapy, are less focused on therapist/patient interaction and more on what goes on in the group as a whole. The work done within an art group can be largely individual or mostly joint, depending on the goals of the group, the nature of the patients, and the bias of the art therapist. The form taken by the different stages in therapy outlined in Chapter 6 is also slightly different with groups than with individuals, but the overall process is the same. What also occurs, however, is a progressive change in the group itself, which starts out as a series of separate individuals linked with a leader and evolves in complex ways into a more integrated unit, developing pairings and subgroups within it. The ways in which groups express resistance and anxiety are especially fascinating, and it helps if the art therapist understands both the developmental and the dynamic aspects of group process. It is especially difficult to be in touch with group process when the group itself is not a consistent one, as is often the case with brief hospitalization. It seems then that there are at least two clusters or levels of group dynamics—those belonging to the people who have worked together before with the art therapist and those belonging to the whole group, which in a sense begins anew each time it assembles.

Families, of course, are a special kind of group, with a long history of interaction with one another. They do not disperse when they leave the therapist like an outpatient group, but have to go home and deal with whatever came up in the art session. To a lesser extent, this is also true of inpatient groups, who live in close proximity on the unit. This fact of living together places a special strain on family art therapy, whether one is seeing the entire nuclear family, the couple, the extended family, or a multiple family group. It is my own feeling that conducting family art therapy over any substantial period of time, especially if it is the sole form of treatment, is as "hot" a clinical situation as art therapists are likely to encounter. Family art therapy is fascinating, challenging,

and requires particularly strong clinical skills and some training in family therapy, or, especially if one is just beginning, a cotherapist with experience in family treatment.

Working in cotherapy is one of the most common forms of collaboration and probably one of the best ways for an art therapist to broaden and deepen her clinical skills. Another way to relate to colleagues is to work in parallel, alongside other clinicians who are also dealing with the same patient(s). In most inpatient work, this usually means that the art therapist is part of a multidisciplinary team, who combine their varied skills to help patients individually, in groups, and sometimes in families. In schools, as in outpatient work, the team concept is not always present or implemented, and an art therapist may be working with an individual who is also being seen by someone else, with little or no contact between the two professionals.

This, in fact, was my own experience when I first worked with children in a psychiatric hospital. Although the director of the unit had told the child psychiatry residents who were seeing children individually of my once-a-week presence, some chose to make contact and share, and some did not. One of the most awkward situations involved a resident who seemed not to know of my existence until the day each of us had to present our work to Erik Erikson in front of a large crowd of local mental health specialists. Since the child had expressed herself much more articulately in art than she was able to in her verbal therapy, the inevitable comparisons made by Erikson were uncomfortable for me and, I suspect, for the resident as well. After that experience, I resolved to overcome my shyness and to be more assertive, at least in making contact with each resident whose child case I saw individually and offering to share what the youngster had done in art.

Although the reader might think I would have learned from that embarrassing incident, I was still rather naive when I started work at the child guidance center several years later. Three child psychiatric residents each requested adjunctive art therapy for a youngster he was seeing individually. I met with each resident to decide on frequency and format. Each one differed slightly according to the resident's perception of the needs of the case, and I thought we were doing a fine job of collaborating. We were, on the surface, but what I was not sufficiently sensitive to was the possible competition and threat for each of these young psychiatrists, new to work with children, of someone else seeing his patient and using another modality. As it turned out, one of the three was quite secure and was able to talk openly and helpfully about how he felt when either of the two patients we shared (a mother and

her child) would disclose something in art therapy not yet expressed in verbal or play therapy. The other two responded in different ways to the children's greater fondness for art therapy. One decided that he should stop seeing the youngster, and that I should become the primary therapist; the other concluded that I should stop seeing the child individually and should put her into an art therapy group. In my own insecurity, I was unable to see beyond my confusion and went along rather meekly with whatever each doctor suggested.

But the lesson was an important one, which I finally grasped, and is highly relevant to anyone doing adjunctive art therapy in any setting. Although competition is probably most loaded in the kind of outpatient situation described above, it exists whenever art therapy is successful and other approaches are not. The ability of other professionals involved to rejoice that something has finally worked seems to be directly proportional to their own feelings of security and competence. As noted earlier, the relative visibility of art therapy seems to have made it more rapidly noticed in our psychiatric hospital (in terms of requests for more services) than any of the other creative modalities, potentially stimulating envy and resentment on the part of the dance, music, and drama therapists. Similar but even more insidious feelings of resentment and jealousy can easily be aroused in other staff members, who try hard but are often less able to reach patients who for one reason or another respond well in art therapy. It is very important for art therapists to be alert to the potential of the modality to evoke such competitive and hostile feelings, so that they can note clues to their emergence and can work to build alliances which will serve to make such feelings less likely and less disruptive.

One of the healthiest ways to build such alliances with other staff is to work together with families or groups, which is also a very dynamic way to learn from someone with more training and experience in either mode. But cotherapy is no bed of roses. It is complicated, demanding, and potentially unpleasant if not carried out carefully. It is vital, from the first, to understand and respect the style and point of view of the other clinician. One way to begin is to observe each other at work, with similar populations if possible. It is then necessary to plan together for each session and to provide time for mutual discussion between each meeting. When I conducted an adolescent art-drama group with a drama therapist and a child psychiatrist, the three of us found that we needed at least two hours a week to collaborate on the two-hour weekly group. One hour was spent discussing what went on, in terms of group process and individual progress, in the presence of a consulting psychiatrist.

The other hour was spent sharing with each other the thoughts and feelings which had been stimulated in each of us by the others' handling of events in the group. Had we not been able to share our discomforts or disagreements, we could probably not have tolerated the intense transferences and countertransferences that developed among us and the members over the two years of the group's existence.

Cotherapy is extremely tricky, since no two individuals have identical styles of working with other human beings, and it is very difficult to monitor and to manage the inevitable complications, such as competition for the patients' affection. Successful cotherapy requires that the partners be at similar levels of clinical development. If one is significantly more advanced than the other, then the roles cannot be equal; rather, one becomes the assistant to the other who functions as the leader. That is fine and may be useful in training, but it needs to be explicitly acknowledged; and it is qualitatively different from a cotherapy situation where the leadership is genuinely shared. When that is the case, great care must be taken to develop an open relationship, as well as an understanding of each other's perspectives, before and throughout the time of working together. Most important is the mutual sharing of feelings about one another, perhaps even more critical at times than collaborating about the patients, though that too is necessary. If the two therapists do not continually express and work out the tensions and differences which inevitably arise between them, then their work with the patients will just as inevitably suffer in some way.

Since it is rather unusual that two art therapists at the same level of development choose to work together in cotherapy, the intense competition likely in such a case rarely occurs. Because both are specialists in the visual arts, the disagreements about how to set up, to motivate, to help, and to reflect could be quite numerous. In my few such experiences, our different notions of what to present and how to relate to the patients created significant tensions for each of us. More often, the art therapist is the acknowledged art specialist of the team, while the partner is the expert in group, family, or a particular type of treatment (e.g., gestalt), or another creative therapy (e.g., dance, drama, or music). Having different and clearly defined areas of expertise is a great asset, since each one has a defined territory in which his or her opinions or wishes are given priority. Nevertheless, there are still inevitable tensions and conflicts when any two people work together, and specialization does not remove all problems. It may minimize them, as when an art therapist agrees to take responsibility for presenting the art experiences to the patients, while the other clinician agrees to lead the discussion

or another activity. Pretty soon, though, as each therapist becomes more familiar and comfortable with the other's modality, each is likely to have more and more opinions about how the modality is being utilized.

I hope that pointing out the pitfalls of parallel therapy or cotherapy will not deter art therapists from trying it. It can be great fun, there is a tremendous amount of learning possible, and it usually increases the potential for growth in the patients when done with care, by offering two possible transference objects, two modalities, and two trained clinicians to help them with their problems. For each therapist, it is possible to discuss patients regularly with another professional who is equally invested in their progress. This makes the work much more tolerable when stressful. It also makes it a much richer experience, from which one can usually learn more than from working alone with the same individual, family, or group.

As with settings and populations, any art therapist beginning work in a new mode, whether couple or family or some other configuration, like brief psychotherapy, ought to find out what has been done in that kind of art therapy by others. With individual patients, the literature is more extensive than with groups and families, though the latter is growing rapidly. Certainly it makes sense, if one has to select, to do so on the basis of similarities on all three dimensions, e.g., the kind of art therapy with the population in the type of setting in which one is involved. Since most of the recommended readings for Chapter 6 (Knowing Therapy) involve individual psychotherapy, I have limited suggested references for this section to a few items in the areas of group, family, and time-limited treatment. But the principle is still important, for no matter how imaginative one may be, it never hurts to find out what has worked for others. Since the literature often deals with theory as well as technique, reports by other art therapists working in the same mode(s) may also help anyone to better understand what is going on.

Making a decision as to which mode is best when options exist is not an easy one, and it takes many years of clinical experience with each in order to choose in an informed way. There are certainly assets and limitations to any particular mode of art therapy, and there is no rule book saying that only one kind may be offered at a time. One of my favorite family art therapy cases also involved individual treatment for two of the children (one in art therapy), and eventually couple therapy for the parents as well. At the risk of oversimplifying, it would seem that, when a problem has been internalized in the patient (has become part of his basic personality structure), then individual art therapy makes the most sense. Group art therapy makes sense as the only mode of

treatment when the individuals involved cannot, for some reason, handle individual therapy, or when their problems are not so much internal as with the external world.

It is naive, however, to think that just because a person has difficulty relating to peers, putting him into a group for treatment will successfully address that problem. If he suffers from a "delusion of uniqueness," discovering that others have similar troubles may, of course, be helpful. Also, if he is able to relate to people with some awareness of their separateness, a group can certainly be a place for him to learn about the impact of his behavior on others. Group therapy as adjunctive is, of course, different from group as the primary mode of treatment, in art or any other form of therapy. The same considerations hold for family art therapy, that the existence of intrafamilial tensions does not necessarily indicate that family therapy is best as the sole or major form of treatment. Many factors need to be weighed, including the perceived needs of the patient(s) and their apparent readiness for one or another mode of therapy. Art therapists are rarely in the position of making decisions about the type of treatment offered a patient. When they are, however, they need to understand not only the nature of each mode, but also those patient characteristics that would make any one the treatment of choice.

When someone is totally unable to use group art therapy, that usually becomes quickly apparent, as in the patient's excessive withdrawal, demandingness, or disruptiveness. Sometimes it is not so much the fault of the mode itself, but rather the size or makeup or length of the particular group, which, if modified, might make it possible for the patient to participate constructively. With the children on the inpatient unit, for example, we found that, because of a larger than usual number with conduct disorders (due to a research study under way there), the projected group size of six was not manageable. Four was a more realistic number, and the art sessions also worked better when shortened in time and increased in frequency. Finally, it was found that screening patients in individual art interviews prior to placing them in groups made it possible to have more functional group compositions. For those few children who were still unable to share the space, materials, or therapist, individual art therapy was made available.

On several adult floors in the hospital, it has been found that making the art therapy groups more homogeneous facilitates the clinician's work, while on others, heterogeneous groupings seem to enhance what happens in the art groups. There are, of course, advantages to both, and it is always necessary to balance the gains and losses in each in order

to decide what will work best for any setting or population. The same kind of reasoning holds true for the room in which the art therapy occurs, and the length of each session. Sometimes a smaller space helps greatly to facilitate interaction, but at other times it can be too close or too intimate for patient comfort. Similarly, a larger space offers options in closeness or distance, which may enable some individuals to function better, while others can be overwhelmed, confused, or lost in too vast a space, especially one with many stimuli.

What probably matters most in regard to knowing different modes of art therapy is that the art therapist become knowledgeable about which-ever one(s) she is called upon to use. Taking a course, doing some reading, getting some consultation or supervision, or even going into that form of treatment oneself are all good ways to learn. Working collaboratively, either parallel or together, has many advantages for learning and for creating a more secure place for oneself in any system. Cotherapy, as noted earlier, is probably the most difficult, yet one of the most rewarding ways to learn and grow, especially if done with a colleague at the same level of professional development. Study groups are also great fun, if organized around topics of mutual interest. De-veloping as an art therapist, in other words, is a lifelong task, if one is to achieve true artistry.

Addendum: Knowing What You Don't Know

This book has been all about what one needs to know if one is to be an effective art therapist. In addition to the basics, about art and therapy and the interface in which they combine to become art therapy, I have added some "extras," for those who deliver indirect as well as direct service. I have also noted some considerations regarding different populations, settings, and modes of art therapy, of which one needs to be aware in order to do any kind of work in the field. I have outlined the knowledge, experiences, beliefs, and ways of being which seem to be necessary for good work in art therapy. A final essential, one of which I become more certain each year, is to be aware of what one doesn't know, and to do something about rectifying it, especially when that seems needed in order to do one's work properly and well.

An attitude of humility is one that fits the present development of our field. Art therapy is young, and we are working in territory which is largely uncharted and not at all well understood. We do not have precise or definite answers about the meanings of art products as much as others would like us to. We also do not have clear and certain answers about optimal art activities, much as many wish that we did. We are, as a discipline, still feeling our way, and we need to acknowledge that fact in our interactions with others, whether patients or professionals. An inappropriate brashness or unwarranted certainty in statements or presentations can do art therapy much more harm than good. We can believe, without ambivalence, in the healing power of art and in the value of the visual image as symbolic speech. We do not need in any way to pretend that we have answers that we simply do not have.

What is needed, therefore, is modesty, both as individuals and as a group; a never-ending attitude of inquiry, of open-mindedness, of flexibility; an ability to try and to err, or to try and to fail. I believe that only such a stance will promote the full development of art therapy, with its thrilling but largely undefined potential for understanding and helping human beings, especially those in pain.

Appendix: Suggested Readings

Since I have made so many specific suggestions in the course of this book about areas in which art therapists need to be knowledgeable, I have appended lists of suggested readings, each one potentially helpful in terms of the subject matter discussed briefly in the chapters. Making such a selection was not easy, since there are many readings that might be useful in each of the areas involved. Like most instructors in most areas, I have generally shared my personal favorites—those books or articles that have helped me to understand something more broadly or more deeply.* I am sure that others could add many useful references of which I am not aware, or with which I failed to connect when I encountered them. So I hope that the reader will not take the lists of suggestions as if they were either the best or the only references in each content area. They are offered as starters, for those who may not have access to other sources of guidance about where to begin.

I hope that the lists will be used in the way suggested in the chapter on teaching: that you will try to integrate your reading with some direct experience, as well as taking the opportunity to reflect upon it in the presence of another. If you can find a guide who is more knowledgeable than you in the area, that is best; but if not, you can extend your learning by arranging to discuss readings with one or more peers who are also interested in understanding more about the subject. Study groups are a most appropriate form of continuing professional development. While they generally occur with people who have reached a fairly advanced level of sophistication, they can also be useful for those who do not have access to an expert or a course in the area they wish to learn about. In any case, it seems appropriate to end a book such as this with ways and reasons to continue to grow, so that one can develop ever better *artistry* in the *art* of *art therapy*.

---

*Because the literature in art therapy itself is so new and still rather limited, I have decided to be inclusive on the lists for Part III, rather than selective, as elsewhere.

PART I. THE ART PART

Chapter 1. Knowing Materials

Alschuler, R.H., & Hattwick, L.W. *Painting and personality: A study of young children* (rev. ed.). Chicago: University of Chicago Press, 1969. (More extensive information available in original 2-volume edition, 1947.)

Berensohn, P. *Finding one's way with clay.* New York: Simon & Schuster, 1972.

Cherry, C. *Creative art for the developing child.* Belmont, CA: Fearon Publishers, 1972.

D'Amico, V., et al. *Art for the family.* Garden City, New York: Doubleday, 1954.

Foley, D.E. *Art recipes.* Dansville, NY: F.A. Owen, 1966.

Grözinger, W. *Scribbling, drawing, painting: The early forms of the child's pictorial creativeness.* New York: Humanities Press, 1955.

Hartley, R., Frank, L., & Goldenson, R. *Understanding children's play.* New York: Columbia University Press, 1952, Chapters 6, 7, 8.

Heberholz, D., & Heberholz, B. *A child's pursuit of art: 110 motivations for drawing, painting, and modeling.* Dubuque, IA: William C Brown, 1967.

Johnston, M.F. *Visual workouts: A collection of art-making problems.* Englewood Cliffs, NJ: Prentice-Hall, 1983.

Langstaff, N., & Sproul, A. *Exploring with clay.* Washington, D.C.: Association for Childhood Education International, 1979.

Linderman, E.W. *Invitation to vision: Ideas and imaginations for art.* Dubuque, IA: William C Brown, 1967.

Linderman, E.W., & Heberholz, D. *Developing artistic and perceptual awareness* (3rd ed.). Dubuque, IA: William C Brown, 1974.

Lord, L. *Collage and construction in elementary and junior high schools* (2nd ed.). Worcester, MA: Davis Publications, 1958.

Lüthe, W. *Creativity mobilization technique.* New York: Grune & Stratton, 1976.

Mattil, E.L. *Meaning in crafts* (3rd ed.). Englewood Cliffs, NJ: Prentice-Hall, 1971.

Mayer, R. *The artist's handbook of materials and techniques* (4th ed.). New York: Viking Press, 1981.

Montgomery, C. *Art for teachers of children* (2nd ed.). Columbus, OH: Charles E. Merrill, 1973.

Morman, J.M. *Art: Of wonder and a world* (rev. ed.). New York: Art Education, 1978.

————. *Art: Tempo of today* (rev. ed.). New York: Art Education, 1978.

Nicolaides, K. *The natural way to draw*. Boston: Houghton-Mifflin, 1975.

Petrie, M. *Modeling*. Peoria, IL: Charles A. Bennett, 1955.

Richards, M.C. *Centering: In pottery, poetry, and the person*. Middletown, CT: Wesleyan University Press, 1962.

Robertson, S. *Creative crafts in education*. London: Routledge & Kegan Paul, 1967.

Shaw, R.F. *Finger painting*. Boston: Little, Brown & Company, 1938.

Sproul, A. *With a free hand: Painting, drawing, graphics, ceramics, and sculpture for children*. New York: Reinhold, 1968.

————. *Teaching art: Sources and resources* (with photographs by John Urban). New York: Van Nostrand Reinhold, 1971.

Wanklemann, W.F., & Wigg, P. *A handbook of arts and crafts* (5th ed.). Dubuque, IA: William C Brown, 1982.

Wilkinson, V.C., & Heater, S.L. *Therapeutic media and techniques of application: A guide for activities therapists*. New York: Van Nostrand Reinhold, 1979.

Chapter 2. Knowing Processes

Anderson, H.H. (Ed.). *Creativity and its cultivation*. New York: Harper & Row, 1959.

Arieti, S. *Creativity: The magic synthesis*. New York: Basic Books, 1976.

Arnheim, R. *Art and visual perception: A psychology of the creative eye*. Berkeley: University of California Press, 1954.

————. *Towards a psychology of art*. Berkeley: University of California Press, 1967.

————. *Visual thinking*. Berkeley: University of California Press, 1969.

Beittel, K.R. *Mind and context in the art of drawing*. New York: Holt, Rinehart, & Winston, 1972.

Brittain, W.L. *Creativity, art, and the young child*. New York: Macmillan, 1979.

Edwards, B. *Drawing on the right side of the brain*. Los Angeles: J.P. Tarcher, 1979.

Ehrenzweig, A. *The psycho-analysis of artistic vision and hearing*. New York: George Braziller, 1965.

————. *The hidden order of art: A study in the psychology of artistic imagination*. London: Weidenfeld & Nicholson, 1967.

Freeman, N.H. *Strategies of representation in young children: Analysis of spatial skills and drawing processes*. New York: Academic Press, 1980.

Gardner, H. *Art, mind and brain: A cognitive approach to creativity*. New York: Basic Books, 1982.

Getzels, J.W., & Cziksentmihalyi, M. *The creative vision: A longitudinal study of problem finding in art*. New York: Wiley, 1976.

Ghiselin, B. (Ed.). *The creative process*. Berkeley: University of California Press, 1952.

Golomb, C. *Young children's sculpture and drawing*. Cambridge: Harvard University Press, 1974.

Goodnow, J. *Children drawing*. Cambridge: Harvard University Press, 1977.

Havelka, J. *The nature of the creative process in art*. The Hague: Martinus Nijhoff, 1968.

Horowitz, M.J. *Image formation and cognition* (2nd ed.). New York: Appleton-Century-Crofts, 1978.

Kubie, L. *Neurotic distortion of the creative process*. New York: Noonday Press, 1958.

Lowenfeld, V. *The nature of creative activity* (2nd ed.). London: Routledge & Kegan Paul, 1952.

McKim, R.H. *Experiences in visual thinking* (2nd ed.). Belmont, CA: Brooks/Cole, 1980.

May, R. *The courage to create*. New York: W.W. Norton, 1975.

Meares, A. *Hypnography*. Springfield, IL: Charles C Thomas, 1957.

————. *Shapes of sanity*. Springfield, IL: Charles C Thomas, 1960.

Milner, M. *On not being able to paint* (2nd ed.). New York: International Universities Press, 1967.

Parnes, S.J., & Harding, H.S. (Eds.). *A sourcebook for creative thinking*. New York: Scribner's, 1962.

Rothenberg, A., & Hausman, C.R. (Eds.). *The creativity question*. Durham, NC: University of North Carolina Press, 1976.

Torrance, E.P. *Rewarding creative behavior*. Englewood Cliffs, NJ: Prentice-Hall, 1965.

Chapter 3. Knowing Products

Billig, O., & Burton-Bradley, B.G. *The painted message*. Cambridge, MA: Schenkman Publishing Company, 1978.

Burns, R.C., & Kaufman, S.H. *Kinetic family drawings*. New York: Brunner/Mazel, 1970.

————. *Actions, styles, and symbols in kinetic family drawings*. New York: Brunner/Mazel, 1972.

Campbell, J. *The mythic image*. Princeton: Princeton University Press, 1974.

Cardinal, R. *Outsider art*. New York: Praeger, 1972.

Delacroix, H., & Tansey, R.G. *Art through the ages*, 2 Vols. (7th ed.). New York: Harcourt, Brace, 1980.

DiLeo, J. H. *Young children and their drawings*. New York: Brunner/Mazel, 1970.

————. *Children's drawings as diagnostic aids*. New York: Brunner/Mazel, 1974.

————. *Interpreting children's drawings*. New York: Brunner/Mazel, 1983.

Eissler, K. *Leonardo da Vinci: Psychoanalytic notes on the enigma*. New York: International Universities Press, 1961.

Freud, S. *Leonardo da Vinci and a memory of his childhood* (1910). New York: W.W. Norton, 1964.

Gardner, H. *Artful scribbles*. New York: Basic Books, 1980.

Gedo, M. *Picasso: Art as autobiography*. Chicago: University of Chicago Press, 1980.

Gombrich, E. *Art and illusion: A study in the psychology of pictorial representation*. Princeton: Princeton University Press, 1960.

Hammer, E.F. (Ed.). *The clinical application of projective drawings*. Springfield, IL: Charles C Thomas, 1958.

Harris, D.B. *Children's drawings as measures of intellectual maturity*. New York: Harcourt, Brace & World, 1963.

Janson, H.W. *History of art* (2nd ed.). New York: Abrams, 1977.

Jung, C.G. *Man and his symbols*. New York: Doubleday, 1964.

————. *Mandala symbolism*. Princeton: Princeton University Press, 1972.

Klepsch, M., & Logie, L. *Children draw and tell: An introduction to the projective uses of children's human figure drawings*. New York: Brunner/Mazel, 1982.

Koppitz, E.M. *Psychological evaluation of children's human figure drawings*. New York: Grune & Stratton, 1968.

Kris, E. *Psychoanalytic explorations in art*. New York: Schocken, 1952.

Lark-Horovitz, B., Lewis, H.P., & Luca, M. *Understanding children's art for better teaching*. Columbus, OH: Charles E. Merrill, 1967.

Levick, M.F. *They could not talk and so they drew: Children's styles of coping and thinking*. Springfield, IL: Charles C Thomas, 1983.

Liebert, R.S. *Michelangelo: A psychoanalytic study of his life and images*. New Haven: Yale University Press, 1983.

Machover, K. *Personality projection in the drawing of the human figure.* Springfield, IL: Charles C Thomas, 1949.

Malraux, A. *The voices of silence.* New York: Doubleday, 1953.

Masters, R. E., & Houston, J. *Psychedelic art.* New York: Grove Press, 1968.

Nagera, H. *Vincent van Gogh: A psychological study.* New York: International Universities Press, 1967.

Neumann, E. *Art and the creative unconscious.* Princeton: Princeton University Press, 1971.

————. *The archetypal world of Henry Moore.* New York: Pantheon Books, 1959.

Pasto, T.A. *The space-frame experience in art.* New York: A.S. Barnes, 1964.

Plokker, J.H. *Art from the mentally disturbed.* Boston: Little, Brown, 1965.

Prinzhorn, H. *Artistry of the mentally ill.* New York: Springer-Verlag, 1972.

Reitman, F. *Psychotic art.* London: Routledge & Kegan Paul, 1950.

————. *Insanity, art and culture.* New York: Philosophical Library, 1954.

Rose, G. *The power of form.* New York: International Universities Press, 1980.

Schildkrout, M.S., Shenker, I.R., & Sonnenblick, M. *Human figure drawings in adolescence.* New York: Brunner/Mazel, 1972.

Schmidt, G., Steck, H., & Bader, A. *Though this be madness.* London: Thames & Hudson, 1961.

Stokes, A. *The image in form.* New York: Harper & Row, 1972.

Thevoz, M. *Art brut.* New York: Rizzoli, 1976.

Volmat, R., & Wiart, C. (Eds.). *Art and psychopathology.* Amsterdam: Excerpta Medica Foundation, 1969.

Waelder, R. *Psychoanalytic avenues to art.* New York: International Universities Press, 1965.

Winner, E. *Invented worlds: The psychology of the arts.* Cambridge: Harvard University Press, 1982.

Chapter 4. Knowing Development

Baldwin, A.L. *Theories of child development* (2nd ed.). New York: Wiley, 1980.

Blos, P. *On adolescence: A psychoanalytic interpretation.* New York: The Free Press, 1962.

Brim, O.G., & Kagan, J. (Eds.). *Constancy and change in human development.* Cambridge: Harvard University Press, 1980.

Bronfenbrenner, U. *The ecology of development: Experiments by nature and design.* Cambridge: Harvard University Press, 1979.

Butler, R.N. *Why survive? Growing old in America.* New York: Harper & Row, 1975.

Carter, E.A., & McGoldrick, M. (Eds.). *The family life cycle: A framework for family therapy.* New York: Gardner Press, 1980.

Cath, S.H., Gurwitt, A.R., & Ross, J.M. (Eds.). *Father and child: Developmental perspectives.* Boston: Little, Brown, 1982.

Dohrenwend, B.S., & Dohrenwend, B.P. *Stressful life events: Their nature and effects.* New York: Wiley, 1974.

Elkind, D. *A sympathetic understanding of the child six to sixteen* (2nd ed.). Boston: Allyn & Bacon, 1978.

Erikson, E.H. *Childhood and society* (2nd ed.). New York: W.W. Norton, 1963.

————. *The life cycle completed: A review.* New York: W.W. Norton, 1982.

Esman, A.H. (Ed.). *The psychology of adolescence.* New York: International Universities Press, 1975.

Fraiberg, S.M. *The magic years: Understanding and handling the problems of early childhood.* New York: Scribner's, 1959.

Freud, A. *Normality and pathology in childhood: Assessments of development.* New York: International Universities Press, 1965.

Gallinsky, E. *Between generations: The six stages of parenthood.* New York: Times Books, 1981.

Garmezy, N., & Rutter, M. (Eds.). *Stress, coping, and development in children.* New York: McGraw-Hill, 1983.

Gould, R. *Transformations: Growth and change in adult life.* New York: Simon & Schuster, 1978.

Greenspan, S., & Pollock, G.H. (Eds.). *The course of life: Psychoanalytic contributions toward understanding personality development* (3 vols.). Adelphi, MD: National Institutes of Mental Health, 1980-81.

Josselyn, I.M. *The happy child: A psychoanalytic guide to emotional and social growth.* New York: Random House, 1955.

————. *The psychosocial development of children* (2nd ed.). New York: Family Service Association, 1977.

Kagan, J., & Coles, R.J. *Twelve to sixteen: Early adolescence.* New York: W.W. Norton, 1973.

Knobloch, H., & Passamanick, B. (Eds.). *Gesell and Amatruda's developmental diagnosis* (3rd ed.). New York: Harper & Row, 1974.

Kübler-Ross, E. *Death: The final stage of growth.* Englewood Cliffs, NJ: Prentice-Hall, 1975.

Lerner, R.M., & Busch-Rossnagel, N.A. (Eds.). *Individuals as producers of their own development: A life-span perspective.* New York: Academic Press, 1981.

Levinson, D.J., et al. *The seasons of a man's life.* New York: Knopf, 1978.

Lewis, M. *Clinical aspects of child development: An introductory synthesis of developmental concepts and clinical experience* (2nd ed.). Philadelphia: Lea & Febiger, 1982.

Lidz, T. *The person: His and her development throughout the life cycle.* (rev. ed.). New York: Basic Books, 1976.

Mahler, M.S., Pine, F., & Bergman, A. *The psychological birth of the human infant: Symbiosis and individuation.* New York: Basic Books, 1975.

Maier, H.W. *Three theories of child development* (2nd ed.). New York: Harper & Row, 1978.

Mussen, P. *The psychological development of the child* (3rd ed.). Englewood Cliffs, NJ: Prentice-Hall, 1979.

Neugarten, B., et al. *Personality in middle and late life: Empirical studies.* Salem, NY: Ayer & Company, 1980.

Osofsky, J.D. (Ed.). *Handbook of infant development.* New York: Wiley, 1979.

Piaget, J. *Play, dreams and imitation in childhood.* New York: W.W. Norton, 1962.

Piaget, J., & Inhelder, B. *A child's conception of space.* New York: W.W. Norton, 1967.

Pulaski, M.A.S. *Understanding Piaget: An introduction to children's cognitive development* (rev. ed.). New York: Harper & Row, 1980.

Sarnoff, C. *Latency.* New York: Jason Aronson, 1976.

Scarf, M. *Unfinished business: Pressure points in the lives of women.* New York: Doubleday, 1980.

Sheehy, G. *Passages: Predictable crises of adult life.* New York: E. P. Dutton, 1976.

Singer, D.G., & Revenson, T.A. *A Piaget primer: How a child thinks.* New York: International Universities Press, 1978.

Smelser, N.J., & Erikson, E.H. (Eds.). *Themes of work and love in adulthood.* Cambridge: Harvard University Press, 1980.

Smith, N.R., & Franklin, M.P. (Eds.). *Symbolic functioning in childhood.* Hillsdale, NJ: Laurence Erlbaum Associates, 1979.

Stern, D. *The first relationship: Infant and mother.* Cambridge: Harvard University Press, 1977.

Stone, L.J., & Church, J. *Childhood and adolescence* (5th ed.). New York: Random House, 1984.

Walsh, P.B. *Growing through time: An introduction to the psychology of adult life*. Belmont, CA: Brooks-Cole, 1982.

Werner, H. *Comparative psychology of mental development* (rev. ed.). New York: International Universities Press, 1970.

White, B.L. *The first three years of life*. Englewood Cliffs, NJ: Prentice-Hall, 1975.

PART II. THE THERAPY PART

Chapter 5. Knowing Dynamics and Deviations

Achenbach, T.M. *Developmental psychopathology* (2nd ed.). New York: Wiley, 1982.

American Psychiatric Association. *A psychiatric glossary* (4th ed.). New York: Basic Books, 1975.

American Psychoanalytic Association. *A glossary of psychoanalytic terms and concepts* (3rd ed.). New York: The American Psychoanalytic Association, 1984.

Anthony, E.J., & Benedek, T. (Eds.). *Parenthood: Its psychology and psychopathology*. New York: Basic Books, 1972.

Bemporad, J.R. (Ed.). *Child development in normality and psychopathology*. New York: Brunner/Mazel, 1980.

Blanck, G., & Blanck, R. *Ego psychology*. New York: Columbia University Press. Vol. I, 1974; Vol. II, 1979.

Brenner, C. *The mind in conflict*. New York: International Universities Press, 1980.

Burton, A. (Ed.). *Operational theories of personality*. New York: Brunner/Mazel, 1974.

Coleman, J. *Abnormal psychology and modern life* (6th ed.). Glenview, IL: Scott, Foresman, 1980.

Cruikshank, W. *Psychology of exceptional children and youth* (4th ed.). Englewood Cliffs, NJ: Prentice-Hall, 1980.

———— (Ed.). *Concepts in special education: Selected writings*. Syracuse: Syracuse University Press, 1981.

Erickson, M.T. *Child psycho-pathology: Behavior disorders and developmental disabilities* (2nd ed.). Englewood Cliffs, NJ: Prentice-Hall, 1982.

Fenichel, O. *The psychoanalytic theory of neurosis*. New York: W.W. Norton, 1945.

Freud, A. *The ego and the mechanisms of defense*. New York: International Universities Press, 1946.

Freud, S. *The interpretation of dreams* (1900). London: Hogarth, 1953.
———. *The ego and the id* (1923). London: Hogarth, 1947.
———. *The complete introductory lectures in psychoanalysis* (1916/17 & 1933). New York: W.W. Norton, 1966.
———. *An outline of psychoanalysis* (1939). New York: W.W. Norton, 1949.
Gedo, G., & Goldberg, A. *Models of the mind*. New York: International Universities Press, 1973.
Hall, C.S., & Lindzey, G. *Theories of personality* (3rd ed.). New York: Wiley, 1978.
Harrison, S.I. & McDermott, J.F. (Eds.). *Childhood psychopathology: An anthology of basic readings*. New York: International Universities Press, 1972.
Kaplan, H.I., & Sadock, B.J. *Modern synopsis of comprehensive textbook of psychiatry* (3rd ed.). Baltimore: Williams & Wilkins, 1981.
Kessler, J.W. *Psychopathology of childhood*. Englewood Cliffs, NJ: Prentice-Hall, 1966.
Lindzey, G., Hall, C.S., & Manosevitz, M. *Theories of personality: Primary sources and research* (2nd ed.). New York: Wiley, 1973.
Millon, T. *Modern psychopathology: A biosocial approach to maladaptive learning and functioning*. Philadelphia: Saunders, 1969.
——— (Ed.). *Theories of psychopathology and personality: Essays and critiques* (2nd ed.). Philadelphia: Saunders, 1973.
———. *Disorders of personality: DSM III: Axis II*. New York: Wiley, 1981.
Mordock, J.B. *The other children: An introduction to exceptionality*. New York: Harper & Row, 1975.
Nagera, H. *The developmental approach to childhood psychopathology*. New York: Jason Aronson, 1981.
Offer, D., & Sabshin, M. *Normality: Theoretical and clinical concepts of mental health* (rev. ed.). New York: Basic Books, 1974.
Pruyser, P.W. (Ed.). *Diagnosis and the difference it makes*. New York: Jason Aronson, 1977.
Rychlak, J.F. *Introduction to personality and psychotherapy: A theory-construction approach* (2nd ed.). Boston: Houghton-Mifflin, 1981.
Shepherd, M., & Zangwill, O.L. (Eds.). *Handbook of psychiatry I. General psychopathology*. New York: Cambridge University Press, 1983.
Thomas, A., & Chess, S. *The dynamics of psychological development*. New York: Brunner/Mazel, 1980.
Walker, C.E., & Roberts, M.C. *Handbook of clinical child psychology*. New York: Wiley, 1983.
Walsh, F. (Ed.). *Normal family processes*. New York: The Guilford Press, 1982.

Wenar, C. *Developmental psychopathology: From infancy to adulthood*. New York: Random House, 1983.

Chapter 6. Knowing Therapy

Auvenshine, C.D., & Noffsinger, A.L. *Counseling: Issues and procedures in the human services*. Baltimore: University Park Press, 1983.

Basch, M.F. *Doing psychotherapy*. New York: Basic Books, 1980.

Beck, A.T. *Cognitive therapy and the emotional disorders*. New York: International Universities Press, 1976.

Belkin, G.S. (Ed.). *Contemporary psychotherapies*. Chicago: Rand McNally, 1980.

Bellack, A.S., & Hersen, M. *Behavior modification: An introductory textbook*. Baltimore: Williams & Wilkins, 1977.

Benjamin, A.D. *The helping interview* (3rd ed.). Boston: Houghton-Mifflin, 1981.

Brenner, C. *An elementary textbook of psychoanalysis* (rev. ed.). New York: International Universities Press, 1973.

Bruch, H. *Learning psychotherapy: Rationale and ground rules*. Cambridge: Harvard University Press, 1974.

Chessick, R.D. *How psychotherapy heals: The process of intensive psychotherapy*. New York: Science House, 1969.

Fromm-Reichman, F. *Principles of intensive psychotherapy*. Chicago: University of Chicago Press, 1950.

Garrett, A. *Interviewing: Its principles and methods* (3rd ed.). New York: Family Service Association, 1982.

Goldfried, M.R. (Ed.). *Changing themes in psychotherapy: Trends in psychodynamic, humanistic, and behavioral practice*. New York: Springer, 1982.

Greenspan, S.I. *The clinical interview of the child*. New York: McGraw-Hill, 1981.

Hammer, E. (Ed.). *Use of interpretation in treatment: Technique and art*. New York: Grune & Stratton, 1968.

Hedges, L.F. *Listening perspectives in psychotherapy*. New York: Jason Aronson, 1983.

Horner, A.J. *Object relations and the developing ego in therapy*. (2nd ed.). New York: Jason Aronson, 1984.

Kell, B.L., & Mueller, W.J. *Impact and change: A study of counseling relationships*. Englewood Cliffs, NJ: Prentice-Hall, 1966.

Lacoursiere, R. *The life cycle of groups: Group developmental stage theory*. New York: Human Sciences Press, 1980.

Langs, R.J. *The therapeutic interaction: A synthesis*. New York: Jason Aronson, 1977.

May, R., Angel, E., & Ellenberger, H.F. (Eds.). *Existence: A new dimension in psychiatry and psychology*. New York: Basic Books, 1958.

Paul, I.H. *The form and technique of psychotherapy*. Chicago: University of Chicago Press, 1978.

Perls, F., Hefferline, R.F., & Goodman, P. *Gestalt therapy*. New York: Julian Press, 1951.

Racker, H. *Transference and counter-transference*. New York: International Universities Press, 1968.

Rogers, C. *Client-centered therapy: Its current practice, implications, and theory*. Boston: Houghton-Mifflin, 1951.

Sampson, E.E., & Matthas, M.K. *Group process for mental health*. New York: Wiley, 1977.

Shaw, M.E. *Group dynamics: The psychology of small group behavior*. New York: McGraw-Hill, 1971.

Singer, E. *Key concepts in psychotherapy*. New York: Basic Books, 1970.

Singer, J. *Boundaries of the soul: The practice of Jung's psychology*. New York: Doubleday, 1973.

Slipp, S. (Ed.). *Curative factors in dynamic psychotherapy*. New York: McGraw-Hill, 1982.

Sullivan, H.S. *The interpersonal theory of psychiatry*. New York: W.W. Norton, 1970.

Weiner, I.B. *Principles of psychotherapy*. New York: Wiley, 1975.

Chapter 7. Knowing Art Therapy (& Related Fields)

American Psychiatric Association, *The use of the creative arts in therapy*. Washington, D.C., 1980.

Anderson, W. (Ed.). *Therapy and the arts: Tools of consciousness*. New York: Harper & Row, 1977.

Avedon, E.M. *Therapeutic recreation service: An applied behavioral science approach*. Englewood Cliffs, NJ: Prentice-Hall, 1974.

Axline, V.M. *Play therapy*. New York: Basic Books, 1947.

Bernstein, P.L. *Theory and methods in dance-movement therapy: A manual for therapists, students, and educators* (2nd ed.). Dubuque: Kendall Hunt, 1975.

———. *Eight theoretical approaches in dance-movement therapy*. Dubuque: Kendall Hunt, 1979.

Erikson, J.M. *Activity, recovery, and growth: The communal role of planned activities*. New York: W.W. Norton, 1976.

Feder, B., & Feder, E. *The expressive arts therapies.* Englewood Cliffs, NJ: Prentice-Hall, 1981.

Fleshman, B., & Fryrear, J.L. *The arts in therapy.* Chicago: Nelson-Hall, 1981.

Frye, V., & Peters, M. *Therapeutic recreation: Its theory, philosophy, and practice.* Harrisburg: Stackpole Books, 1972.

Gardner, R.A. *Therapeutic communication with children: The mutual storytelling technique.* New York: Science House, 1971.

Gaston, E.T. (Ed.). *Music in therapy.* New York: Macmillan, 1968.

Hopkins, H.D., & Smith, H.L. *Willard & Spackman's occupational therapy* (6th ed.). Philadelphia: Lippincott, 1983.

Kraus, R. *Therapeutic recreation service.* Philadelphia: Saunders, 1973.

Krauss, D.A., & Fryrear, J.L. (Eds.). *Phototherapy in mental health.* Springfield, IL: Charles C Thomas, 1983.

Leedy, J.J. *Poetry therapy.* Philadelphia: Lippincott, 1969.

———. *Poetry the healer.* Philadelphia: Lippincott, 1973.

Lerner, A. (Ed.). *Poetry in the therapeutic experience.* New York: Pergamon, 1978.

McNiff, S. *The arts and psychotherapy.* Springfield, IL: Charles C Thomas, 1981.

Mosey, A.C. *Activities therapy.* New York: Raven Press, 1973.

Moustakas, C.E. *Children in play therapy.* New York: Ballantine Books, 1953.

Nickerson, E.T., & O'Laughlin, K. (Eds.). *Helping through action: Action-oriented therapies.* Amherst, MA: Human Resources Development Press, 1982.

Nordoff, P., & Robbins, C. *Creative music therapy: Individualized treatment for the handicapped child.* New York: T.Y. Crowell, 1977.

Plach, T. *The creative use of music in group therapy.* Springfield, IL: Charles C Thomas, 1980.

Reed, K.L. *Models of practice in occupational therapy.* Baltimore: Williams & Wilkins, 1983.

Reed, K.L., & Sanderson, S. *Concepts of occupational therapy* (2nd ed.). Baltimore: Williams & Wilkins, 1983.

Schaefer, C.E. (Ed.). *Therapeutic use of child's play.* New York: Jason Aronson, 1976.

Schattner, G., & Courtney, R. (Eds.). *Drama in therapy. Vol. I. Children, Vol. II. Adults.* New York: Drama Book Specialists, 1981.

Shivers, J.S., & Fait, H.F. *Therapeutic and adapted recreational services.* Philadelphia: Lea & Febiger, 1975.

Shorr, J.E., et al. (Eds.). *Imagery, Vol. 3.* New York: Plenum, 1983.

Singer, J.L., & Pope, K.S. (Eds.). *The power of human imagination: New methods in psychotherapy.* New York: Plenum, 1978.

Tyson, F. *Psychiatric music therapy: Origins and development.* New York: Creative Arts Rehabilitation Center, 1981.

Winnicott, D.W. *Therapeutic consultations in child psychiatry.* New York: Basic Books, 1971.

PART III. THE INTERFACE

(DOING ART THERAPY)

Edited Collections of Miscellaneous Papers

American Art Therapy Association: Conference Proceedings
   1976: *Creativity and the art therapist's identity* (Ed. R.H. Shoemaker & S.E. Gonick-Barris)
   1977: *The dynamics of creativity* (Ed. B.K. Mandel, R.H. Shoemaker & R.E. Hays)
   1978: *Art therapy: Expanding horizons* (Ed. L. Gantt, G. Forrest, D. Silverman, & R.H. Shoemaker)
   1979: *Focus on the future: The next ten years.* (Ed. L. Gantt & A. Evans)
   1980: *The fine art of therapy* (Ed. L. Gantt & S. Whitman)
   1981: *Art therapy: A bridge between worlds* (Ed. A.E. DiMaria, E.S. Kramer, & I. Rosner)
   1982: *Art therapy: Still growing.* (Ed. A.E. DiMaria, E.S. Kramer, & E.A. Roth)

Jakab, I. (Ed.). *Psychiatry and art.* New York: S. Karger. Vol. I, 1968; Vol. II, 1970; Vol. III, 1971; Vol. IV, 1975.

———— (Ed.). *The personality of the therapist.* Pittsburgh, PA: American Society of Psychopathology of Expression, 1981.

Roth, E.A., & Rubin, J.A. (Eds.). *Perspectives on art therapy.* Pittsburgh: Western Psychiatric Institute and Clinic, 1978.

Ulman, E., & Dachinger, P. (Eds.). *Art therapy in theory and practice.* New York: Schocken Press, 1975.

Ulman, E., & Levy, C. (Eds.). *Art therapy viewpoints.* New York: Schocken Press, 1980.

General Books on Art Therapy

Capacchione, L. *The creative journal: The art of finding yourself.* Chicago: Swallow Press, 1979.

Hill, A. *Art versus illness.* London: George Allen & Unwin, 1945.

————. *Painting out illness*. London: George Allen & Unwin, 1951.

Keyes, M.F. *The inward journey*. Millbrae, CA: Celestial Arts, 1974.

Kwiatkowska, H.Y. *Family therapy and evaluation through art*. Springfield, IL: Charles C Thomas, 1978.

Landgarten, H. *Clinical art therapy*. New York: Brunner/Mazel, 1981.

Lucas, X. *Artists in group psychotherapy*. New York: Brunner/Mazel, 1982.

Lyddiatt, E.M. *Spontaneous painting and modeling*. London: Constable & Co., 1971.

Naumburg, M. *Dynamically oriented art therapy: Its principles and practice*. New York: Grune & Stratton, 1966.

Paraskevas, C.B. *A structural approach to art therapy methods*. New York: Collegium, 1979.

Pickford, R.W. *Studies in psychiatric art*. Springfield, IL: Charles C Thomas, 1967.

Rhyne, J. *The gestalt art experience*. Monterey, CA: Brooks/Cole, 1974.

Robbins, A., & Sibley, L.B. *Creative art therapy*. New York: Brunner/Mazel, 1976.

Robbins, A., et al. *Expressive therapy: A creative arts approach to depth-oriented therapy*. New York: Human Sciences Press, 1980.

Virshup, E. *Right-brain people in a left-brain world*. Los Angeles: Art Therapy West, 1978.

Wadeson, H. *Art psychotherapy*. New York: Wiley, 1980.

Art and Therapy With Children

Anderson, F. *Art for all the children*. Springfield, IL: Charles C Thomas, 1978.

————, Colchado, J., & McAnally, P. *Art for the handicapped*. Normal, IL: Illinois State University, 1979.

Bender, L. (Ed.). *Child psychiatric techniques*. Springfield, IL: Charles C Thomas, 1952.

Cane, F. *The artist in each of us*. New York: Pantheon Books, 1951.

Clements, C.B., & Clements, R.D. *Art and mainstreaming*. Springfield, IL: Charles C Thomas, 1984.

Fukurai, S. *How can I make what I cannot see?* New York: Van Nostrand Reinhold, 1974.

Kearns, L.H., Ditson, M.T., & Roehner, B.G. (Eds.). *Readings: Developing arts programs for handicapped students*. Harrisburg: Arts in Special Education Project of Pennsylvania, 1981.

Kramer, E. *Art therapy in a children's community*. Springfield, IL: Charles C Thomas, 1958.

————. *Art as therapy with children.* New York: Schocken Press, 1971.

————. *Childhood and art therapy.* New York: Schocken Press, 1979.

Lowenfeld, V. *The nature of creative activity.* London: Routledge & Kegan Paul, 1952.

————. *Creative and mental growth* (3rd ed.). New York: Macmillan, 1957.

————. *The Lowenfeld lectures* (Ed. J.A. Michael). University Park: Pennsylvania State University Press, 1982.

Petrie, M. *Art and regeneration.* London: Paul Elek, 1946.

Read, H. *Education through art* (3rd ed.). New York: Pantheon Books, 1958.

Robertson, S. *Rosegarden and labyrinth: A study in art education.* New York: Barnes & Noble, 1963.

Rubin, J.A. *Child art therapy: Understanding and helping children grow through art* (2nd ed.). New York: Van Nostrand Reinhold, 1984.

Schaeffer-Simmern, H. *The unfolding of artistic activity.* Berkeley: University of California Press, 1948.

Silver, R.A. *Developing cognitive and creative skills in art.* Baltimore: University Park Press, 1978.

Singer, F. *Structuring child behavior through visual art.* Springfield, IL: Charles C Thomas, 1980.

Uhlin, D.M. *Art for exceptional children* (2nd ed.). Dubuque, IA: William C Brown, 1979.

Williams, G.H., & Wood, M.M. *Developmental art therapy.* Baltimore: University Park Press, 1977.

Case Studies of Art and Therapy

Axline, V.M. *Dibs: In search of self.* New York: Ballantine Books, 1964.

Barnes, M., & Berke, J. *Mary Barnes: Two accounts of a journey through madness.* New York: Harcourt Brace Jovanovich, 1973.

Baruch, D.W. *One little boy.* New York: Dell Paperback, 1983.

Betensky, M. *Self-discovery through self-expression.* Springfield, IL: Charles C Thomas, 1973.

Eng, H. *The psychology of children's drawings: From the first stroke to the coloured drawing.* (2nd ed.). London: Routledge & Kegan Paul, 1954.

————. *The psychology of child and youth drawing: From the ninth to the 24th year.* New York: Humanities Press, 1957.

Fein, S. *Heidi's horse.* Pleasant Hill, CA: Exelrod Press, 1976.

Harris, J., & Joseph, C. *Murals of the mind.* New York: International Universities Press, 1973.

Klein, M. *Narrative of a child analysis.* London: Hogarth, 1961.

McDougall, J., & Lebovici, S. *Dialogue with Sammy: A psycho-analytical*

contribution to the understanding of child psychosis. New York: International Universities Press, 1969.

Meares, A. *The door of serenity.* London: Faber & Faber, 1958.

Milner, M. *The hands of the living God.* New York: International Universities Press, 1969.

Naevestad, M. *The colors of rage and love: A picture book of internal events.* London: Whitefriars Press, 1979.

Naumburg, M. *Studies of the "free" art expression of behavior problem children and adolescents as a means of diagnosis and therapy.* Nervous & Mental Disease Monograph No. 71, 1947 (*Introduction to art therapy.* New York: Teachers College Press, 1973).

————. *Schizophrenic art: Its meaning in psychotherapy.* New York: Grune & Stratton, 1950.

————. *Psychoneurotic art: Its function in psychotherapy.* New York: Grune & Stratton, 1953.

Schreiber, F.R. *Sybil.* New York: Warner Books, 1974.

Sechehaye, M. *Symbolic realization.* New York: International Universities Press, 1953.

Selfe, L. *Nadia: A case of extraordinary drawing ability in an autistic child.* New York: Academic Press, 1978.

Ude-Pestel, A. *Betty: History and art of a child in therapy.* Palo Alto, CA: Science & Behavior Books, 1977.

Wysuph, C.L. *Jackson Pollock: Psychoanalytic drawings.* New York: Horizon Press, 1970.

Bibliographies

Gantt, L., & Schmail, M. *Art therapy: A bibliography.* Washington, D.C.: National Institutes of Mental Health, 1974.

Hanes, K.M. *Art therapy and group work: An annotated bibliography.* Westport, CT: Greenwood Press, 1982.

Kiell, N. *Psychiatry and psychology in the visual arts and aesthetics: A bibliography.* Madison: University of Wisconsin Press, 1965.

Moore, R.W. *Art therapy in mental health.* Washington, D.C.: National Institutes of Mental Health, 1981.

Journals

American Journal of Art Therapy (formerly *Bulletin of Art Therapy*). Published and edited by Elinor Ulman (Box 4918, Washington, D.C. 20008).

The Arts in Psychotherapy (formerly *Art Psychotherapy*). Published by An-
    kho International, New York City.
Confinia Psychiatrica. Published from 1958 to 1980 by S. Karger, Swit-
    zerland.

PART IV. INDIRECT SERVICE

Chapter 13. Knowing Teaching

Abels, P. *The new practice of supervision and staff development*. New York:
    Association Press, 1977.
Benjamin, H. *The saber-tooth curriculum*. New York: McGraw-Hill, 1939.
Bibring, G.L. (Ed.). *The teaching of dynamic psychiatry*. New York: Inter-
    national Universities Press, 1968.
Bruner, J. *The process of education*. Cambridge: Harvard University Press,
    1961.
————. *On knowing: Essays for the left hand* (rev. ed.). Cambridge: Harvard
    University Press, 1979.
Ford, C., & Morgan, M. (Eds.). *Teaching in the health professions*. St. Louis:
    C.V. Mosby, 1976.
Knopke, H.J., & Diekelmann, N.L. (Eds.). *Approaches to teaching in the
    health sciences*. Reading, MA: Addison-Wesley, 1981.
Lauffer, A., & Sturdevant, C. *Doing continuing education and staff devel-
    opment*. New York: McGraw-Hill, 1978.
Lewin, B., & Ross, H. *Psychoanalytic education in the United States*. New
    York: W.W. Norton, 1960.
Lowy, L., et al. *Integrative learning and teaching in schools of social work*.
    New York: Association Press, 1971.
Mager, R.F. *Preparing instructional objectives* (2nd ed.). Belmont, CA: Fea-
    ron Publishers, 1975.
Miller, G.E., et al. *Teaching and learning in medical school*. Cambridge:
    Harvard University Press, 1961.
Smith, R.A. (Ed.). *Aesthetic concepts and education*. Urbana, IL: University
    of Illinois Press, 1970.
————. *Aesthetics and problems of education*. Urbana, IL: University of
    Illinois Press, 1971.
Towle, C. *The learner in education for the professions*. Chicago: University
    of Chicago Press, 1954.
Tyler, R.W. *Basic principles of curriculum and instruction*. Chicago: Uni-
    versity of Chicago Press, 1950.
Ulich, R. (Ed.). *Three thousand years of educational wisdom: Selections from*

great documents (2nd ed.). Cambridge: Harvard University Press, 1954.

Whitehead, A.N. *The aims of education.* New York: New American Library, 1957.

Zabarenko, R.N., & Zabarenko, L.M. *The doctor tree: Developmental stages in the growth of physicians.* Pittsburgh: University of Pittsburgh Press, 1978.

Ziegfeld, E. (Ed.). *Education and art: A symposium.* Paris: UNESCO, 1953.

Chapter 14. Knowing Supervision

Austin, M.J. *Supervisory management in the human services.* Englewood Cliffs, NJ: Prentice-Hall, 1981.

Boyd, J., et al. *Counselor supervision: Approaches, preparation, practices.* Muncie, IN: Accelerated Development, 1978.

Cogan, M.L. *Clinical supervision.* New York: Houghton-Mifflin, 1973.

Ekstein, R., & Wallerstein, R.S. *The teaching and learning of psychotherapy.* (rev. ed.). New York: International Universities Press, 1972.

Fleming, J., & Benedek, T. *Psychoanalytic supervision: A method of clinical teaching.* New York: Grune & Stratton, 1966.

Goldhammer, R., Anderson, R.H., & Krajewski, R.J. *Clinical supervision* (2nd ed.). New York: Holt, Rinehart & Winston, 1980.

Hess, A.K. (Ed.). *Psychotherapy supervision: Theory, research and practice.* New York: Wiley, 1980.

Kadushin, A. *Supervision in social work.* New York: Columbia University Press, 1976.

Kaslow, F.W., et al. *Supervision, consultation, and staff training in the helping professions.* San Francisco: Jossey-Bass, 1977.

Mueller, W.J., & Kell, B.L. *Coping with conflict: Supervising counselors and psychotherapists.* New York: Meredith Corporation, 1972.

Munson, C.E. (Ed.). *Social work supervision.* New York: Free Press, 1979.

————. *An introduction to clinical social work supervision.* New York: Haworth, 1983.

Pettes, D.E. *Staff and student supervision: A task-centered approach.* London: George Allen & Unwin, 1979.

Schuster, D.B., Sandt, J.J., & Thaler, O.F. *Clinical supervision of the psychiatric resident.* New York: Brunner/Mazel, 1972.

Semrad, E.V., et al. *Teaching psychotherapy of psychotic patients.* New York: Grune & Stratton, 1969.

Shulman, L. *Skills of supervision and staff development.* Itasca, IL: F.E. Peacock, 1982.

Wallerstein, R.S. (Ed.). *Becoming a psychoanalyst: A study of psychoanalytic supervision.* New York: International Universities Press, 1981.

Whiffen, R., & Byng-Hall, J. (Eds.). *Family therapy supervision: Recent developments in practice.* New York: Grune & Stratton, 1982.

Wilson, S. *Field instruction: Techniques for supervisors.* New York: Free Press, 1981.

Chapter 15. Knowing Consultation

Argyris, C. *Intervention theory and method: A behavioral science view.* Reading, MA: Addison-Wesley, 1970.

Beisser, A.R. *Mental health consultation and education.* Santa Monica, CA: Institute Press, 1972.

Bennis, W.G., Benne, K.D., & Chin, R. (Eds.). *The planning of change: Readings in the applied behavioral sciences* (3rd ed.). New York: Holt, Rinehart & Winston, 1976.

Caplan, G. *The theory and practice of mental health consultation.* New York: Basic Books, 1970.

Cooper, S., & Hodges, W.F. (Eds.). *The mental health consultation field.* New York: Human Sciences Press, 1983.

Fairweather, G.W., et al. *Creating change in mental health organizations.* New York: Pergamon Press, 1974.

Gallesick, J. *The profession and practice of consultation.* San Francisco: Jossey-Bass, 1982.

Goodstein, L.D. *Consulting with human service systems.* Reading, MA: Addison-Wesley, 1978.

Greenblatt, M., Sharaf, M.R., & Stone, E.M. *Dynamics of institutional change: The hospital in transition.* Pittsburgh: University of Pittsburgh Press, 1971.

Ketterer, R.F. *Consultation and education in mental health: Patterns and prospects.* Beverly Hills: Sage Publications, 1981.

Mannino, F.V., et al. (Eds.). *The practice of mental health consultation.* New York: Gardner Press, 1975.

Newman, R.G. *Psychological consultation in the schools.* New York: Basic Books, 1967.

Chapter 16. Knowing Research

Anderson, F. *A review of the published research literature on arts and the handicapped, 1971-1981.* Washington, D.C.: National Committee, Arts for the Handicapped, 1982.

Barron, F. *Artists in the making*. New York: Seminar Press, 1972.

Beittel, K. *Alternatives for art education research*. Dubuque, IA: William C Brown, 1973.

Berlyne, D.E. *Aesthetics and psychobiology*. New York: Meredith Corporation, 1971.

———— (Ed.). *Studies in the new experimental aesthetics*. New York: Wiley, 1974.

Best, J. *Research in education* (4th ed.). Englewood Cliffs, NJ: Prentice-Hall, 1981.

Borg, W.R. *Applying educational research: A practical guide for teachers*. New York: Longman, 1981.

Borg, W.R., & Gall, M.D. *Educational research: An introduction* (4th ed.). New York: Longman, 1983.

Burns, R.C. *Self-growth in families: Kinetic family drawings (KFD): Research and application*. New York: Brunner/Mazel, 1982.

Butterworth, G.E. (Ed.). *The child's representation of the world*. New York: Plenum, 1977.

Cartwright, D., & Zander, A. (Ed.). *Group dynamics: Research and theory* (3rd ed.). New York: Harper & Row, 1981.

Cox, R.C., & West, W.L. *Foundations of research for health professionals*. Laurel, MD: Ramsco Publishers, 1982.

Davis, D.J. (Ed.). *Behavioral emphasis in art education*. Reston, VA: National Art Education Association, 1976.

Fried, E. *Artistic productivity and mental health*. Springfield, IL: Charles C Thomas, 1964.

Gardner, H. *The arts and human development*. New York: Wiley, 1973.

Goldman, L. (Ed.). *Research methods for counselors: Practical approaches in field settings*. New York: Wiley, 1978.

Gurman, A.S., & Razin, A.M. (Eds.). *Effective psychotherapy: A handbook of research*. New York: Pergamon, 1977.

Hardyck, C.D., & Petrinovich, L.F. *Introduction to statistics for the behavioral sciences* (2nd ed.). Philadelphia: Saunders, 1976.

————. *Understanding research in the social sciences*. Philadelphia: Saunders, 1976.

Hare, A.P. *Handbook of small group research* (2nd ed.). New York: Free Press, 1976.

Hatterer, L.J. *The artist in society*. New York: Grove Press, 1965.

Hersen, M., & Barlow, D.H. *Single case experimental designs: Strategies for studying behavior change*. New York: Pergamon Press, 1976.

Kazdin, A.E. *Research design in clinical psychology*. New York: Harper & Row, 1980.

Kensler, G. (Ed.). *Observation: A technique for art educators.* Washington, D.C.: National Art Education Association, 1971.

Machotka, P. *The nude: Perception and personality.* New York: Irvington, 1979.

Mattil, E.L. (Ed.). *A seminar in art education for research and curriculum development.* University Park: Pennsylvania State University, 1966.

Morris, D. *The biology of art: A study of the picture-making behavior of the great apes and its relationship to human art.* New York: Alfred A. Knopf, 1962.

O'Hare, D. (Ed.). *Psychology and the arts.* New Jersey: Humanities Press, 1981.

Perkins, D., & Leondar, B. (Eds.). *The arts and cognition.* Baltimore: Johns Hopkins University Press, 1977.

Pickford, R.W. *Psychology and visual aesthetics.* London: Hutchinson, 1972.

Polit, D.F., & Hungler, B.P. *Nursing research: Principles and methods* (2nd ed.). Philadelphia: Lippincott, 1982.

Pope, K.S., & Singer, J.L. (Eds.). *The stream of consciousness: Scientific investigations into the flow of human experience.* New York: Plenum Press, 1978.

Selfe, L. *Normal and anomalous representational drawing ability in children.* New York: Academic Press, 1983.

Journals

Empirical Studies of the Arts. Published by Baywood Publishing Company, New York.

Imagination, Cognition, and Personality. Published by Baywood Publishing Company, New York.

Journal of Mental Imagery. Published by the International Imagery Association, New York.

Scientific Aesthetics (Sciences de l'Art). Published by Plenum Press, New York.

Studies in Art Education. Published by the National Art Education Association, Reston, Virginia.

Visual Arts Research. Published by the University of Illinois Press, Urbana, Illinois.

Chapter 17. Knowing Theory

Blatt, S.J., & Blatt, E.S. *Continuity and change in art: The development of modes of representation.* New York: Analytic Press, 1984.

Erikson, E.H. *Toys and reasons: Stages in the ritualization of experience.* New York: W.W. Norton, 1977.

Freud, S. *On creativity and the unconscious: Papers on the psychology of art, literature, love, religion.* New York: Harper & Row, 1958.

Gedo, J.E. *Portraits of the artist: Psychoanalysis of creativity and its vicissitudes.* New York: Guilford, 1983.

Goodman, N. *Languages of art* (2nd ed.). Indianapolis: Hackett, 1976.

Grolnick, S.A., & Barkin, L. (Eds.). *Between reality and fantasy: Transitional objects and phenomena.* New York: Jason Aronson, 1978.

Kreitler, H., & Kreitler, S. *Psychology of the arts.* Durham, NC: Duke University Press, 1972.

Kris, E. *Psychoanalytic explorations in art.* New York: Schocken Press, 1952.

Kuhns, R. *Psychoanalytic theory of art.* New York: Columbia University Press, 1983.

Langer, S.K. *Philosophy in a new key.* Cambridge: Harvard University Press, 1942.

———. *Feeling and form.* New York: Scribner's, 1953.

———. *Problems of art.* New York: Scribner's, 1957.

Lewin, B.D. *The image and the past.* New York: International Universities Press, 1968.

Meerloo, J.A.M. *Creativity and eternization.* New York: Humanities Press, 1968.

Peckham, M. *Man's rage for chaos: Biology, behavior, and the arts.* New York: Schocken Press, 1965.

Phillips, W. (Ed.). *Art and psychoanalysis.* New York: Meridian Books, 1957.

Pruyser, P.W. *The play of the imagination: Toward a psychoanalysis of culture.* New York: International Universities Press, 1983.

Schneider, D.E. *The psychoanalyst and the artist.* New York: International Universities Press, 1950.

Winnicott, D.W. *Playing and reality.* New York: Basic Books, 1972.

PART V. APPLICATIONS

Chapter 18. Different Populations

Children and Adolescents

Esman, A.H. (Ed.). *The psychiatric treatment of adolescents.* New York: International Universities Press, 1983.

Foster, G.W., et al. *Child care work with emotionally disturbed children.* Pittsburgh: University of Pittsburgh Press, 1971.

Ginott, H.G. *Group psychotherapy with children*. New York: McGraw-Hill, 1961.

Haworth, M. (Ed.). *Child psychotherapy: Practice and theory*. New York: Basic Books, 1964.

Meeks, J.E. *The fragile alliance: An orientation to the psychiatric treatment of the adolescent* (2nd ed.). New York: Krieger, 1980.

Mishne, J. *Clinical work with children*. New York: The Free Press, 1983.

Morris, R.J., & Kratochwill, T.R. (Eds.). *The practice of child therapy*. New York: Pergamon Press, 1983.

Moustakas, C.E. *Psychotherapy with children*. New York: Ballantine Books, 1959.

Ross, A.O. *Child behavior therapy: Principles, practices, and empirical basis*. New York: Wiley, 1981.

Slavson, S.R., & Schiffer, M. *Group psychotherapies for children*. New York: International Universities Press, 1975.

Speers, R.W., & Lansing, C. *Group therapy in childhood psychosis*. Chapel Hill: University of North Carolina Press, 1965.

Steinberg, D. *The clinical psychiatry of adolescence: Clinical work from a social and developmental perspective*. New York: Wiley, 1983.

Adults and Geriatrics

Anthony, E.J., & Benedek, T. (Eds.). *Depression and human existence*. Boston: Little, Brown, 1975.

Arieti, S. *Interpretation of schizophrenia* (2nd ed.). New York: Basic Books, 1974.

Bellak, L. (Ed.). *Disorders of the schizophrenic syndrome*. New York: Basic Books, 1979.

Brink, T.L. *Geriatric psychotherapy*. New York: Human Sciences Press, 1979.

Butler, R.N., & Lewis, M.I. *Aging and mental health: Positive psychosocial approaches* (3rd ed.). St. Louis: C.V. Mosby, 1983.

Freeman, T. *A psychoanalytic study of the psychoses*. New York: International Universities Press, 1973.

Frosch, J. *The psychotic process*. New York: International Universities Press, 1983.

Giovacchini, P.L., & Boyer, L.B. (Eds.). *Technical factors in the treatment of the severely disturbed patient*. New York: Jason Aronson, 1982.

Hartocollis, P. (Ed.). *Borderline personality disorders: The concept, the syndrome, the patient*. New York: International Universities Press, 1977.

Kernberg, O. *Borderline conditions and pathological naricissism*. New York: Aronson, 1975.

Kohut, H. *The analysis of the self*. New York: International Universities Press, 1971.

McNeil, E.B. *Neuroses and personality disorders*. Englewood Cliffs, NJ: Prentice-Hall, 1970.

———. *The psychoses*. Englewood Cliffs, NJ: Prentice-Hall, 1970.

Masterson, J.F. *The narcissistic and borderline disorders: An integrated developmental approach*. New York: Brunner/Mazel, 1981.

Pao, P-N. *Schizophrenic disorders: Theory and treatment from a psychodynamic point of view*. New York: International Universities Press, 1979.

Paykel, E.S. (Ed.). *Handbook of affective disorders*. New York: Guilford Press, 1982.

Scheflen, A. *Levels of schizophrenia*. New York: Brunner/Mazel, 1981.

Schlossberg, N.A. *Counseling adults in transition: Linking practice and theory*. New York: Springer, 1984.

Searles, H.F. *Collected papers on schizophrenia and related subjects*. New York: International Universities Press, 1966.

Sheehan, S. *Is there no place on earth for me?* Boston: Houghton-Mifflin, 1982.

Whitehead, J.A. *Psychiatric disorders in old age: A handbook for the clinical team*. New York: Springer, 1979.

Handicapped and Disabled

Buck, P. *The child who never grew*. New York: John Day, 1950.

Burlingham, D. *Psychoanalytic studies of the sighted and the blind*. New York: International Universities Press, 1972.

Cutsforth, T.D. *The blind in school and society: A psychological study*. New York: American Foundation for the Blind, 1951.

Eissler, K.R., Kris, M., & Solnit, A.J. (Eds.). *Physical illness and handicap in childhood*. New Haven: Yale University Press, 1977.

Evans, D.P. *The lives of mentally retarded people*. Boulder, CO: Westview Press, 1983.

Fraiberg, S. *Insights from the blind: Comparative studies of blind and sighted subjects*. New York: Basic Books, 1977.

Gardner, H. *The shattered mind: The person after brain-damage*. New York: Vintage Books, 1974.

Garrett, J.F., & Levine, E.S. (Eds.). *Psychological practices with the physically disabled*. New York: Columbia University Press, 1962.

Gliedman, J., & Roth, W. *The unexpected minority: Handicapped children in America*. New York: Harcourt Brace Jovanovich, 1980.

Goffman, E. *Stigma: Notes on the management of spoiled identity*. Englewood Cliffs, NJ: Prentice-Hall, 1963.

Hunt, P. (Ed.). *Stigma: The experience of disability.* London: Geoffrey Chapman, 1966.

Lindemann, J.E. *Psychological and behavioral aspects of physical disability: A manual for health practitioners.* New York: Plenum Press, 1981.

Marinelli, R.P., & Dell Orto, A.E. (Eds.). *The psychological and social impact of physical disability.* New York: Springer, 1977.

Samuels, S. *Disturbed exceptional children: An integrated approach.* New York: Human Sciences Press, 1981.

Seligman, M. *The family with a handicapped child: Understanding and intervention.* New York: Grune & Stratton, 1983.

————. *Group psychotherapy and counseling with special populations.* Baltimore: University Park Press, 1982.

Stubbins, J. *Social and psychological aspects of disability.* Baltimore: University Park Press, 1977.

Wright, B.A. *Physical disability: A psychological approach* (2nd ed.). New York: Harper & Row, 1984.

Chapter 19. Different Settings

Bayes, K. *The therapeutic effect of environment on emotionally disturbed and mentally subnormal children.* London: Unwin Brothers, 1967.

Beigel, A., & Levenson, R.I. (Eds.). *The community mental health center.* New York: Basic Books, 1972.

Bettelheim, B. *Love is not enough.* New York: The Free Press, 1950.

————. *A home for the heart.* New York: Alfred A. Knopf, 1974.

Brendtro, L., & Ness, A. *Re-educating troubled youth: Environments for teaching and treatments.* New York: Aldine Press, 1983.

Canter, D., & Canter, S. (Eds.). *Designing for therapeutic environments: A review of research.* New York: Wiley, 1979.

Cumming, J., & Cumming, E. *Ego and milieu.* New York: Atherton Press, 1962.

Goffman, E. *Asylums.* New York: Anchor Books, 1961.

Heacock, D.R. (Ed.). *A psychodynamic approach to adolescent psychiatry: The Mount Sinai experience.* New York: Marcel Dekker, 1980.

Holahan, C.J. *Environmental behavior: A dynamic perspective.* New York: Plenum Press, 1978.

Langsley, D.G., Berlin, I.N., & Yarvis, R.M. *Handbook of community mental health.* New York: Excerpta Medica, 1981.

Luber, R.F., & Anderson, C.M. (Eds.). *Family intervention with psychiatric patients.* New York: Human Sciences Press, 1983.

Mahlmann, J., & Jungels, G. (Eds.). *Art in the lives of persons with special needs*. Reston, VA: National Art Education Association, 1981.

Moos, R.H., et al. *The human context: Environmental determinants of behavior*. New York: Wiley, 1976.

Ostroff, E. *Humanizing environments: A primer*. Cambridge, MA: The Word Guild, 1978.

Ostroff, E., & Tamashiro, R. *Transforming institutions with play, the arts, and environmental design*. Boston: Massachusetts Department of Mental Health, 1975.

Polsky, H., Claster, D.S., & Goldberg, C. (Eds.). *Social systems perspectives in residential institutions*. East Lansing: Michigan State University Press, 1970.

Proshansky, H.M., Ittelson, W.H., & Rivlin, L.G. (Eds.). *Environmental psychology: Man and his physical setting*. New York: Holt, Rinehart & Winston, 1970.

Rossi, J., & Filstead, W. (Eds.). *The therapeutic community: A sourcebook of readings*. New York: Behavioral Publications, 1973.

Schulberg, H.C., & Baker, F. *The mental hospital and human services*. New York: Behavioral Publications, 1974.

Sederer, L.I. (Ed.). *Inpatient psychiatry: Diagnosis and treatment*. Baltimore: Williams & Wilkins, 1983.

Yalom, I.D. *Inpatient group psychotherapy*. New York: Basic Books, 1983.

Chapter 20. Different Modes

Baruth, L.G., & Huber, C.H. *An introduction to marital theory and therapy*. Monterey, CA: Brooks/Cole, 1983.

Bellak, L., & Small, L.S. *Emergency psychotherapy and brief psychotherapy* (2nd ed.). New York: Grune & Stratton, 1978.

Cohen, R.G., & Lipkin, G.B. *Therapeutic group work for health professionals*. New York: Springer, 1979.

Erickson, G.D., & Hogan, T.P. (Eds.). *Family therapy: An introduction to theory and technique* (2nd ed.). Monterey, CA: Brooks/Cole, 1981.

Goldenberg, I., & Goldenberg, H. *Family therapy: An overview*. Monterey, CA: Brooks/Cole, 1980.

Gurman, A.S., & Kniskern, D.P. (Eds.). *Handbook of family therapy*. New York: Brunner/Mazel, 1981.

Haveliwala, Y.A., Scheflen, A.E., & Ashcraft, N. *Common sense in therapy: A handbook for the mental health worker*. New York: Brunner/Mazel, 1979.

Hoffman, L. *Foundations of family therapy*. New York: Basic Books, 1981.

Jones, S.L. *Family therapy: A comparison of approaches*. Bowie, MD: Robert J. Brady Company, 1980.

Lambert, M.J. (Ed.). *Psychotherapy and patient relationships*. Homewood, IL: Dow Jones-Irwin, 1982.

Mullen, H., & Rosenbaum, M. *Group psychotherapy: Theory & practice* (rev. ed.). New York: The Free Press, 1978.

Naar, R. *A primer of group psychotherapy*. New York: Human Sciences Press, 1982.

Satir, V.M., et al. *Helping families to change*. New York: Aronson, 1976.

Small, L.S. *The briefer psychotherapies* (rev. ed.). New York: Brunner/Mazel, 1979.

Wolberg, L.R. *Handbook of short-term psychotherapy*. New York: Thieme-Stratton, 1980.

Yalom, I.D. *The theory and practice of group psychotherapy* (2nd ed.). New York: Basic Books, 1975.

Index